MIRACLE ON 33RD STREET

The New York Knickerbockers'
Championship Season, 1969-70

PHIL BERGER

FOUR WALLS EIGHT WINDOWS, New York/London

TO MY FATHER AND MOTHER
(1970)

TO MY DAUGHTER JULIA
(1994)

© 1994 Phil Berger

Published in the United States by:
Four Walls Eight Windows
39 West 14th Street, room 503, New York, N.Y., 10011

U.K. offices:
Four Walls Eight Windows/Turnaround
27 Horsell Road, London, N51 XL, England

First printing January 1994.

Library of Congress Cataloging-in-Publication Data:
Berger, Phil,
Miracle on 33rd Street/Phil Berger.
p.   cm.
ISBN: 1-56858-008-8
1. New York Knickerbockers (Basketball team). I.Title.
GV885.52.N4B4   1994
796.323'64'097471—dc20
93-39326
CIP

Printed in the United States

INTRODUCTION
by Marv Albert

TAKE IT FROM a guy who was there: Phil Berger's *Miracle on 33rd Street* is not just another book about the New York Knicks. Sure, it goes without saying that the 1969-70 championship season was not just another basketball schedule being played out. It was a remarkable year for a special team. But a lot of typewriters started making noise after that final buzzer was drowned out by the din of screaming Garden fans. Check the out-of-print listings if you really want to know how many books were written about the '69-70 Knicks—the simple truth is that while great teams are not easily forgotten, books written about them usually don't stand the test of time. In *Miracle on 33rd Street*, however, Phil Berger has written a beautiful—and revealing—book that will continue to enthrall lovers of the game as long as the game itself exists.

Phil took a lot of us by surprise when *Miracle on 33rd Street* was first published, in 1970. He had accomplished something still new to sports journalism: a timeless book. In so doing, he joined a select group that included boxing writer A.J. Liebling, baseball writers Jim Brosnan and Jim Bouton (whose *Ball Four* also came out in 1970), and *Paris Review* editor George Plimpton, who successfully joined the ranks of American sportswriters with *Paper Lion* in 1965.

You'll notice from the first page that Phil doesn't cheat his readers. After all, he didn't decide to write *Miracle on 33rd Street* after the season had ended, or even midway through. Nor did he, in the Fall of '69, decide to travel with the Knicks for an entire season with the hope that they would win it all and lay history at his feet.

Phil is a writer in the truest sense. He went after the whole story: the busses, the hotels, the personality conflicts—the endeavor of surviving the rigors of a single season. It's a story that hadn't been told in any previous book about basketball.

Of course, it didn't hurt that the Knicks did win it all in the Spring of 1970. And Garden fans, among the most intelligent and devoted in the country, deserved that first Knickerbocker championship as much as did Bill Bradley, Dick Barnett, Dave DeBusschere, Willis Reed, and Walt Frazier. (One thing I'll always remeber about the fans in '69 was they they exhibited full appreciation even for role players coming off the bench, guys like Mike Riordan, whose entrance always meant we could expect a strategic intentional foul, and soon... but I'll let Phil tell the stories.) That team commanded respect, and New York fans gave it to them. It stands to reason, then, that Knick fans will appreciate this thorough account by Phil Berger.

Marv Albert
New York City, 1993

♛ CHAPTER ONE

Asofsky has always been fanatic about his sports.

He used to hide in the latrine on Saturdays for the New York Rangers, a hockey team. This was at the old Madison Square Garden on Eighth Avenue and Forty-ninth Street.

In the mornings, Howard Cann's New York University basketball team split into red- and blue-jerseyed contingents and scrimmaged. Afterward, there was an industrial league game—teams like Gimbels, Macy's, Lewyt Vacuum Cleaners. Patrons of the morning's events were permitted to remain for the matinee in which the professional Knickerbockers were the attraction.

Then Asofsky used to hide in the latrine.

Quiet as a monk, he waited while Garden personnel made the place over. The basketball court was disassembled like pieces of a jigsaw puzzle, 140 slats of 3-by-10s carted away on ten trucks. The ice plant then pumped brine at a frigid 11 degrees through pipes and up to the floor; the floor was sprayed five times and the ice built to a thickness of five eighths of an inch. Just before the final spray, it was painted white to make the puck more visible. Around Asofsky's special pew downstairs, maintenance people mopped and scrubbed. They never bothered him. "The security guys were the ones you had to fear," Asofsky remembered. "You didn't have to fear the workmen. They felt if you earned your spot, stay in there."

Even then Asofsky had fan's blood. Other kids from Brooklyn got their kicks running bases in Betsy Head Park, doing sneakered

7

pirouettes on playground courts, miming Sugar Ray. But for him
it was a big deal to cop a hockey seat. "I was a rare kid," he has
said. "I loved to watch people play."

The Ranger business, of course, bothers him. These days Stanley Asofsky is, you see, strictly a basketball man, a Knickerbocker
superfan, in fact. Cazzie Russell has drunk papaya juice with him;
Nate Bowman points him out to other players during games; and
once a former Knick named Freddie Crawford warned black mili-
tants at the Rucker's Tournament in Harlem to lay off Asofsky. On
occasion, Don Dejardin, the general manager of the pro Carolina
Cougars, has called long distance for advice on schoolyard prospects. So zealous is Asofsky that in the offseason he will travel
anywhere in or out of the city to see a basketball game.

The summer before this season he and big Fred Klein spent
weekends at the Rucker's, a summer competition where amateurs
and sometimes Knicks competed and which was, for Asofsky and
Klein, a preseason rite long before it became fashionable among
nouveau basketball people. This summer they had photographer's
stools bought at a rummage sale expressly for the Rucker's so they
could sit front row and not obstruct views, a very savvy move.

For nine years, Asofsky and Fred Klein and sometimes Bernie
Brosniak and Al the Plumber sat first row floor level, directly behind the basket at the old Garden. The tickets were purchased in
the name of an acquaintance and fellow aficionado, Bill Bierman.
When the Garden shifted to its present Thirty-third Street site,
just above Pennsylvania Station, the group lost its vantage in the
administrative bungling that attended transition.

The prospect of no season tickets for 1969–70 prompted Asofsky
to fire off a three-page letter to Mr. Edward (Ned) Irish, president of the Knickerbocker organization, in which he raised the
ghosts of past Knickerbocker notables from Ossie Schectman to
Brendan McCann, commended his own allegiance to the team,
and spoke of the seats' "leveling effect in this turbulent society."

Apparently Irish succumbed to this suasion. The tickets—Section R, Row 1—were dispatched to all members of the party save
Bierman. This was inadvertent but was not regarded as tragic by
the group, the sentiment being best expressed by Fred Klein, who
said, "Bill Bierman used to come to the Garden and all he wanted

to do was clap his hands for Richie Guerin and eat candy. 'Maybe you guys want a piece of Nestle's Crunch?' And we were always on diets and we'd say, 'Get away with Nestle's Crunch.' Actually, you can't take this guy. He's the kind of fan that's so nice that you want to hit him in the head with a truck. We're sort of hard-core fans."

There was no scarcity of New Yorkers now claiming such passion for the home team. Actor Zero Mostel, for instance, had nearly driven Stanley to distraction in the playoffs, banging a cane backside Asofsky's seat at Knickerbocker moments, a ploy calculated to spare his stage voice. New fans like Zero had enthusiasm but most of them had arrived at their fervor without the sobering toll of nonsense that die-hards like Asofsky had endured.

Granted, there was some cause for optimism, notably the cataclysmic change in Knickerbocker fortunes the past season with the arrival of Dave DeBusschere, a 6-foot 6-inch forward. DeBusschere had come to the New York organization from Detroit in a trade for the Knickerbockers' 6-10 center Walter Bellamy and 6-1 guard Howard Komives, a pair whose effect on the team was considered pernicious. When DeBusschere appeared in the city, the team was mediocre (its record: 18 wins, 17 losses), a situation his presence and, just as surely, the departure of Bellamy and Komives helped repair. From that point on, the Knickerbockers proceeded to win 36 of 47 games, the most successful record in the National Basketball Association over the period.

The rousing finish was tonic for New Yorkers who had grown accustomed to a certain kind of Knickerbocker denouement, countless games commencing in artful propriety only to be reversed by godalmighty clinkers whose cumulation night after night turned accountants and poets alike into seriocomic mourners or, worse, football fans. All that was changing.

The vogue in antiheroic expired. Knickerbocker success apparently was easier to bear; season ticket sales for the new campaign doubled from the year previous (8,000 seats already sold for the 19,500-capacity arena), and Knickerbocker faces became box office. Willis Reed for Equitable insurance. Walt Frazier for Supp-Hose sox. Cazzie Russell for Ideal board games. Frazier and De-Busschere contracted for books.

The demand for Knick games led drinking bars in the city to install cable television so their clientele could watch home contests. Manhattan Cable Television reported its business had grown from nine bars at last year's playoffs to eighty-five in the new season, and a bar owner in an area not yet serviced by the company was threatening to sue. For games in which bars were crowded, fans had taken to phoning the Manhattan Cable warehouse to enquire whether they could join the sales force there to watch the action.

For fadhoppers and corporate vaudevillians, the team was turning into jockstrap *Hello Dolly*, the newest plaything in town. Naturally, none of this impressed hard-core guys like Asofsky, Klein, Brosniak or Al the Plumber. They had their reasons.

The Knickerbockers had had a competitive existence of twenty-three years in which time the team had not won a single league championship. Their ineptitude in the past decade was at times so transparent that a former New York player named Darrall Imhoff carried his travel bag in such a way that the embossed name of the team was illegible, and Bill Bradley could recall being spat upon by the disenchanted at the old Garden as the club traversed to and from the locker room. The memories of authentic supporters, then, were like a bad home movie, laughable were they not so personal.

"We used to call Carl Braun 'Mary Braun' and Kenny Sears 'Sara Sears' because we felt that they didn't have that all-out fight," Fred Klein remembered. "Same for Willie Naulls, who we called 'Harry Belafonte' because he didn't get involved either. I remember once, Cleveland Buckner—he was about six feet nine inches, had a crazy way of shooting—he came down once, the Knicks were losing by about forty at the half to someone—he came down and stole the ball in midcourt and went running in and running in and running and threw a dunk shot and tore the house down. But he walked about forty steps on it. He ran, literally ran, from half-court to the basket, physically ran forty feet, without dribbling the ball, he must have forgot. Then there was Whitey Bell, we called him Popeye, he looked like Popeye, he had a tattoo on each arm, no teeth, blond hair, he looked like about fifty years old. He was horrible. And then they had [Holy Cross great] Jack Foley, Jack *the Shot* Foley. I think his arms only came from his shoulder to his elbow, he had no arms, you know, and he could never get a shot off.

"It would be so bad that we'd get on the refs for lack of anything better to do. But even that had a way of backfiring. I was screaming at this ref, Sid Borgia, one night and Borgia turned around and said, 'I'm going to call a technical foul on the Knicks because of you.' Like that. And the Knicks coach, Fuzzy Levane, jumped off his chair screaming, 'What do you want from me?' And as he jumped up, he knocked the seat over and they called a technical foul on Levane because Borgia thought he was throwing the seat or something like that."

Things were in such a state that when the Knicks went seeking a big pivotman, and found a Harlem Globetrotter who seemed to fit the role, it turned out that the player, Willie Gardner, had a heart condition. In those years, New York was required to take help anyway it could, which allowed one player, Ernie Vandeweghe, to work both in hospital wards and at the old Garden.

"We used to call the space behind the Knick bench 'Ernie Vandeweghe Avenue,'" Asofsky said, "reason being that Vandeweghe came late to ball games after making intern rounds, and used to warm up running up and down the floor in back of the Knick bench, even while the game was on—wind sprints and such. And on time-outs, he was the only ballplayer I've ever seen on time-outs to shoot baskets to get set."

Nights like those in the Forty-ninth Street Garden had a tempering effect on roseate visions; at the promise of quicksnatch golden rings on the sporting-go-round, history was still instructive. Yet if greatness sprang from a peekaboo and wink at Olympus, then the stretch run the Knicks had made in 1968-69 provided sufficient grounds for them to dare it. In sweeping four championship playoff games from Baltimore, New York had beaten a team whose record over the 82-game regular-season schedule was the best among the pros, and whose style was the very antithesis of the Knickerbockers', having a permissiveness that let each man dribble to his own drummer. In a confrontation of playtime postures, New York had emerged from the series assured that old-fashioned team virtues could work against even the helter-skelter best. Nor did the Knicks' subsequent elimination from the playoffs by Boston (aided by Frazier's prohibiting groin injury) likely diminish their conviction at preseason.

The training camp of the Knicks was at the State University of New York in Farmingdale, Long Island, 380 grassy acres on which the main business was agricultural and technical education —courses in greenhouse management, turf-grass culture, COBOL programming, highway design and so forth. The college maintained a herd of dairy cattle (Holsteins, Ayrshires and Guernseys), a herd of beef cattle (Angus), a few swine and sheep. The State University motto was "Let Each Become All He Is Capable of Being."

The players were sheltered two-to-a-room at the nearby Pickwick Motor Inn in Plainview, where a sign read, *Welcome NY Knicks / Sauna Right in Room Healthful and Relaxing / 2 for $4.44 in the Camelot Restaurant and Lounge.* A Knickerbocker who did not indulge in the 2-for-$4.44 special was Willis Reed, who came to his abstinence one night when team trainer Danny Whelan pointed out a man whose aproned outfit appeared to have come from the university's barn down the road.

"Get a look at the chef, Will," said Whelan.

"Be seeing you," replied Reed.

Reed had spent the summer as one of New York State's larger (6 feet 9 inches, 245 pounds) boys' camp proprietors, a position not in keeping with his more spirited sporting image. Reed's coach at Grambling College, Fred Hobdy, recollected the time in Kansas City when Reed knocked down "a little white boy" who was apparently up to no good in the backboard territory Reed considered his domain. A teammate of his from Grambling, Jimmy Jones, said that whether it was white boy or black boy, it made no difference. He remembered a pivotman from all-black Southern University breaking Reed's nose with an elbow and ending up quite useless for the remainder of the game when Reed promptly flattened him with one punch.

As a pro, Reed's game was just as straightahead. There were no frills to it. The Cap'n, as his Knick teammates called him, worked the boards with the kind of cruel insistence that Marciano put on a man. There was often inelegance to his art—a weary Reed ran like a girdled damsel—but his body was like that of an overweight tapdancer, capable of surprises. Reed striding across the lane, his chest inflating, limbs stretching, had a kind of striking majesty.

Dave DeBusschere was like Reed in his absence of flair. Whatever poetry there was in his game was not calculated; he was a thoroughgoing pragmatist, the house efficiency expert. No strange psychic embers lit his performance; there were no freaky bends in his mind. He was a professional: grace, muscle, cortical buttons night after night, that was DeBusschere.

He would never qualify for sports page exotic, as DeBusschere did not go in for the ruffles of nicknames and rituals and labyrinthian personal visions. The only thing remotely odd about him was a historic need for a cold beer; he had guzzled since he was a lad of seven, a deed less culpable for his father's having been a distributor.

Neither Reed nor offseason stockbroker DeBusschere (these two were the muscle of the New York team) was weary from summer play, each having taken his leisure while he could. Training camp offered no idle prospects for the players, a fact that DeBusschere acknowledged by saying, "It's a necessary evil because you have to get yourself in shape, and the only way you're going to do it is by your being pushed. And no matter how much you work out by yourself, you never push yourself enough. That's why you have to have camps. I hate them. Just the thought of it . . . it's 'God, here we go again.' "

There was little *joie de vivre* in preseason—too much of blurred time and repetition and nothing for kicks in return, no moments when great spoils were at stake. The regular season at least had the edge of these combats to diminish the deadening rituals of the in-between, the limbo of hotels and TV soaps and room service and social beer or cheer or lady things. But even the regular season, 100 games or so in an eight-month span, could be exhaustive, so much so that a gung-ho like Frazier needed a sabbatical.

Frazier had the kind of entranced joy inside the game's rhythm that surfers are said to have in a wave's curl. If there was such a thing as a hedonist in sport, Frazier was it. The roar of a Garden crowd juiced him, often setting him off on his most productive binges. Even Knickerbocker practices moved him; he took pleasure in berating the second team—"chumps" he mockingly called them. But for all that, Frazier laid off in the summer. "I want to make myself miss it," he said. "I want to be hungry for the game."

So Frazier would wander about town or idle in his room on the twenty-ninth floor of the Hotel New Yorker, content in this narrow rectangle of space to let humping soul rhythms or mere silence surround him, not even curious enough to eye onto Eighth Avenue below, serene as a Buddha was he in that room. Nighttimes, he might slip into a wide-brimmed hat and a wide-lapeled suit—1930s fashions which had given the Knicks to tag him Clyde, for Clyde Barrow—and glide off to places where there were drinkables and/or women, to Jock's in Harlem, or Nepentha on the East Side. And sometimes, late at night he would return to his room alone and be struck by an uneasy sense of disconnection. Lacking a basketball, he was out of socket. He ended up buying barbells for such midnight and rainy-day deadends.

The impasse that Dick Barnett was approaching was founded not on disjointed days but rather on stark years. Barnett, at thirty-three, was the old man of the team, a goateed black man whose hooded lids and sleepwalker's gait gave him an oracular aspect that suggested his basketball skills owed as much to mystical faculties as to a refined motor ability. Had it been so, Barnett no doubt would have been pleased to pass a lingering summer in Gary, Indiana. As it was, the fallibility of his bones had been shown him.

The summer before he had practiced his unconventional shots on his own rather than against defenders, a policy that had adversely affected his shooting touch in the early going of last season. So this summer Barnett shot his odd left-handed jump and contorted drives against Chicago-area professionals like Bob Boozer, Jim Washington and Flynn Robinson, and came to camp in the pink, looking younger in fact than before, with a new dental plate that stoppered a front gap in his mouth and, as Barnett put it, got his image *to-gethuh.*

The image of another Knickerbocker, Bill Bradley, was intact once again, too, having suffered only slightly in the transition from amateur athlete-scholar to working stiff. As a Princeton undergraduate, the image of Bradley was that of the disciplined achiever whose moral and spiritual underpinnings were solid.

Regimenting mightily, he became the best college basketball player in the nation and an accomplished thinker, the combination of which earned him a Rhodes scholarship and the regard of America. The image that accompanied all this brought Bradley some fifty letters a day, many of the sort that wind up in the mail pouch of Dear Abigail and forced him to hire, at age nineteen, a part-time secretary.

Bradley's image had tarnished only after he returned from his two years at Oxford and chose to play professional basketball for a four-year contract of an estimated half-million dollars. In part, public regard for Bradley declined because he elected to make his wages in a game rather than in more anointed precincts and, to a greater degree, because he did the unthinkable and failed to succeed in the game's commercial version. Bradley did not make it as a pro until one of New York's starting forwards, Cazzie Russell, broke his ankle in the middle of the 1968–69 season and forced coach William (Red) Holzman to switch Bradley from guard to forward, a change that allowed him to move unencumbered by the ball to vacant areas on the floor from where he could launch a remarkably quick and accurate one-hander against larger but less nimble frontline opposition. Free of handling the ball against quick-footed backcourtmen, his entire game improved, reaching an artistic peak in the playoffs, where he both scored and defensed in a professional manner.

Modest success did not diminish in Bradley a spartan streak about which his college coach, Bill van Breda Kolff, once remarked, "I think Bradley's happiest whenever he can deny himself pleasure." Bradley's training started in mid-July when he returned to New York from Washington, where he had worked as a volunteer in the Office of the Director of Poverty. Afternoons in the city, he ran in old cuffed suit pants and a tee shirt along Riverside Drive, pausing at Ninty-sixth Street for calisthenics, then resuming the run on its downtown leg. Sometimes, at the insistence of schoolyard players around Seventy-fourth Street, he would stop to shoot baskets on the macadam courts for their pleasures. Evenings he spent at places like the Downtown Athletic Club or the Ninety-second Street YMHA with a basketball.

Twice a week he took an afternoon Penn Central coach to Philadelphia and then taxied to ghetto neighborhoods where street-corner walls were spray-painted with names like *Mighty Zulu Nation* and *Peanut* and *Crow* and *Little Duke* and where the games of the Charles Baker League were played. Bradley was on the roster of the Jimmy Bates B-Bar team. The Kent Taverneers had NBA stars Hal Greer and Chet Walker. Gaddie Real Estate had a pro named Earl Monroe whose moves were a mix of jive and cunning that one night drove a tall beauty in an Afro to shriek, "Ooooh, Earl, you're my baby."

Bradley said, "It was a casual kind of organized basketball. In some places, there was no ventilation, it got over a hundred degrees. Your basketball shoes became so wet you were running in puddles of water. I'd take the eleven forty from Philadelphia back to New York and get in about one thirty."

There was no pay for Baker League play, but there were profits in it for Bradley. Even though he was more efficient in the corners of the floor, he worked out of the backcourt for Bates B-Bar, to acquire the dribble as another means of transport to the open shot, his specialty. "I wasn't confident with the ball, that I could control it," he said. "I needed the work."

It was not by chance that of the starters Bradley and Barnett were busiest in the summer break. Bradley did not have the brawn of Reed or DeBusschere in the frontcourt to compensate for a shot gone bad. Barnett could not depend on quickness the way Frazier could. They were more of opportunists, the mathematics of their game was more rigid.

But however ready they were, training camp was not so crucial for the starters. The uncommon communion they'd had at the tail end of the previous season ensured each of them of primary status at least until sufficient reversals in a new season nullified the advantage of their history. Training camp was more crucial to benchmen trying to secure reputations that would be negotiable later in playing time, the source of all sporting gains, fiscal or spiritual. But even on this level, the camp had a foregone quality.

There was small chance, say, that rookies would make waves. Some Knickerbockers, it can be noted, had been to camps of character in the past. Reed was at one when Harry Gallatin was New York's coach. Gallatin ran his camp as if he were in charge of the Green Bay Packers. He would roll a ball on the floor and direct his high-priced athletes to dive for it, a kind of Blue Cross steal-the-bacon. He had his players run up fieldhouse steps, work on isometric racks and even had piggyback races in which Reed might lumber downcourt with Jim (Bad News) Barnes on his back. Bad News was 6 feet 8 inches, 240 pounds.

That was nothing stacked against the Detroit Piston camp of Charley Wolf's that DeBusschere had attended. Wolf was the American Gothic of pro basketball coaches: He did not smoke, drink, gamble or curse. His concept of leadership was that of the headmaster of a boarding school. At St. Clair, Michigan, Wolf rented a big house for the Pistons; and to keep that house in order, players were not permitted out of the backyard after six, lights out was at ten. For transport to and from practice, the players rode bicycles.

Wolf forbade card games for money for the sake of team spirit ("Somebody might lose," he said), so bootleg card games sprang up under blankets and in dark corners. He espoused celibacy and was, of course, ignored. "One time on the day of an exhibition game," DeBusschere said, "Wolf saw one of the players with his girl—he wasn't seen in his room, but he was seen with the girl the day of the game. Well, needless to say, the guy didn't play for about two weeks and the guy was a starter. Everybody knew why."

For exhibition games, Wolf gave each player a clipboard and pencil. "You were supposed to keep a record," DeBusschere said, "of the guy who you were competing with for the same job—what he did in this particular exhibition game . . . how many rebounds . . . how many shots he took, and all. You'd walk on the floor, everybody had their own clipboard. Guys from the other team would look at you, they'd all laugh, you felt like a jerk. It was goofy because no one was serious about it. And if you're going against your competitor—the guy might have eight rebounds, you put down four, see, so he comes back and he'd put a 'one' in front of it, it became a fourteen."

Lacking these absurd circumstances, Knick comic relief fell perforce to reserve center, Nate Bowman, whose laughs had proceeded in the past as much from sheer effrontery as from wit. There was the night, for instance, when a bus driver made a wrong turn and headed down a highway lost, a plight that brought only insults from Nate's Knick soul brothers. When the abuse did not let up and the driver became flustered, Bowman rose to help the man out. "Don't take that shit from those black bastards," he advised.

Another time, the chairman of the board of Madison Square Garden Corporation, Irving Mitchell Felt, was at courtside for a game when Bowman spied him.

"Oi-ving. Hey, hello, Oi-ving, what are you doing?" he remarked.

Felt looked up blankly, and did not respond.

"You call him Oi-ving?" teammate Don May asked.

"Yeah," said Bowman. "He calls me Nate, I don't mind."

Bowman rode along the edge of the sporting life. In pregame warmups, he might wink at pretty courtsiders. On the road, he devised a long-armed solution to institutional pay toilets. He was the Knicks' own Marx Brothers movie. *Psychedelic Sid* was the name Frazier gave him.

The trouble for the Knicks was that Nate's humor was, too often, indistinguishable from his basketball. As Psychedelic Sid, in foppish hats and smoking lean cigars, he had a silky grace moving down airport corridors, a stylish ease of motion that vanished when he set his 15-D feet onto a court.

Then his movements proceeded from some tortured music in his head. Bowman passing a ball, elbows raised up and out, looked like a man pushing through the swinging doors of Wyatt Earp's favorite saloon; the force with which those passes arrived caused Barnett to term them *facebreakers* or *Walter Kennedy Specials*, Kennedy being the NBA commissioner whose name was reported to be imprinted on a man's face when Nate threw a pass. Shooting a jump shot, Bowman's head nestled at the shoulder and, from the other direction, his right arm shot out, as if in some militant political salute, and the ball would go riding off on a zeppelin journey; the whole thing seemed choreographed by the shotputter Parry O'Brien.

Bowman's virtues as a defender were springy legs and a physical toughness to contest the league's biggest men in relief of Reed, but he lacked control of the triggers. He was wont to foul when airborne, as if his offense gave him an unquenchable need to compensate through that god-given gift for bounding into the air. There *were* occasional nights when he managed his instincts and defensed and rebounded like a prince; those nights and his blessed size (6-10, 220) had given him tenure in the NBA. Nor did Holzman take Nate's comic gifts lightly; he considered him the greatest thing since George Gipp for morale, the coach's feeling being that the team that brayed together played together.

That may have been. But for Don May and Bill Hosket, scrubs with dimmest prospects, the laughs were of a distinctly darker nature. May and Hosket had played basketball on the same Dayton (Ohio) High School team and, as rookies the year before, suffered through a season and a city, their entry into New York society being of sufficient hardship to prompt their being called the *Dayton Sissy Mothers.*

Hosket had come to New York straight from the 1968 Olympics in Mexico, where he had been on the US of A basketball team. "I must have been a sight," he said, "arriving at the Hotel New Yorker at two thirty in the morning in a red-white-and-blue blazer. I had souvenirs, suitcases and so forth. I probably looked like a one-man band. There was construction taking place in the lobby. And a sign that said, 'Please excuse our mess.' A Hungarian acting group was just checking in. There were four or five different languages being spoken. My reservation had been misplaced, and I had to wait a long time. Nobody seemed to give a damn. Finally, they got it straightened out, and I got my keys. There was no bellboy around, so I lugged my bags to the elevator. Then I got to the door of the room, opened it up and there was a guy in bed with his wife, covers around them up to their shoulders which were bare. The guy looks at me and says, 'Who the hell are you?' I couldn't give the guy an answer. I just stood there."

Eventually, Hosket acquired the presence to leave the couple to their bed, and weeks later, he and his own wife were in residence in Freeport, Long Island. Bachelor May, in that time, had become a permanent guest at the New Yorker. "I'd walk out onto Eighth Avenue," he said, "and bums would ask me for money. They'd have no shoes, no shirt. Sometimes I followed them. They'd just walk around in circles. Go five feet farther and there was some other bum. I'd wonder where they stayed and how they lived. It depressed me."

Like Frazier, May stayed a lot in his parcel of space high up in the New Yorker, and let the city go by, unmoved by its popular entertainments or even the temptations of Joanie of the Crucifix, St. Joanie. "She used to be in the lobby all the time," he said. "Then once she came up to me and told me her name was Joanie and she was a Catholic. She was dark-haired, pleasantly plump, average looks. She said she wanted to come up to my room to say some prayers or something to my crucifix. It was kind of funny. I said, 'No, sorry,' and I walked away. Anyway, I found out later she was Jewish."

Meantime, out in Freeport, Hosket was still in a state of cultural shock. "When we moved into our place on the island," he said, "we did a lot of shopping. Store clerks were edgy, completely different from what we were used to. I imagine we gawked around. People must have thought we were a couple of farmers. We found that the New Yorker was a more sophisticated human being. There's so much exposure to media. You'd get in a conversation and at times it would make you feel ignorant. I overreacted. I'd think, 'My gosh, I just came here to play ball.'

"I remember seeing *Midnight Cowboy* in Ohio. People there took it as something unreal, exaggerated. No place could be like that. Then months after I'd settled into New York, I was coming out of Gallagher's with my wife and son and saw this guy with his head against the curb, bloody and dirty. Things like that used to stop me when I first came to the city. I'd want to get help. This time we just passed him by and I thought, 'My god, I've become oblivious to it all, too!' The New York environment consumes you. I went to see *Midnight Cowboy* again with Riordan, who's a New Yorker. He laughed at all the opposite things. When Dustin tells these demonstrators to get a job, Mike laughed. People didn't get it in Ohio.

"I had a car, a gold Buick Wildcat, Ohio license plates. It was hit five times that first season, and not once did somebody bother to leave a note. The first time was after the first practice I went to. Another time after practice, somebody had written in the dust on the car, 'Hayseed, Farmboy.' "

Life was not much more bearable on the court for Hosket or May. "The first night I played in the Garden," said Hosket, "I looked up at the scoreboard and it flashed a message that said, 'Welcome *Bob* Hosket, number 20.' They couldn't even get my name right. I knew then that all that All-America and Olympic stuff didn't mean a thing.

"Coming off the bench to play was a different experience, going against guys with years of experience, guys I'd watched so many years on television. Some nights I'd hit three baskets in a minute and a half and think, 'I'm on my way.' Other days, nothing. What happens is your mind plays tricks, you start to wonder if you can play the game.

"And the New York crowds. Say DeBusschere got in foul trouble you could feel the crowd overreact . . . because you're coming in. The crowd would be loud, then an uh-oh when DeBusschere got the foul. When we'd be making the change, me for DeBusschere, it'd become quiet. They were worried I was coming in. I could talk to Dave as if only a thousand people were in the Garden. You could feel the added pressure. It was like all eyes were upon you."

There were pressures from within. "If I got into a game," May said, "it was only for a couple of minutes. You get beat and you're in the doghouse. If you had playing time, you wouldn't have to be nervous and worry. So you try to get shots up when you can. If I didn't get shots up, there'd be no noticeability about what I can do. You want to feel like you're contributing something. If you make a basket, that's something positive. Anybody likes to see that, even Red. The big thing for any guy coming off the bench is to hit your first shot or make a good defensive play. That loosens you up. Otherwise, if you do bad, Red starts screaming at you."

Those onerous circumstances made for the perverse vision the

Knick substitutes had of their situation. A kind of jailhouse
camaraderie arose among them in 1968–69 that led to the creation
of what was called the "scumbag tradition."

"This is how it got started," said Hosket. "One time Mike Riordan called Don May a scumbag for one thing or another, and
Donnie didn't know what it meant at the time. He had never
heard the term. You don't use it much back in Ohio. And he wrote
home to his mother that he wasn't shooting very well, he was the
scumbag of the team. And I guess this upset his family. They all
gather around to read the letters coming from Don and, you
know, his brothers knew what it meant and wondered what had
gotten into Don since he went to New York. Then, of course, we
were down to nine players last year—all we had on the second
string was four guys [Bowman, Riordan, May and Hosket]—so
the starters called us the scumbag squad and Mike was the scum
coach. It just kind of fit Mike; he always tried to coach us in practice."

Under Riordan's guidance, the scum institution soon acquired
its own rituals. "I got to reading about football's game ball," Riordan said, "and came up with the scumball, which was a spoof of
the football one. It was awarded to the guy who made the silliest
play, but only when the team won. From there it was a logical
step to the mythical scum all-star game. We named players and
everything. Everything associated with the game had to be of
scum quality. For instance:

—*The national anthem* . . . "Cincinnati's hands down. Our
guys were impressed by the one their cub scouts put on, not that
we're slamming the cub scouts. But these kids didn't have the spit
and polish that people expect. One boy had a hole in his shoe.
This one was no contest."

—*Caterer* . . . "The Coney Island something or other in Detroit, a few blocks from the Sheraton-Cadillac Hotel, known as
Ptomaine Tommy's to the guys. It's a dirty dingy all-night place
that specializes in chili dogs. After eating there, you don't feel too
good at night. You got the gremlins coming out."

—*Lighting effects* . . . "The Georgia Tech Fieldhouse, home
playing court of the Atlanta Hawks. This is just about the only
place in the league where you need a candle to find your way to

the court. It's so bad there's not enough light to have color telecasts of the games."

—*Official residence* . . . "The Madison Hotel in Boston, a narrow choice over our own New Yorker. The Madison had elevators that sometimes didn't run, telephones from the 1890s. You could pick up and wait five minutes for an operator."

—*Airline* . . . "Allegheny. No comment necessary."

—*Arena* . . . "Chicago Stadium. A great place for the Dartmouth Winter Festival."

The heyday of the tradition was short-lived. The attention the press gave it made it too public. "The press," said Hosket, "couldn't call it scumbag, so they changed it into scrummy or some goofy term, some fabrication that really hurt our pride." And the change in its bench circumstances made the name invalid. New York had reserves that other teams coveted for starters.

There was, for one, Cazzie Russell, whose idiosyncrasies in physical culture had given the Knicks to call him variously Muscles Russell, Cockles 'n' Muscles, Wonder Boy and Stillman's Gym, and whose traveling bag so abounded with vitamins and food supplements that roommate Barnett advised visitors that admission to their place was by pharmaceutical note only.

Russell's concern for body's welfare derived from his high school coach, Larry Hawkins. Hawkins' practices at George Washington Carver High School in Chicago included fitness drills that had the *William Tell Overture* as orchestration and agility-inducing ballet runs. Hawkins acquired a disciple in Cazzie. Russell now percolated tea in the locker room before a game; kept his mattress on a floor rather than a bed when he slept; bore his personal stock of wheat germ and honey to restaurant counters; maintained a fitness armament of skip ropes, hand-squeezers and a waist-slimming device teammates referred to as *the wonderwheel;* adapted health aids such as the papaya juice Asofsky recommended and which Cazzie took to buying by the quart; and swabbed his body with enough therapeutic oils and lotions to earn still another nickname—Max Factor.

When Russell was at Fort Dix, New Jersey, for basic military training, he even fretted about scoring the maximum points on the army's physical training test. "The night before the PT test," he

said, "our company got off at five thirty. At seven, I went out to
the testing area. First I found some old broken grenades; then I
got into this pit and threw the grenades out toward these concen-
tric circles they use for scoring. Then I worked on the horizontal
bars. My hands being as big as they are, they would slip sometimes, so I worked to get a rhythm. Then there was something
called the dodge and jump, a kind of obstacle course. . . . Yeah,
I maxed the test."

Summer workouts—rubber-suited runs, golf and basketball—
were calculated to build up the ankle he had broken, but Russell
claimed that minute adhesions, particularly in the Achilles tendon,
limited his shape. "I'm not in race horse form," he said. "There's
no oxygen debt, it's just the zip that's missing." Whether or not
Russell's spirits were in decline at his reserve predicament he was
not saying, but he still did recall a particularly galling night
shortly after he had left the hospital. "I was coming out of the
Garden and was signing autographs," he said. "The guys had
played real well that night. I remember there was this one kid
who made it a point to come up to me and say, 'We don't need
you anymore.' I had given him my autograph before being injured. I told him I didn't appreciate that. It makes you wonder
what makes people tick."

No speculation existed about what animated the Knicks' Mike
Riordan. He was in possession of an accelerated metabolism for
which he required workouts on days that games were scheduled
to "come down," and jogs around his block at night so that he
might sleep. Teammate Don May said, "The first thing Mike does
when he walks into a hotel room is tear the bedspread off because
he doesn't want it on there for some reason and then checks the
heat to make sure it's down pretty low, say sixty. That's pretty
chilly for normal people. One time he was in a room, the TV was
on, the radio was on, and Mike was laying in bed reading a book.
When someone turned the TV off, Mike said, 'I'm watching it,
leave it on.' "

Riordan's presence on the New York roster was an accident of
the sort that is supposed to happen to movie starlets in Schwab's
Drugstore. Selected by New York on the eleventh round of the
1967 draft of college talent, he did not figure to be invited to the

club's training camp and was, in fact, planning to study for a master's degree in history that fall at Providence College. Then Bradley signed with the Knicks and a workout was arranged so that the media could make an assessment. For lack of enough players —the season already had ended—Riordan, a Long Islander, was brought in. He did well enough to be asked to training camp.

He did not make the team in 1967, ended up instead in the Eastern League, a weekend enterprise whose casual organization, it is said, once led a player to demand at gunpoint his game wages from a team owner, and from time to time occasioned rumors of playoffs being drawn out to take full benefit of a per-game basis of payment. (NBA playoff funds for the players are drawn from the first four games only.)

Strange things often happened in Eastern League cities, places like Wilkes-Barre, Wilmington, Asbury Park and at Allentown, where Riordan played. "There were some looney-tune fans in some of those places, coal miners in overalls and hayseed hats, chomping on straws," he said. "To get to the locker rooms in those places, you had to walk beneath a balcony. They'd spit at you and throw popcorn. Anytime you won an away game, you traveled as a group.

"Even the refs were too much. One time a ref called a foul on this guy, Bob McIntyre—he'd played at St. John's—for pushing. A guy on the other team had ripped Bob's pants at the side seam. You could see flesh up to the hipbone. Bob pointed to the rip and said, 'What about this?' The ref said, 'Fuck you, man.' And afterward he wanted to fight."

It was, for Riordan, not like any game he'd played before. "I was used to playing to win," he said. "But the thing there was to fight your own team for the ball. The league had a three-point rule for shots made from twenty-five feet out. One time a guy shot from twenty-five feet on a fast break, missed, followed his shot, got it and dribbled out to twenty-five feet and shot it again. What happened was that a buddy of mine on the team, Jay Neary, and I had our own plays. It was the only way to survive. We had a bunch of two-man plays, consisting of pick and rolls, backdoor plays, inside picks. We had head and hand signals for calling them."

The sense of the ludicrous that Riordan acquired at Allentown served him well as a rookie with the Knicks in 1968–69. Holzman sent him into games for the so-called *give-one* foul, the intent of which was to limit the opposition to a one-point free throw opportunity and create a mathematical advantage at the other end of the court where New York would have a chance to score two points on a regulation goal. The situation ceased when a team collected six fouls in a quarter; at that juncture every foul automatically was worth two shots.

So Riordan was used to absorb these extraneous fouls, coming into the game long enough to apply a restraining blow to a dribbler and then leave. Teams would plot to avoid the foul—long passes downcourt and a quick shot—but Riordan was aggressive at pursuing the ball, and the vigor with which he did it soon became a sideshow at the Garden. "I guess it seemed funny at first to the people," he said. "After a while they loved it. It was like a Roman Circus, Christians thrown to the lions. Even the guys on the bench would laugh when I came off the court. Red could feel the attitude and he'd say, 'This bother you? You don't feel I'm trying to make an ass of you?' I didn't care what the reaction in the stands was. It was a way to get a little experience."

When Bradley's shift to forward created a need for a backup guard, Riordan got into ball games more regularly and startled the public. "The people were surprised that I could make a jump shot or a decent pass," he said. "One fan said to me, 'Hey, I didn't know you could shoot.' Tell you the truth, I didn't care what people thought."

Seeking increased stature on the team, Riordan worked out all summer, lost ten pounds on the chance that it would make for greater footspeed and, like Russell, anticipated enough playing time to validate the effort. But had there been no prospects at all for them both Riordan and Russell would have put out the same energy. Their demons had that kind of need.

There was one other veteran Knickerbocker in training camp. His name was Dave Stallworth and, at twenty-seven, he had had enough in adversity to rival Job for patience. In older godforsaken Knick days his bobbing locomotion had been one of the few sources of kicks for New York fans. Then, in the 1966–67 season, he had had what doctors diagnosed as a heart attack and his career was said to be finished.

By his own recollection, Stallworth was in the hospital for 34 days, 2 hours and 27 minutes, none of it very painful. The commotion in his chest was, in his memories, more like a peptic ache than a hurt of disabling magnitude. He evoked the image Hemingway once had used for oncoming death, that of a presence crouched lightly over him.

The heart condition, he said, "flabbergasted" him, but he took it gracefully. And when a Knickerbocker teammate, Emmette Bryant, checked into the same hospital for an operation, they were a pair of katzenjammers at secreting wheelchairs and riding about the wards as if it were some kind of weird roller derby the place was running.

There were for Stallworth precedents in pain that helped him through his situation. He said the only time he had cried was at age twelve, when a younger sister died, an experience that left him, in his own words, "an upset young man."

The life in the Oak Cliff section of Dallas, where he was raised, did little to help settle Stallworth. His adolescence was a rough-and-tumble one in which he was alternately the hunter and hunted on the streets of Oak Cliff and the alien turf of South Dallas, crosstown. Trips to South Dallas required guerrilla wit: he recalled parties there where knives flashed and scars were inflicted (Stallworth had one in his lower back) and routine walks that became chases in the night. "I'll say this here," said Stallworth, "it wasn't funny then and it's not funny now, 'cause this was real, you know what I mean. This was strictly for life, because during this time guys thirteen, fourteen, fifteen years old'd carry knives, guns, and they would use these things.

"I've carried a knife, I've carried a gun. But . . . believe this here, I wasn't carrying it to start anything. We might get a gun—twenty-twos you know, twenty-five automatics and this type of thing—we find a lot of these because you see . . . you see some of the older guys they used to carry those guns, and it's a graveyard up on the main part of town, Eighth Street, where the movie house is, and a lot of these guys . . . like the police would come up there a lot and the guys would drop the guns or throw them in the trash cans or throw them in the graveyard and this type of thing. We found a lot of this stuff over there. That's how I came into possession of this gun."

Stallworth carried the gun, he said, as protection for the trips to South Dallas, where his school, James Madison High, was located and where Oak Cliff brethren were viewed with suspicion. One night, leaving Madison, there was trouble.

"We were walking along outside the locker room, along the wall there, because we had to go along the wall to get out to the main street. And this guy Gene Williams was fairly close to the wall where a bullet hit about two feet in front of him. So Gene says, 'Those guys shooting, man.' So we duck, they kept on shooting. I guess there were about four or five of the guys—you know, they were using pistols, they were moving in—so I turned around, and told the guys, 'Man, I'm not running anymore.' And I started firing back, you know. All of a sudden it ceased. Nobody was hit on either side."

The two years he was away from pro ball, Stallworth spent in Wichita, Kansas, where he had been an All-American in basketball at Wichita State University. He worked for the city's park department as a recreation supervisor, often seeking out troubled young blacks he thought he could help. In that time, he brought some dozen or so "out of the dumps," sometimes with unconventional methods. In particular he remembered "this one little cat, Pinky," a six-three, fourteen-year-old who shrank with fear from women, compensated by bullying his peers and apparently had an authority hangup to boot. At lunchbreak one afternoon, he threatened Stallworth. "My philosophy has always been, see, anytime a kid is large enough to swing on me, he's large enough to get his butt kicked.

"Well, I thought the kid was joking, so I said, 'Let's come out in the gym'—the gym is right next to the office. We come out. I had my back turned to this kid and I turned around and I saw this huge fist coming at me. I ducked. I threw my hands up and ducked. 'I'm gonna have to drop this young kid.' So I hit him a couple, three blows and dropped him right quick. He found out I wasn't joking. So I laughed at him, this type thing. This really hurt him. He got to tell me, 'You don't have to be laughing at me, Mr.

Stallworth.' So I said, 'Man, why don't you just shut up and act a man, be a man, crying like a baby, look at you.' 'I'm not crying, I'm not crying.' This type thing. And he was really cracking me up, but I couldn't really break down and cap on him that way. I said, 'Well look here, Pinky, why don't you just be cool, you don't have to go through all this to prove to the fellows that you dig them, to prove to the fellows that you're regular. All the fellows know that you're a regular guy and you're OK people. You're losing more friends than you're gaining going around slapping people upside the head.' He seemed so scared, I told him there's nothing to be afraid of, you'll be just like us. If you can't communicate with each other like men, then all of us need help."

In his recuperative period, Stallworth did not experience any of the postcardiac effects—dizzy spells, fatigue, blackouts—that doctors told him he would, and he began to work out for increasing lengths of time on basketball courts. Eventually, his Wichita physician, Dr. Lillia Rodriguez-Tocker, wondered whether he had had a heart attack at all. (An inflammation of the outer membrane of the heart called pericarditis, doctors claim, can mimic the symptoms of a heart attack.) Examinations in Wichita and later in New York gave him clearance for a return to the pros. In preparation, Stallworth ran up and down the steps of Wichita Stadium University Fieldhouse to burn off a good-times excess of 25 pounds and reach his playing weight of 220 pounds, and on outdoor courts he set up chairs around which he would maneuver and then shoot his jump shot. He did it so often that his shoulders would ache afterward.

There was in training camp a stranger as well, a recreational player whose college days had ended with a banked forty-foot shot in the last second of his last game, a glorious finish to a rather ordinary varsity life. Since then, he had dabbled in the game, in city leagues where players wore headbands to keep hair out of their eyes and ran ragged to keep past childhoods in their minds.

As a prosewriter by profession he was dispatched every so often by sporting journals to locker rooms where basketball professionals made him privy to "inside" confidences. But now at Farmingdale, he was just another guy with a notepad; the casual eyes Knicks laid on him marked him for an outsider. Trying to fathom faces and place was a dizzying personal experience, and when he retired to bed that first night it was with a piercing migraine.

What connection he was to make those early days in camp came through the Knick reserves, fellows whose neglect by chroniclers in the past made each in his own way sensitive to any attentions. Bowman, delivering a punch line, might turn to see if it had gone over with the outsider. Hosket noted with some chagrin his name spelled wrong on a notepad. May spoke of his situation in so wry a manner as to suggest he was referring to somebody else. Later in the season, in that ironic way of his, May would ask the writer, "Do you think I could become more sensitive?"

The outsider's only previous acquaintance among Knicks was with Bradley, whom he had interviewed when he was breaking into the NBA. At the start of that session Bradley had read his mail, mumbled answers and forced his interrogator to ask about cinema and books rather than sport to get his attention. Even then, Bradley answered cautiously lest, it seemed, he be charged with excessses of conceit. Now, seasons later, he responded more directly and in a logical manner, breaking down questions into alphabetical parts.

Drawing answers from Barnett was trickier business. Barnett affected boredom with all subjects save money. The humor suggested by previous written accounts about him was nowhere evident to the stranger. Holzman was as drab and, it turned out, less reliable a source. Certain questions, credibility questions, did not evoke from him answers that corresponded to already known facts. Holzman was tight-lipped and suspicious. One time he asked, "If you saw a guy coming in at four in the morning, you wouldn't write that, would you?"

The associations the stranger had with these Knicks and the rest did not reassure him. For a long while he felt like an intruder in their midst, and no doubt walked about like one. That tippytoe habit earned him a nickname from Barnett that other Knicks picked up on. Barnett called him Sly.

Red Holzman was no Gallatin at bloodletting, but there was considerable business in the two workouts a day. One fine torture was a drill in which players had to fetch a ball rolled upcourt, dribble it the length of the floor to score, and then turn and do it again. The drill was run like revolving doors, players moving to both baskets at once. The tempo of it was enough to discomfort some.

Don May suffered in his legs, which were more accustomed to marching than running. He had won a trophy as soldier-of-the-cycle at Fort Polk, Louisiana, in the summer, but military training filled him more with torpor than patriotic zeal. "When I came out, I was sort of a zombie," he said. "You know how the army does that to you. I spent the short time before training following around my fiancee—to the caterer, the florist, the church. I should have run some, but I didn't. I reported to camp in no shape." A few days into the camp, May pulled a chest muscle. Shortly after, he left to get married.

May's Dayton compatriot, Hosket, had barely recovered from a knee operation when it was time to go to camp. Exercise was a shock to his legs. For others, the dues were psychological. "It's the boringness that gets you," said DeBusschere. "Here we go. Every day the same gym, the same smelly clothes you put on. It's still beautiful weather at the time you're working out, and you know damn well you don't want to be in this gym. You don't feel like it. Basketball is a winter sport and here you are in September and the temperature is eighty degrees and sun shining and everybody is sitting out on the grass and you're going inside, sweating in a stuffy gym."

Holzman's camp was, at least, more sane than Charley Wolf's. It had (unlike the regular season) an 11:00 P.M. curfew but no totalitarian flashlighted enforcements. Under Wolf, players were required to wear jackets to practice. Knickerbocker attire was more casual. Stallworth showed up sometimes in a black Yancey Derringer cowboy hat. Bradley might wear shoes without sox, a sight more remarkable for the fashion of his footwear—the "boxcar look," it was designated by teammates. Even polo shirts were suitable at Farmingdale. And players went to and from practice not on bicycles but in cars.

Holzman had small regard for mickey mouse. The Knick coach was not a fusser, he did not meddle with players beyond the gym. His own life was dedicated to creature comforts, to bottled scotch and good cigars and sirloin, and he brought to the dinner table a homespun soul that offered for edification these precepts:

"A broad-beamed bus driver is a good bus driver."

"Never get your hair cut by a bald-headed barber. He has no respect for your hair."

"Never talk about money with your wife at night."

"Never worry about anything you have no control over."

"Never accidentally raise your hand when the check is coming."

"Never take medical advice from a waiter."

Holzman affected the same casual air about coaching. He would say, "I never thought getting an ulcer made you a more dedicated man. Is a fighter better because he has a cauliflower ear?" Or, "What do you want to talk to me for? I don't do anything special as a coach." His pronouncements rivaled the saints' for self-effacing virtue.

Q: What have you done to help your team's success?
A: Some stuff I have done has evidently appealed to them.
Q: What do you mean, "stuff"?
A: Offensive and defensive stuff.

A Philadelphia writer listened to such blarney and said, "Holzman's as funny as cold oatmeal." Another, columnist Ira Berkow, fantasized in public print the gradual disappearance of Holzman in clouds of his own ineffable modesty. In home quarters, the coach fared better. New York writers made him into a bourgeois hero of mythical proportions for whom a pastrami sandwich was a prerogative. That, surely, was a simplification, for there was method to Holzman's muteness.

Carl Braun, one of several New York coaches for whom Holzman scouted college talent, said, "Red is as dumb as he wants you to think he is. He's dumb like a fox. Red is the type of guy who . . . I always get the feeling looking in Red's eyes that he's right on top of everything but he's not saying anything.

"I don't think Red ever wanted to be a coach. He found a niche as scout. He was going to be there for a long time, and he was a most accurate and adequate scout, did an excellent job for me. He was the type of guy that would stand up to Ned Irish or anybody. I asked him an opinion once which was completely contrary to what I knew Irish thought, but I did it quite honestly because I wanted to see if Red would stand up in front of Ned.

"I wanted Johnny Egan [in the college draft]. Johnny Egan was coming out of Providence. Whitey Martin was coming out of St. Bonaventure. As I remember these were the two names. Well [Vince] Boryla, who was the general manager, and Irish wanted Whitey Martin and they got their way. But I said I think Egan is the better ballplayer, and I asked Red's opinion right at the draft meeting, right in front of Irish, and he stood right up and was counted.

"Here's what's interesting. When I asked him the question he answered it, but it wasn't a case where he was ever going to volunteer. He would have sat there and not said a word, believe me, when we were discussing this. It was like the three of us discussing and Red sitting there. He never said a word, but when I looked over, 'Hey, Red, what do you think?' now you got to answer. Then he stepped right up. He said, 'I think Egan without a doubt.'"

Holzman was like the poker player who kept confidences to himself, tabulated all the news on the table and only paused for chit-chat on his way out the door with the stakes in his pocket. There was never any bluffing him. "My first year in scouting," said Jerry Krause, now with the Chicago Bulls, "I'm going to Oklahoma City and I'm seeing Flynn Robinson from Wyoming against Oklahoma City University, and there's a game at Wichita the same night down the road. I get on a plane after the game and I go into Kansas City. It's four thirty in the morning in Kansas City and here's Red sitting there, and Red looks at me and I look at Red, and Red says, 'Where you been?' I said, 'Down the road,' and he looks at me and he says, 'Son, I want to tell you something. I know where you've been and if you got any brains in your head you know where I've been, so let's cut the bullshit out and let's be friends.'"

Even after he won acclaim as a professional coach, it was scouting, not coaching, that Holzman fancied. "He said something to me," said Krause, "before this season started. We're sitting there talking and I said, I'm itching to get going. He said, 'I bet you are. Nice to get back on the road again, isn't it? You can do what you want and when you want, you're your own boss on the road,' and I think he really likes that."

Holzman's thoroughness as a coach was said to derive from his scouting. "Red never scouted from the motel," said Krause. "See, you go into a town, what do you do? Let's say you get there early in the morning. Got a game that night. A lot of times, if you're smart, you go out to the college and you say to the coach, 'Look, if you got a room with a projector and some of your game film . . .' You sit there and you watch for five or six hours, you're not in the motel sitting on your ass. You're out working and you're getting a little extra than the other scouts in the league. You're stealing a little. That's the way Red was. Our coach at Chicago, Dick Motta —used to coach at Weber State College—he said Red was the only scout to come to a practice. Red would go see a guy and if he'd like him, he'd keep going back. He wanted to see him in as many different situations as he could.

"He was exact. He always made sure on a kid's height. He'd stand close to him. Like the other night in New York I stood next to this kid from Niagara, Cal Murphy. I wanted to make sure. Murphy don't know who I am. But I wanted to know who he was, understand what I mean? I got that from Red.

"This was how meticulous he was. We're up in the air and we're going someplace and we got to get there a certain time and it becomes apparent we can't land. Red hauls the little airline book out—the little book with all the schedules—gets all the alternate schedules out and he asks the stewardess. He said, 'Will you please check on these flights for me?' He was all prepared to get us to this other place because he was the only scout in the game who had the airline book with him. He never made a show of all this, he just did the job."

Holzman's practices bore his mark. There was nothing of ball-handling arabesques or flashy doo-dah. Function rather than aesthetics concerned him. If football camps had banshee fevers,

Holzman's had instead the working calm of Degas' practice rooms.

Morning practices, Knicks went up the court in successive waves, handling the ball, passing it and then retreating against passes thrown the length of the court. Holzman stood on the sidelines, in windbreaker, bermudas, white sox and black ripple-sole shoes, hands in pockets, a trim freckled man with thinning hair who shouted, over and over, SEE THE BALL, CLYDE. SEE THE BALL, DAVE. SEE THE BALL, NATE. SEE THE BALL, BRADLEY. SEE IT. SEE IT.

The idea was for one of the backpedaling New Yorkers to intercept or deflect the ball before it got through to its imagined receiver. More than that, it was intended to create a reflex that would turn players into defenders the instant a score was made, and reverse a natural inclination to relax at the transitional moment.

Holzman's chief scout and predecessor as coach, Dick McGuire, or the team's director of public relations, Frank Blauschild, would take the ball as it came through the basket and lob these long passes in the other direction and the Knicks would go chasing after them. All the while, Holzman played the querulous maestro: SEE THE BALL, CLYDE. SEE THE BALL, DAVE. SEE THE BALL . . . SEE THE BALL DAMMIT. SEE IT. SEE IT.

Holzman was crazy for his defense. He had been raised in a basketball era when the game was played closer to the ground and was full of ball handling and subtle motions—men feinted and moved their defenders and eyed for collaborators, the court was laid with foxy ruses, it was a game that taxed a defender's wits. The game changed with the advent of the jump shot, which allowed the player to spring into the air and shoot from elevated vantage rather than with his feet planted on the ground. Suddenly, rather than delicate conspiratorial patterns and nurtured moments of freedom in which shooters lofted precise arcing set shots or, if trickery accomplished it, uncontested lay-ins at close range, there were all these free-form solos anywhere on the court.

Some claimed the game had a lobotomy, others that it simply became more visceral; in any case, it was the difference between the minuet and the boogaloo.

As basketball accelerated, players went to the basket with more and more expertise. They could twist and turn in air like goosed sorcerers, and when access to such maneuvers was blocked, the jump shot bailed them out. All this made a defensive man's lot more difficult. What happened was that defense became a virtue honored only in the abstract; on professional floors *laissez faire* was the policy, scoring totals got higher and higher, and by 1955–56 teams averaged 99 points per game, or 31.3 more than in 1946–47, the league's first season.

Then a bearded black with the elongated tensile body of an El Greco figure came into the league to play with the Boston Celtics, and the skill with which this 6-10 man, Bill Russell, could swat away shots helped his team win eleven championships in thirteen years. The Celtic defense was a unique creature, relying for its effectiveness on Russell's faculty for nullifying its mistakes. He allowed teammates to make gambles on defense they would not have dared without him. The resultant defensive swarm did not give the free-form specialists the leisure needed for success.

In a way, then, the game turned back to its origins. Basketball people saw that the confusion a defense created could defuse the shooters, and special pains were taken to get personnel who could pressure a ball handler. To cope, some teams resorted to smaller and quicker forwards; men who stood 6-5, 6-6 replaced those 6-8, 6-9 in the corners of the floor.

Not all clubs reverted. But Holzman's did—most notably with defense. Red sought to impose chaos on the foe, to panic every dribbler, and to do this without an ultimate nullifier like Bill Russell but rather with an organism whose amoebic knack for reassembling would self-correct. Congregate awareness replaced the freak of genius.

Such a defense needed to be expertly tuned by a head coach. And so Holzman promoted collective attention at every juncture, in drills whose purpose was to get players to refocus the instant a score was made, or in the controlled circumstances that would follow such a drill, competitive two-on-two, three-on-three, or red-and blue-shirted fives.

SEE THE BALL! SEE THE BALL!—jackhammer words to drive Knick defenders from their own petty defensive concern into a more communal fix. New Yorkers had to know where the ball was, had to see it, see it, so that when Frazier made one of his darting thrusts for the ball, and forced his foe to lurch like a man caught in wind, each of his teammates moved to that station on the floor that would make Clyde's move pay off. Barnett would come peeling in from behind the man to frisk the ball, he and Frazier working like a pair of classy muggers, and the rest of the defense rotated so that when the panicked man sought to be freed of the onus of incompetence and threw the ball to places where his conditioned tubes told him his people would be, Bradley or DeBusschere or Reed was there instead to steal the ball. And it would all happen because each man had seen the ball.

Other teams shared neither New York's methods nor purpose on defense. They engaged an offense like partners in a robust polka and went round and round, energetic and together and without embellishment. The concern of individual defenders on these clubs was to stay the number, no more, no less. Many did it with great vigor, but gave not a hoot for the next guy. There was no overall tactical intent here.

Defense was charlady's drudgery, the flash was in the shot. It took some doing to turn the gratification totem around; Holzman's plaint was a means by which he could make it happen, dunderheads would get no comfort from him, he exposed them, SEE THE BALL DAMMIT! SEE IT! SEE IT! At the more egregious oversights his lips would curl at the corners and his teeth would show: GET YOUR ASS BACK ON DEFENSE! PICK UP, DAMMIT. NOBODY GETS AN OPEN SHOT!

Knick defenders did not swing to their places like automatons. There was a network of communication, voices, the gargling basso of Russell, the foggy reverberations of Barnett, Frazier's sugary drawl, DeBusschere's folksy midwest tones, Bradley's gruff reminders. There were constant telegrams being sent out. GOT MINE, I GOT YOURS; STAY, STAY, YOU'RE ALL RIGHT;

BALL, GET THE BALL. Frazier would be working in the open
floor against the dribbler and might speculate on the treacheries
shaping behind him. WHICH WAY? TALK TO ME, he'd say.
And DeBusschere would see that there was nothing there and
he'd say, YOU'RE ALL BY YOUR LONESOME, CLYDE. And
Frazier would know he could work his man without fear of being
run into another man, a screen it was called.

Morning sessions lasted an hour and a half, two hours, most of
it on the defense. Offense at Farmingdale was a breather, the
Knicks would go through their patterned plays, calling them by
names like "trap" or "Barry" or "D" or "33," each player timing his
move to make combined prefigurations from which a particular
man would emerge for the clear shot. When it did not happen, the
team did not become grounded; there were options for stalled
situations off each play.

Other times, Holzman would break the club into four groups
for shootouts, two units at each basket competing in jump-shot
marksmanship. These were occasions for some levity; the border-
lines from which shots were launched might be transgressed, a
peccadillo viewed with outrage by all. CHUMPS! was the standard term of derision. LOOKIT THESE CHUMPS! And as each
competition drew to its close the voodoo chants and obscuring
stunts increased. MISS IT, CHUMP. Holzman would smile and,
with mock severity, warn them not to quibble. When deceptions
became excessive, Bowman was apt to step forward, like an indig-
nant statesman, and say to his coach: "Red, lookit this shit." Once,
when Nate's team won its contest, he glanced to the other end,
where the shooting was still going on, and snidely remarked, "Flip
a coin, Red, so we can get on with practice." It was like Kate
Smith criticizing Mae West for being a few pounds over.

There were scrimmages in the evening. In most training camps
these were occasions on which rookies made smoke and won jobs.
There was, however, scant chance of that happening with the
Knicks. Eleven veterans had signed contracts, and were secure in
their jobs. Even 'bag men Hosket and May had no-cut multiyear
contracts. The twelfth and final spot on the roster was said to
belong to John Warren, a local boy (Far Rockaway High School,
St. John's University) who had also signed a multiyear contract. It

would take a performance on the magnitude of Biblical miracles
for any other rookie to make the breakthrough.

Unlike football training camps where rookies were hazed or
even had their heads shaved, there was a roaring indifference to
them at the Knicks' training grounds. "I'll be honest with you, said
DeBusschere, a seven-year veteran, "I don't know their names, I
don't know they're there. Why become attached to somebody
when you have a good idea they're not going to be around?"

Frazier knew their names. "I remember when I was a rookie,"
he said. "If a guy called my name—God! he knows me—this makes
you feel good. So I do the same thing for other rookies. You know,
I couldn't just go around and play like I don't know a guy."

Of the rookies, Milt Williams of Lincoln University in Jefferson
City, Missouri, was showing the most. His flair for driving past his
man made defenses swing to him, leaving men free for the shot.
Consistently Williams was able to penetrate the defense and then
pass the ball to the open man, a habit a team with as many accurate shooters as the Knicks had could find useful. In the summer,
Williams had worked as a community organizer for the Beacon
Neighborhood House in Chicago. Each morning at six, before
going on the job, he would throw on a sweat suit and run laps in
the Gladstone playground near his residence. The press
designated Williams the dark horse of the camp, and fans like
Asofsky back home envisioned Farmingdale as a battleground.

The only resemblance the camp did bear to combat was the
effect it had on rookies; they had the shakes that recruits do in
war. Even John Warren, known as "The Iceman" in college for his
composure in heated situations, was unnerved in the pros. He
confessed, "I'm playing scared. I'm nervous, I'm not at ease. I go
to practice and tell myself, 'Be cool.' I keep telling myself I'm
pretty good. I've mentioned it to other players that I was scared.
They told me, 'Don't worry, everything will come.' " It did not
come right away for Warren. In practices, his eyes showed uncer-
tainty, and if he made a mistake, he would stare at the floor and
shake his head.

For the veterans, the problem was acclimation of another sort.
There was boredom at Farmingdale, practices did not vary, and
there was a holding game in reputations. The camp was bloodless,

there was never sufficient moment for warm leisures. The Knicks away from the court either conceded satisfactions and slept, or pursued them like soldiers on a weekend crash, storing in those interludes whatever was sweet to their needs in whatever manner possible, a hotbox existence that allowed a motel maid endearingly known as The Fireplug to win considerable acclaim in the camp. Her short-order exploits were recounted with comic genius by Knickerbockers who had access to her, a group whose exclusiveness was limited only by desire. "They were killing the maids around there," said Frazier.

A celebrated case of the social tactics employed at Farmingdale was that of Cazzie Russell. Just prior to a squad cut, Russell happened to meet a co-ed friend of rookie Ken Moorehead's. When he suggested a date to her and she mulled it, Cazzie did not hesitate to remind her that he would be at Farmingdale the next week and Moorehead would be gone the following day, a forecast that proved both accurate and persuasive. Russell's approach became locker room lore the rest of the season; this piece of con was to be recalled whenever he and teammates bid for ladies' attentions, the line directed to Cazzie, in mock warning, being, "Look here, Cazzie, I'm no Ken Moorehead."

Russell got his just deserts when attention was drawn to his sleek Continental, a vehicle whose portals were protected by a burglar alarm. "I ran over to his room," Bowman said, "and I said, 'Man, somebody threw a brick through your . . . through your car window.' And he said, 'What? Man, you're kidding.' And like he was almost crying, y'know. So he jumped right out of bed and slipped on a pair of pants, and it was cold, man, and he didn't have no shoes, or no shirt or nothing, and run downstairs. . . . Oh, man. And . . . uh . . . and the window wasn't broke, I was just kidding, but I really shook him up. . . . He wasn't really angry. . . . He thought I had set the alarm off, but I didn't. I don't know who did."

All this became, in time, the stuff of Dick Barnett's dinnertime narrations. In his monotone Remus voice, he could remark on anything from an ill-fitting mackintosh of DeBusschere's ("London Fog? That sucker cover all of London") to the fickle regard

Reed had had for a lady ("Back in New York you act like you don't know her; out here like she was Hedy Lee-mar or something"), more often than not harking back to the mild cruelties Knickerbockers visited on each other.

The pro game itself was not run on philanthropic principles; a reminder of that at Farmingdale was 6-foot 8-inch Phil Jackson, who came to camp in a back brace, just to have a look. Healthy, Jackson was a Knick forward whose anatomically odd shoulders—they were perpendicular to the rest of his torso, without even the faintest slope—had given him to be called "Coathangers" and "Head 'n' Shoulders." His specialty was defensive pressure. When his long arms began turning like windmills and he came at a dribbler in his awkward way, he was apt to deflect or intercept a basketball.

But Jackson had been in the back brace since last season and would not remove it until November. The brace was necessary for the complications that set in after he had suffered a leg injury that management, in its competitive lust, compounded.

The leg injury had caused Jackson to favor his other leg to the disadvantage of his back. The ache there increased when one night he came down from a jump shot and landed heavily on his heels. He herniated two discs in his vertebrae, a condition so painful he didn't sleep for two nights. Jackson went into traction, and was given muscle-relaxing shots. The shots diminished muscle tone; his right leg was an inch to an inch and a half smaller in diameter when he left the hospital, and he even lost the power to rise on his toes.

"At San Diego, before I went into traction, the doctor there suggested I have an operation," he recollected. "I have a feeling the Knicks wanted me to try to play on it. They wanted me around just in case, particularly after Cazzie broke his ankle. If I had had the operation, I probably could have come back this year. I understand management's view, but from my point of view it's different. The whole thing was typical of professional athletics and I accept it."

Jackson's summer was spent, then, recovering from the operation he had had late in April. "I wasn't able to lift things," he said.

"I couldn't drive or have sex for six months. I talked to [hockey player] Rod Gilbert about the sex. He'd had the same kind of operation. He said you could cheat, but you had to be careful.

"I ended up going back to the University of North Dakota, where I took a reading course in counseling-guidance. Part of the course was group therapy, three times a week. You'd sit in an easy chair, an hour and a half. Regular therapy goes deeper, but it was very good for me anyhow. It gave me more a mirror of what my personality is like. You know Cooley's looking glass theory; we have an idea how we appear that's not always consistent with how we do appear. For example, I'm verbally quite aggressive, not loud but assertive; some people might be frightened. In past years, I was an active being, now I was completely inactive. I had a lot of aggression pent up. Therapy did a lot for getting rid of anxieties built up."

The Knicks got rid of any strangeness that Jackson and Stallworth might have felt about their medical problems. When Stallworth arrived in training camp, Bowman looked at him and asked, "You got tape over your heart?" For Jackson, the players wondered aloud whether he had gotten a chastity belt for his wife. "Got her chained to the bed," Jackson told them.

Jackson and Stallworth got no special attention from Holzman in briefings or homilies. It did not surprise them. Personalized touches were not in Holzman's style; for him business was business. In fact, when Jackson showed up late for the second practice of the camp, Red came up to him and said, "If you're gonna be part of this, be here on time."

Jackson, who had come only to see what the Knicks were planning for the new season, nodded and said, "Yes, sir."

He stayed a few days, and then left.

For casualties like Jackson, the Knickerbockers had in their employ a sharp-witted Irishman, Daniel J. Whelan, the team trainer. He had not started out to be a trainer; he had been a baseball prospect good enough to be sent to St. Mary's College for infield education by the Boston Red Sox. Then came World War II and Whelan ended up stateside in charge of a naval special services program.

Returning to civilian life, Whelan found it was too late to be a baseball player. Having worked as a clubhouse boy with the Pacific Coast League San Francisco Seals before the war, he was able to persuade the Seals' president to make him assistant to the team trainer. Whelan became the Knick trainer in 1967–68, charged with attending the minor aches and pains of the players, a job he undertook with enough flourish to be called Big Time Danny Whelan. It was an apt name for him. A Knick rookie might walk into the locker room for his first time, see seven players taping themselves and Danny sitting in the middle of the locker room on a folding chair with his hands clasped behind his neck and a cigar in his mouth. And there would never after be any question whether or not Whelan was Big Time.

Whelan's grandiose manner was a pose that enlivened the locker room and kept the players loose. He relished the give and take of locker room repartee, and could snap off a line in a side-of-the-mouth Leo Gorcey voice that humbled the saltiest of wise guys. And if he did not have the medical knowhow of Albert Schweitzer, that too was part of his charm. "There was one time I had an injury," recalled a player, "and the doctor told Danny the only thing I could do to try to keep the strength in the leg was to work on my quadriceps and he named a few other muscles and Danny nodded in agreement that he would get me on those exercises right away. And then the doctor left the room and Danny went over to the chart and was looking up on the anatomy of the human body all the muscles he had just named. He had no idea what doc was talking about."

In his own workaday sphere, where no latinate musculature confounded a man, Whelan had a practical knack at keeping athletes together. He fished up his magics from a large black satchel he carried. When he talked about the contents of that bag, he sounded like a street-corner pitchman. "We have right here," he said, "salt tablets, aspirins, murine for the eyes, cold tablets, baby powder, Vaseline, Heet—it's liquid heat, gives you instant heat, a guy like Frazier uses it on his big toe because it's a little arthritic and this here steams him up. Also some pain-killers if someone is in excruciating pain. It's a Darvon compound that the doctor prescribes and he gives it to me and tells me who to give it to and how much to give. And what else . . . there's a tabasco sauce, that's for me. A lot of times when you're on the road and you have room service, it's surprising some hotels, motels don't have tabasco sauce and that drives me crazy because I like tabasco sauce on my eggs. So I carry it along just in case."

Whelan ministered to Knick morale in another way. When the team finally went on the road for preseason exhibition games—the veterans and rookie survivors John Warren and Milt Williams—it was the trainer whose tales helped revive the sense of continuity in Knickerbocker professional lives.

Occasionally the players would goad him to tell a particular tale, calling out names the way nightclub patrons do when a band asks for requests. On a bus speeding through small-town Michigan night, the sentiment was strong for one called Jack Downey. Bowman poked Stallworth in the ribs and grinned anticipating it, and Stallworth moved to the front of the bus for a listen.

"Jack Downey," Whelan said, "was the trainer for the Sacramento Solons baseball team in the Pacific Coast League, and he was an old-time fighter who'd fought a draw against Jack Dempsey in a three-, four-round exhibition. Naturally, Jack Dempsey being the champion of the world and a fellow like him standing on his feet for four rounds and they calling it a draw, it was like a victory for Jack Downey. Anyhow, in those days the trainers were all rough and they weren't educated. Their main source of taking care of any athletes was a bottle of iodine and a roll of tape and maybe a couple of gauze bandages and that'd be about it.

"Now Jack was very proud of his medical bag. It was a doctor's bag, yeah, a satchel, and in those days it was a funny thing, any time an injury came about they would run out on the field with this medical bag. Well if a person had a severe cut or if a person had something else, you couldn't work with them on the field, because his leg would be dirty and you'd have to wash it and such. And so there was really no purpose of running out there with a bag, you can't do anything out there with a bag no matter.

A doctor would have to bring him in to the hospital to clean him and to do all the work on him he was to do no matter what happened. But anyway that was their trait at that time. So this day here they emptied out Jack's bag while Jack wasn't looking and the game was to start. The players did this and around the third inning someone slid into second base and laid there for a while, was spiked. And all of a sudden Jack grabbed his bag and ran out on the field. Now he was gonna dress this cut right out on the field, and he opened up his bag and there it was, there was a ham and cheese sandwich in the bag and nothing else."

The exhibition itinerary was like that of a second-rate carnival —Saginaw, Grand Rapids, Paterson, Trenton, Bethlehem, Bangor, Utica. The pros went to the sticks in preseason, to draggy byways in which there had been franchises early after World War II when the league was formed. In those times there were the Waterloo Hawks, Sheboygan Redskins, Anderson Packers; the league had the raunch and steam of the midway then and for some time after. Games were played in smoky arenas whose cramped quarters allowed fans the proximity to become *engagé.* Syracuse was, in the 1950s, known to the Knicks as The Zoo; the crowd at the Fairgrounds there sat close enough to hold the player's trunks or flick out cigarettes against their legs, or rattle the guidewires that were attached to the backboards when a New Yorker was at the foul line. Some could remember a woman who used a hatpin on visiting players. Referees fared no better. "We had a fan," recalled Dolph Schayes, a former star at Syracuse, "a big three-hundred-pound fellow who one time grabbed the referee by the throat. The policemen came, but the fan left a few marks on the ref's throat and the ref didn't want to come out in the second half. But they prevailed upon him to do so." Carl Braun, the Knicks best scorer those years, recalled, "I saw a guy one night come out and give one of the refs a kick right in the behind, right on the court. They probably walked the guy under the stands and gave him a free beer, the way things went in Syracuse."

Syracuse fans were not the only notorious ones. The gallery at Philadelphia's Convention Hall in the 1950s was so injudicious with its remarks that the Knicks plotted a way to get even. "These

were all bettors," remembered Braun, "and they could be pretty
raw because they had their ten dollars on the game or something.
They all sat together, they were very vocal. I mean it was concen-
trated, twenty, thirty voices. And what we'd do, if I had the ball
and if someone was really being—I don't mean someone just saying, 'You bum,' but someone might be referring to your wife, I
mean these guys get pretty low—if we had the game locked up, or
where it didn't make any difference near the end, we'd send one
of our guys cutting right down the court in front of this guy. I was
an ex-baseball pitcher, I could throw that ball real hard, and I
want to tell you, it could break your nose or do a lot of things to
you if it hit you square. I got one guy on the top of the head one
night—if I hit him in the face, I would have hurt him, so it was
probably just as well I didn't—but I want to tell you it stunned
him. That ball went up about forty rows. But they weren't sure
that it was intentional. It looked like our guy was actually trying
to catch it."

Makeshift circumstances prevailed in the league then. The first
Baltimore franchise played in an arena where the showers backed
up so that the last man in would have six inches to a foot of dirty
water to tread through. The Chicago Stags played in a building
where the dressing rooms were separated from the floor by a parking area, and players would traipse through carbon monoxide
fumes and onto the floor. Barnett could recall from his early days
that heaters were placed over teams' benches whenever there
were games in Providence, the arena there having been built for
hockey. In Rochester, there were two doors behind one basket
that led to an alley. One night a Knick named Goebel Ritter drove
in for a layup, ran into the iron bar which depressed the doors
outward, and finished his shot in a snow bank.

To keep teams solvent in those strange times, an owner resorted
to rigid budgetary measures. Teams were known to use warmup
balls until they resembled pumpernickels, or to deny visiting
teams a bar of soap. The owner of one franchise, Ben Kerner, one
year sent a Christmas card to a sportswriter friend that another
owner had sent him, and attached a shoestring in way of explana-
tion. Flimflam carried over to the court: New Yorkers swore that
the Minneapolis Lakers played funny with their own baskets so

that they were the official 10 feet off the floor at the front rim and
9 feet 11 inches at the rear, a kind of artificial cup for the hook
shots the Lakers' star pivotman, George Mikan, liked to bank off
the board. It was an era of pennypinching and gross inadequacies
and nobody knew it better than Knickerbocker president Ned
Irish. He refused to put such teams as the Tri-City Hawks and
Sheboygan Redskins on the Garden marquee; on those nights it
simply read, PROFESSIONAL BASKETBALL HERE TO-
NIGHT.

The Knicks' exhibition season, then, was a gypsy tour through
the heartlands, rearview mirror of the game's shabby nights
long ago. There was the feeling of caravan life rolling in and
out of these nowhere places—cheeseburger hotel motel deserted
neon night streets sadness stasis. Sweat and dribbleball were
trotted out for the customers and then stashed away for the
next town. Whatever kicks there were were self-contained, as with
a tightknit jazz group among strangers. The players insulated
themselves in Holiday Inn T.V. of cowboy 'n' Carson. Or in
printed matter: Reed read *Deer Hunter's Guide* and *How to
Raise Money for Your Small Business;* DeBusschere *Psychocyber-
netics;* Milt Williams *Harlem Underground.* Or in quick eats or
treats: Riordan was the king of counter gourmets, and was said to
lack the patience for a sitdown meal; Hosket played IQ on an
airport juke (Q: What author's play was responsible for *My Fair
Lady* . . . Choices: G. B. Shaw   Pinter   Albee   Miller). And
everywhere there was a sense of waiting. THESE GAMES ARE
BOOOLSHIT, Barnett said to Frazier, and Clyde back to him, I
WANNA PLAY FOR REEE-UL.

The dressing quarters became waiting rooms in time. On some
of their walls were posted slogans that were intended to inspire.
In Bethlehem it was a high school football locker room, cement
floor, tackling dummies in the corners, and these:

BLUFF CANNOT TAKE THE PLACE OF ABILITY.
MAKE GOOD OR MAKE ROOM.
THE BIGGER A MAN'S HEAD GETS, THE EASIER IT IS TO
   FILL HIS SHOES.
100%ERS ONLY.

CONDITIONING MEANS STAMINA. STAMINA DEMANDS
TRAINING. TRAINING SPELLS SACRIFICE. SACRIFICE
IS THE HIGHWAY TO DESIRE. IF YOU ARE TRAVEL-
ING ANOTHER ROAD, WE DON'T WANT YOU AROUND
THIS FALL.

Such hoo-hah had no visible effect on the Knicks. The games
were not for reee-ul, adrenal tricks were superfluous. Bradley sat
isolated between rows of lockers reading Adam Smith's *The
Money Game*, Frazier worked a big push comb through his hair at
a mirror, Whelan ambled down a hallway in boxcar shoes, floral
BVDs and an orange Knick warm-up shirt, and voices took on
falsetto pitch in reenactment of great love scenes. Holzman did
not mind the jive. There would be time, time to prepare a face to
meet the faces; the coach considered nonsense functional. Even
outside the dressing room it could be a great distancing dance, a
way to encounter the cosmos on Knickerbocker terms, to retreat
from moms 'n' dads, the well-meaning strangers.

In a Saginaw take-out restaurant:

DAD: Did you guys play tonight?
(Silence.)
BOWMAN (to Reed): How big are you, man?
REED (squaring away like John Wayne): I'm as big as they make
'em in Texas, man. . . . You guys beat the Knicks?
BOWMAN: Uh-huh.
REED: Hey, you Walt Bellamy?
BOWMAN: No, I'm Bill Bradley.

In an airport:

MOM: Are you the Harlem Globetrotters?
REED: No.
MOM: Oh, I thought you might be. You're so big and . . .
REED: These are the Knickerbockers.
MOM: Oh, I thought you were the Globetrotters.
REED: No, not us, but he is (points to DeBusschere).

The Knickerbockers did not court anonymity. Wherever they went they were a road-show spectacle. A veteran like Barnett could cope, he chilled people's smiles with a click of the eyeball. He did not so much avert as pervert their recognition. Where other Knickerbockers might turn away self-consciously, Barnett did not. He hit them direct with the optic freeze that Sonny Liston popularized, a street-corner look whose significance was STAY OFF ME WITH YOUR BOOLSHIT. What moves the man had collected in his career. Others lacked his mastery of the sullen, or his Garboesque regard for privacy, particularly the team's big men—their bodies gave them an aspect of lovable freakishness.

The Reeds, Bowmans, Hoskets and Phil Jacksons had ways to cope, perhaps not so distancing a dance as Barnett's, but big men had means. The classic was that of the celebrated seven-footer who when asked the musical question "How's the weather up there?" spat on his interrogator and said, "It's raining."

Ask Bowman that question and he'd say, "You look like a monkey, climb up here and see."

Speculate whether Reed was a ballplayer, the Cap'n would say, "No, I'm a jockey. I ride elephants."

And let a stewardess wonder how tall Jackson or Bowman was, and either would retaliate by asking for the duration of the trip, "What size is the cup in your bra?"

"People never kid a short guy or a fat guy," said Hosket. "They never say, 'Boy, that guy is short' or 'That guy is fat,' but they feel like any tall guy they can come up and talk to, like anytime. It seems when you're in a confined area such as an elevator or standing in line for movie tickets or something like this, some jerk will come up and say, 'Put your arm out, shorty.' He'd want to walk underneath it. It just gets to you after a while."

"A lot of people," said Bowman, "look at a tall guy and say . . . I mean, like a little short guy or something, like a lot of times I can be just standin' around or something, and a little short guy, say five-seven or five-eight, will walk up to me . . . 'What you looking at, you big . . .' Y'know, I mean, little guys just react to big guys in a odd way, y'know because, uh, I guess because they're not big. A lot of guys just walk up to you and say things to get you to . . . to fight 'em or somethin'. Man, I don't know what'll be on their mind, but I'm not gonna just jump up and just sock every guy that just run up and look at me funny y'know . . . 'd be crazy."

Men of Bowman's size were used to problems. Jackson's adolescent hormones made him black out from time to time. Hosket was unable to fathom the logic that allowed others to beat on him with immunity and did not permit him to retaliate; the boundaries of boyhood bullyism were, for him, confining. And nobody had heard the remarks longer than Reed had: as a ninth-grader in Bernice, Louisiana, he was 6 feet 5 inches tall. There were logistical problems as well. Big men found that props did not always accommodate: beds, restaurant counters, headrests, automobiles. Jackson was forever bumping into pneumatic doorstops. It was nothing new to them.

"As a kid," said Bowman, "I couldn't dress the way I would have liked to dress. A lot of my pants, they didn't fit me the way I wanted them to fit. Y'know, they'd be too short or something like that. I remember one time, um, a guy used to tell me, used to say, y'know, 'You should put sugar in your cuffs to talk your pants down to your ankles . . . to sweet talk 'em, to sweet talk your pants down to your ankles.' Another thing, down in [Fort Worth] Texas, y'know, we used to have gang fights, stuff like this. We could be running through backyards or anything man, I'd get my neck caught on the clothesline, man, it'd really hurt."

The preseason odyssey was calm, but there was a blurred quality to it, as if the mind's eye did an artsy time and motion speedup, not out of aesthetic concern but as a favor. The trip was, after all, a succession of amateur nights. The Knicks' presence in these places was surreal, the way a tuxedoed patron's at an all-night diner is. There was a sense of mismatch

to

these

places

TRENTON
    Civic Center TAKE STOCK IN AMERICA BUY US SAVINGS BONDS AND FREEDOM SHARES *Kiwanians in their fraternal*

*headwear that resemble short-order cooks' hats The Hamilton
Jewelers ("Serving Delaware Valley Since 1912") offer a dollar a
point to Ki-wanis Charitable Fund Trenton*

　*is Bradley Country WHEN WE PASSED PRINCETON in-
tones Reed YOUR HEART MUST HAVE blah blah blah IS
THAT RIGHT, BILL? . . . BILL, BILL, WHERE'S BRAD-
LEY strangers busting into locker at half time Holzman dealing in
strategy and these guys WHERE'S BRADLEY GOTTA TALK
TO and Bradley who doesn't know them quite naturally embarrassed as hell*

　*it's HOT Whelan has salt tablets on the bench DeBusschere
wrings shirt out at the half only Cunningham of opposition Philadelphia doesn't run dry spits in the eye of rookie official Jerry
Loeber and draws a technical*

　Knicks win and have bag lunches on the bus afterward.

PATERSON

　*The place is called John F. Kennedy High School a prelim
game team SOUL BROTHERS dark when fuses blow then Whelan gets the night's supply of towels trouble is they're dish towels
wouldn't dry Reed's hands*

　*hah Phil Foster in the Knick entourage the comedian tells of
nightclub date Chicago and going on radio and knocking the Cub
Bleacher Bums the next night they picket his show and Foster
pickets back his sign reads THEY'RE FULL OF SHIT Windy
City paparazzi ask him to turn it around good feature but gotta
keep it*

　*lean make the corned beef lean Foster and writers before game
in Knicks locker eating deli when in comes Holzman and spies the
publicity man of the Detroit Pistons George Maskin WHAT THE
HELL ARE YOU DOING HERE?/WE DON'T HAVE A JEW-
ISH COACH HE DOESN'T UNDERSTAND CORNED BEEF
Holzman*

　*fuse fixed but mike turns staticky Detroit's van Breda Kolff who
coached Bradley at Princeton SHUT THAT MIKE van Breda
Kolff has a passion for the running soliloquy most of which dedicated to the referees keeps bounding off the bench getting cuffs of
pants stuck on tops of wool sox aspect of knickered chap aloud*

*FRAZIER'S BACK IN THE GAME I JUST READ IT IN THE
NEW YORK PAPERS HE NEVER DOES ANYTHING
WRONG . . . HOW MANY FOULS ON WILLIS. NONE?
TIME OUT. I NEED A MINUTE'S REST*
  Knicks win.
  Q: Which way to Bethlehem?
  A: Follow the star.

BETHLEHEM
  Pictures of old football teams on locker room wall court lighted
by 36 mercury 1000-watt bulbs like sunlamp the players have a
ghostly look as dancers do in the silvery stop and go glare of dis-
cotheque strobes
  a maintenance man tells writer Leonard Lewin of New York
Post SUPERSCOOP in training camp Lewin had own locker with
SUPERSCOOP magic-markered on tape anyhow tells Lewin get
rid of cigar and when he tries to argue it the guy says he doesn't
care where you people are from a case of geographical inferiority
complex
  van Breda Kolff suffers similar affliction is convinced that
officials favor the team from Gotham the sight of Reed sets him
grumbling WILLIS REED, MMMMM again he's on and off the
bench no wool sox tonight one time the officials miss a foul a
violent smacking foul heard throughout the gym van Breda Kolff
turns to crowd and asks DID YOU ALL HEAR IT?/ YEAH/
OKAY
  another consolation: Detroit wins
  later at airport Blauschild asks Barnett DO YOU WEAR A
HENWAY WITH AN ASCOT?/ WHAT'S A HENWAY?/ A
HEN WEIGHS FIVE SIX POUNDS.

BANGOR
  The game is being promoted by a Boston Celtic player name of
Don Nelson has been doing it for a few years and earning
sufficient money to continue
  he Bradley a Celtic named Henry Finkel and Boston's coach
Tom Heinsohn go over to TV studios in the afternoon to promote
game Nelson warning Bradley on the way not to use long words
says THESE PEOPLE ARE FROM BANGOR

Heinsohn talks about the time he was a sports announcer
THERE WAS THIS GIRL SHE RODE HYDROPLANES
QUITE A PRETTY GIRL WE WENT OVER THE INTER-
VIEW BEFOREHAND SHE WAS TERRIFIC THEN GET ON
THE AIR AND SHE FREEZES I'M IN A LITTLE PANIC
TRYING TO FIGURE HOW TO PROLONG THE INTER-
VIEW TO FILL THE SPOT SO I'M ASKING QUESTIONS
AND WHILE SHE ANSWERS I'M LOOKING OVER THE
OTHERS FIGURING WHICH ONE MIGHT DRAW HER
OUT ALL OF A SUDDEN I REALIZE IT'S SILENT AND
SHE'S JUST ANSWERED THE LAST QUESTION I ASKED
SO I SMILE AND SAY THAT'S NICE JESUS THEN I SEE
THE EXPRESSION ON HER FACE AND REALIZE I ASKED
HER ABOUT THE TIMES SHE'S BEEN HURT AND SHE'S
RUN DOWN HER ACCIDENTS AND BROKEN BONES FOR
ME SO I SAY "WHAT I MEAN IS THAT IT'S NICE YOU'RE
STILL IN ONE PIECE AND WHAT A LOVELY PIECE THAT
IS"

*meanwhile in the studio the announcer asks Bradley whether
Knicks will be up there again Bradley ponders the whereabouts of
"there" says if means in the thick of the fight then he presumes
that etc. etc. then big Finkel a seven-footer is asked what's it like
to play for the team's new coach he says it's a great experience
and off camera Heinsohn nods and smiles*

*as for the game the Knicks win and on the return to motel Bar-
nett is heard to say not too many brothers at the game they probably got one in the whole state and he's working the kitchen back
at the motel.*

So on, so forth.

There were 10 preseason games in all. The Knicks won 6, lost 4.
The results were of no account to Holzman. Training period gave
him a chance to experiment with his personnel, and if he did not
tinker to the extent he had the previous year, he had his reasons.
Holzman was priming the team for a fast start and he wanted the
players on whom he would rely to be ready.

Like Stallworth. Dave the Rave, as he was called, was prosper-
ing. He had a problem with making his dribble do elusive work

when he was crowded by a defender, but in those moments there was frenzy on the court, then Stallworth could do wonders. He would come bobbing up the floor, his madonna medal flying up from beneath his jersey, and move into the open lanes, where with airborne turns of the body he would ease by defenders and, unimpeded, send the ball spinning toward the basket. When the game got hopped up, Stallworth was just fine.

Milt Williams, on the other hand, was in trouble. Neither he nor John Warren managed much in the exhibitions. Each suffered from nerves. But if Warren could afford it, Williams could not. Milt knew it. Miscues brought a frown to his face; he had a sense of the arithmetic of his survival—so many mistakes and it would be over, Allentown. He did not say much. In rooms or on transport he sat quietly, like a patient suspecting the worst.

The team, however, was not smitten by doubt. There was a feeling that its late-season success the year before had been no accident of chemistry and moment but rather a phenomenon as inevitable as nature and that it had staying power.

The Knickerbockers' recent history was striking proof that professional rapport was a fragile piece; most of the present players had been together on New York clubs that Dick McGuire had coached, teams on which office politics often was more spirited than court play.

McGuire was to blame. He was miscast as a coach, he did not have the temperament to direct others. At Farmingdale, he would shoot baskets after practices with Sly, and remark on the pleasure he still got playing with kids in the schoolyards. All who knew him regarded him as a very decent man, but he made that trait a liability as a coach. "If the fans booed a guy and wanted him out of the game," said publicity man Blauschild, "McGuire was more apt to leave him in the game. If a player pouted when he *was* taken out of the game, there was a good chance McGuire would put him back in."

What happened to McGuire's approach was a blow to righteousness. The Knicks came to ignore all his entreaties for togetherness, exploited his charity and, in the process, became hacks at their work. "Ballplayers would go out there," remembers Phil Jackson, "and play one-on-one and Dickie would say, 'Come on, let's run some patterns.' And they'd go out and do the same thing, knowing what else can he do, pull me in? What's gonna happen? They're gonna boo him and back I'll go. So in effect you're paying ballplayers sixty, seventy, eighty thousand dollars, you're paying the coach twenty-five thousand. He was more expendable than the players were, which isn't right. Not that they're being overpaid, but the ballplayers can't be more valuable to the team than the coach. A coach has got to be the one that makes the ballplayer expendable or makes the ballplayers toe the line, and that was just what wasn't happening."

Nights in the Knick locker room were full of lunacy. "The old Garden," said Cazzie Russell, "had a hot-dog stand called Nedicks and they would toast the bun and put the hot dog on and put that horse mustard or horse relish or whatever it was and Fred Crawford and Nate Bowman would eat a hot dog, send the ballboy out to buy hot dogs or soda—before the game and at half time. The guys would say, 'Man, run out and get me a couple of dogs at half,' and the guy would sit them between his locker and eat them while McGuire was giving his pep talk. I tell you, man, it was unbelievable and I'm a rookie, you know, and I'm quite impressed, I'm really impressed with the NBA world.

"Oh, man, listen, listen, hot dogs at half time, orange sodas . . . When I say 'McGuire' I just think about a million things. Guys would put on a record, you know, a Ray Charles 'Here We Go Again,' that's what we'd put on before we leave our room, you know. Come on, let's go put in a couple of hours and come on back to the room."

Knickerbocker apathy sank to record depths on a night in Seattle, when it was discovered that one of the players was not with the proceedings. "You know, we got up to go, like in the huddle during time-out," recalled Bowman. "And, uh, y'know, the fans are hollering, they were laughing like I don't know what. We looked around and one of our players was asleep on the bench. Freddie Crawford. He had fallen asleep, y'know. 'Freddie, wake up.' Man, they really cracked up. He woke up and he saw us standing up there and the fans were on him pretty hard. 'Uh, hey,

Crawford, get in the game' or something like that. I don't remember the exact words. All the guys knew about it. McGuire probably knew about it, too. He didn't say anything."

On the court things were not nearly so funny for McGuire.

"If you made a mistake," said Frazier, "McGuire wouldn't tell you, but take it out on himself. [McGuire confesses he had stomach trouble and was unable to sleep during the time he coached. He also became prone to arguments with his family.] McGuire wouldn't like to hurt anybody's feelings. I think he was the wrong guy to be in coaching, because a coach has to bawl you out every once in a while, but he couldn't do this, it wasn't his personality. Guys liked him as a person, but didn't respect him as a coach. Near the end you could see no one respected him anymore. He'd tell a guy, 'Do this,' and the guy would start talking back to him. You could just see the whole thing blowing up right there. When I first came there, if he told the guy to do something, he would do it. But we started losing and then they started talking about a change in coaching. You could just see the guys weren't listening to what he was saying. They wanted something different. It was like they were saying, 'We can't win with this guy.' This seemed like the attitude. And we couldn't win a game, period, the way things were going. Seemed like everything we did was wrong. We'd blow leads and everything. You could just see the ship sinking."

As the situation worsened, personal antagonisms on the team grew, in particular that between Cazzie Russell and Howie (Butch) Komives. Komives was remembered as having an intense dislike of Russell, the origins of which were recalled by a former Knick from those years, Neil Johnson:

"Let me tell you about Cazzie. Now there's a funny character. Because Cazzie was, of course, an All-American and came over with a lot of publicity but he had these . . . I guess you could call them idiosyncrasies, things like staying in shape and also things like the tea and honey. He used to go down to the YMHA on 92nd Street and practice an awful lot, and in practice we all started shooting around. We'd have five, six balls shooting around and Cazzie would only have his ball, and if somehow his went through and you wanted to throw yours back to him or somebody, yours wasn't really yours. He would always come back and get his ball.

"Like, I guess Cazzie rubbed you the wrong way about his type of perfection. I guess that's what he did. He wanted to be such a perfectionist about his workout and that ball of his and I guess his All-American image that he brought in. He always carried this attache case with all these thousands of papers in it, and he would come on the trips and spread his paper work on the planes and, real businesslike, always mention about all these deals he had going with Wilson Sporting Goods and always drop a line here that he was endorsing Wilson. And I remember when he got to training camp he was always telling me about his golf game. He used to go out in the afternoon to practice his golf game and he'd come back with his golf hat on and his golf clothes and his big golf bag with *Wilson* on one side and the other side *Cazzie Russell*.

"When you come in being an All-American, guys want you to prove it, and they don't want to hear all this crap about how great you are till you really prove it, and even then they kind of resent that kind of stuff. On one hand, Cazzie didn't prove it right away and also didn't let up with this crap.

"Now, Butch Komives is a very uptight guy and he is very tense, and he doesn't like to see that stuff happen when a guy comes in, it rubs him the wrong way. Not me, I tend to laugh at it. Butch tends to scowl at it. Butch and him were always arguing—just like I say, he would rub you the wrong way. Things like that, they were magnified. Like we were practicing, so Cazzie pushed Butch a little in the flow of a practice, gave him a little push or an elbow. This would infuriate Butch, and Butch would really look for him downcourt and clobber him, and stuff like that, and Cazzie was, like, gun-shy, so this doesn't impress anybody. If you are in the game you can't be that way.

"Butch would start really getting upset if Cazzie did something, you know, came on with his—come in with his National Guard uniform on, all starched and pressed. And Cazzie would start rapping about what a great army man he is and stuff like that. Butch would start getting uptight, you know, you could see it. He would look at Cazzie and just—just start squinting and really get pissed off.

"I think Cazzie was aware of it. Sometime it could be, like, Cazzie would say to Butch, 'Come on, Butch, throw your passes up a little higher.' Butch would look at him and say, 'Fuck you,' or something like that. This is like I'm trying to say, this is Butch's personality."

The conflict between Komives and Russell became exacerbated to the point, Knicks say, where Komives often would not pass the ball to Russell when he was clear for the shot. McGuire, it is remembered, never confronted the feuding players, but even had he elected to confer with them, there remains considerable doubt he could have repaired the problem.

Moreover, that was not the extent of Knick dissension. In his own inscrutable way, pivotman Walter Bellamy did as much to sabotage the collective sanity of the Knicks as anybody else. Bellamy was 6 feet 10 inches, 245 pounds, a man whose fitful use of impressive skills was a puzzle. When he chose to, Bellamy could play his position with as much ability as anybody; the nub was consistency. More often than not, particularly against the lesser names of pivotry, he seemed to receive the game on delayed tape.

Good nights or bad, Bellamy went through them with an abstracted expression, as if he were party to private thoughts of deep import at all hours. That appearance of impenetrability and the contrast in his performance drove people to distraction. A coach of his once banged at Bellamy's door in a drunken stupor and berated him in outrageously racial terms, offering to transport him back to Africa if an adequate replacement could be found that evening.

As a Knickerbocker, Bellamy did not undergo miracles of transformation. One player said, "If Komives was like a thorn, Bellamy was like an anchor tied to a sailing ship in the America Cup five minutes after the race begins. The team would say, 'Let's go, let's go,' and he would say nothing. Yet he was terribly sensitive and I don't think he sensed there was respect for him as a player from the guys on the team."

Whether innuendoes preceded or proceeded from performance

is unclear; the fact remains that Bellamy was Bellamy in New York. "I don't think anybody ever had any antagonisms against Walt Bellamy," said Phil Jackson. "Walt was the most honest guy on the club. He wasn't fooling anybody. He got paid his seventy, eighty, ninety thousand dollars—whatever he was getting paid—came, played basketball, went home and that was it. It didn't ever enter his mind that he wanted to win a national basketball championship, I don't think. And he was honest about it, you know, he didn't play defense, he wasn't going to play defense and that was it."

All things considered, the firing of Dick McGuire was no surprise, but it did have a strange effect on the team. "There was an attitude of the ballplayers," Jackson recalled, "that we really hadn't done Dick McGuire justice, we really had much more talent than we'd shown. We were ashamed of ourselves the day they fired Dick. He said as a final speech, 'I just want to thank you guys for all you've done for us.' You know, that was enough to make us sit there and wanna cry or laugh or whatever, it was so black humor-y. You know, we hadn't listened to him, we hadn't done anything. So I think there was a basic attitude, 'Say what the hell, let's try to get together a little bit.' "

When Holzman replaced McGuire in 1967–68 he was able to turn the season into a respectable one, but elements that had broken the team under McGuire had not vanished by the beginning of the 1968–69 season. For one thing, Komives still bore a grudge against Russell. On the ride from the Garden to the training camp, Komives downgraded Russell in an indoctrination talk with rookie Don May. "All the way out he talked about Cazzie," May said. "How I'd hate him, how obnoxious and loud he was."

In Holzman's defense-conscious operation, Bellamy's refusal to function on defense was more blatant. Teammates would take a gamble and have Bellamy watch their mistakes go by with his habitual bemused look. It had the effect of subverting the whole aggregate concept. There was a revival of the madness that had plagued McGuire's team. "Butch wouldn't throw to Caz," said one player, "or Bellamy wouldn't put out, or Willis was unhappy in the corner, and guys would complain when they were substituted for. They didn't like coming out. Bill Bradley was upset that too

many guys were going one-on-one. We had a situation where
Walt Frazier was playing third guard, and you know everybody
wanted to know a way to correct the situation, but if you took a
guy like Butch out of the lineup he would squawk forever. He
would create so many problems not starting—like, talk of favorit-
ism or not paying for performance."

The team lost 13 of its first 19 games in 1968–69 and the situation deteriorated to the point where team meetings were called at
the Madison Hotel in Boston. "We were going really terrible,
really horseshit," said a player. "And [Eddie] Donovan shows up,
general manager, gives us a talk and says if you have any gripes, I
want to hear them. And Butch [Komives] says, 'Well, goddammit, I don't care what you say about paying for performance and
let's go out and do a team job and let's do the job, what we're
doing up here is playing for points.' You know, he was upset because Cazzie's contract was so huge evidently and he'd been mad
ever since Cazzie signed for all that money and then Butch, I
guess, went in and tried to get more. Even though he had a better
year than Cazzie he couldn't do anything. They gave him a raise
but . . . you know Butch wanted the world. He wanted to com-
pare everything to this one guy, and so Donovan said they were
paying for performance, and you know anything you say to the
contrary is untrue, seemingly telling Butch, 'We realize you play
good hard-nose defense and you do your job and that's what you
get paid for.'

"And then we had another meeting about the same time in Boston—and this is unbelievable. We had this meeting, we went
around the room and aired out troubles, what was wrong with this
team. It was the first time I ever heard Bill Bradley use . . . say
the word *fuck*. He really shocked me, because I talked to Bradley
a little bit but he never would say anything like that—and he used
it, I could tell later, to get our attention, to get everybody listening
to him, because this makes everybody respond. He was all upset
and was giving his plea, how some guys play one-on-one and Red
keeps telling them that they were going to play team ball but Red
doesn't put in the guys that are gonna play team ball. Nate was
complaining he didn't get to play enough and he didn't like to go
into the game and not shoot—it doesn't say in his contract he can't

shoot. See, Red was putting him in games telling him to just control the ball, just do this, do that. Nate was pissed off because he wasn't allowed to shoot. So it was all small things. Frazier wanted to play more. Then they asked Riordan what he thought—and he'd only been with the Knicks nineteen games and everybody was thinking, 'He's lucky to be on the club, eleventh-round draft choice'—he looked around and said, 'I think it's horseshit.' You know, everybody thought, what is this guy? Then Mike went on in detail, he went on a three-minute spiel about all the things that were wrong with the club, pretty fair analysis.

"As it turns out every guy alluded to the fact that you couldn't go in the league without a good big man, and we had come into Boston that morning and Bellamy had missed the plane—and Walter comes in and explains to Red—it's about the middle of the meeting, you know—he comes in and sits right by the door, we started at the other end—the guys are really blasting him till he shows up. Now they're still talking about him but it's kind of, you know, 'the big man.' Before it was 'Walt's not doing this' and 'Bellamy ain't doing this.' Well, now it's 'our center,' you know, 'we gotta have consistency up front,' and all those other terms. So in rolls the big Bell and explains to Red that he was in the john reading *The New York Times* and the plane took off, flew over the restroom in the airport. And, you know, so then we go on with the meeting and it comes Bell's turn to talk and he says, 'I've only been here briefly. I think we can all make the assumption that sixty percent of the reason for us being here is my play.' You know, he just was completely honest and everyone was expecting Bell to try to bullshit Red, but he just comes right out and said, 'If Walt Bellamy goes out and kills Bill Russell tomorrow night, Walt Bellamy gets compensated for it, but if Walt Bellamy goes out and gets thirty points and thirty rebounds against Connie Dierking, does Walt Bellamy get compensated?' Walt never said paid, he was always saying 'compensated.' "

New York left future compensation to the management of the Detroit Pistons, the team to which both Bellamy and Komives were transported for Dave DeBusschere. And if the deal was for one organization the best of emancipations since Lincoln, there was no saying that the situation was righted for good.

Teams treasured the magic that collaborative concern could bring one year, and then abandoned it the next. Up and down they went in the standings like the standard Duncan yo-yo, the reasons being as complex and as elusive as the men who played the games.

Basketball was peculiarly fitted for flux. It did not have the role hierarchy of football where the lean and quick were stars and the bulkier men were not; basketball did not have as corporate a concept of the individual's worth. The NBA pro was not geared to function and fit but to his own moment and so was more apt to concentrate on the shot and ignore the other departments. When such men were stars and abundantly compensated, as Bellamy would have it, the tendency of others was to emulate them. And so teamwork was screwed.

Only victory could persuade changes, but there came the crisis of precedents. Lacking success to begin with, what was there to make a team change? The Knickerbockers no longer had that sort of problem. They had only to keep the rats out of the closet. Simple enough. But there were no guarantees in games or other forms of reality.

Milt Williams found out: he was cut a day before the season was to begin.

♛ PHOTOGRAPHS

2. There were days when Willis Reed, 19 (racing Atlanta's Bill Bridges, 32, to the ball) was not the superstar he is today. Recalled his college coach, Fred Hobdy: "We played Savannah State in New Orleans. The team whipped us, and I told Reed that night, I said, 'Boy, you'll never play basketball.' And I think he cried a little that night, you know."

1. Stallworth, in midair, lets shot fly. His freewheeling game had origins in his boyhood. "I've carried a knife, I've carried a gun. But . . . believe this here, I wasn't carrying it to start anything."

3. *Barnett dribbling downcourt on a twisting drive of his. Not until recently
has his game become appreciated. "Sportswriters can make a monster out of
you, and they can make shit out of you. As long as I'm rewarded financially,
that's the main thing now. I'm past caring."*

4. Says a teammate about Bradley (right): "He comes in timeouts and hollers like an insane man. He's such a perfectionist."

5. Cazzie Russell, 33, whose idiosyncrasies in physical culture have given the Knicks to call him variously Muscles Russell, Cockles 'n' Muscles, Wonder Boy and Stillman's Gym, and whose traveling bag so abounds with vitamins and food supplements that roommate Barnett advises visitors admission to their place is by pharmaceutical note only.

6. *DeBusschere, with a puffed lip, argues the call with referee Jerry Bannan.*

7. *Riordan, 6, drives against Bailey Howell, 18, on a characteristically intense move. That feeling for the game has prompted the Knicks' Phil Jackson to say, "I can't remember ever a day going by where he had an opportunity to work out that he didn't do it. He's a very intelligent kid, Mike is, but without basketball he'd be crazy."*

8. *Reserves Don May, left, and Bill Hosket, right. Hosket: "One night some people asked us for our autographs and we gave them to these boys and as they were walking away one said to the other one, 'Man, we really got all of the big autographs tonight.'"*

9. *Frazier (right): "I could remember when I was a kid, I'd put on my father's shoes and try his shirts on, like I'm eleven or twelve maybe, but they were all too big. I could remember watches and rings that he had and I couldn't wait 'til I got big enough to wear 'em."*

10. *Cazzie Russell, stylish now, has remembered when he was not. "Okay, now here's a girl. She's going to crawl on the floor back to my seat to put lipstick on me, see. So I said if you put that lipstick on me, I'm going to slap you, you know. This is seventh grade, man. And I said, 'The devil doesn't like ugliness, and if you do that something terrible is going to happen to you.'"*

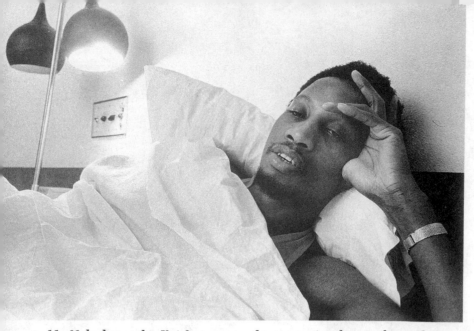

11. Nobody on the Knicks conveys the sense of isolation players have as Barnett does. "Like I want to see Sly and the Family Stone, like the white players, they aren't hip to that, that's not in their world, you know, they're apart from it, they might go see Johnny Cash, I can't dig him. There are so many things. Like most white players don't dance . . . in our world, they're considered squares. . . . I mean like it's what do you have in common except playing basketball?"

12. DeBusschere, left, has a historic need for a cold beer; he has guzzled since he was a lad of seven, a deed less culpable for his father's having been a distributor.

13. *Stallworth welcomed back on opening night. Recalling the ovation, he has said, "You feel like doing something other than standing there, but you also feel that anything you do, it might be out of place. I felt like screaming, I really did, I felt like screaming, just screaming along with them, I really felt that good."*

14. Reed, 19, Holzman, and Frazier, 10. Frazier on Holzman: "Yeah, I've had run-ins with him. It got to a point (one game) where I told him, 'Fine me or something. It's like I get tired of you always calling me, like I'm always screwing up the defense. . . .' Well, he got heated too, you know, told me to shut up, stuff like that."

15. Referee Mendy Rudolph, Barnett, 12, and Knick coach Holzman.

16. *The bench (from left to right)*: *Bowman, Stallworth, Warren, Russell, Hosket.*

17. *Frazier in pregame. "Like if you're a Knick," he said, "you can get (a certain) chick. Like really I've gotten out of that bag. . . . So I set my sights on something different. Maybe she's really beautiful, maybe she can help me in some kind of way, you know. . . ."*

18. *Volleyball at Manhattan Beach, California, on an offday of playoffs. Moustached Phil Jackson dives for the ball, teammate May awaits play. Riordan and book's author ready for return shot.*

19. *Cigar-smoking Fred Klein and aggrieved Stanley Asofsky, die-hard Knick fans. Asofsky: "I yell, I'm verbose, I stand up. I don't do it for David Merrick or theatrics, I do it for myself. And like one time this girl I took, Françoise, I sensed her thinking, 'Like this is the real you, you're on your best behavior when you're in a restaurant with me, but this is the real you . . . you have an orgasm in the Garden.'"*

♟ CHAPTER TWO

THE LAST thing the Knickerbockers saw when they left their locker room before each game was a burlap cloth that showed a bird perched at the end of a rifle held by a pioneer, and beneath which was this rough-lettered inscription:

THERE'S A LITTLE MEANNESS IN EVERYBODY.

A former carnival caricaturist named Chick Green drew it. Green's associate at Rita and Eddie's Professional Movie Co., a man named George Lawrence, thought it appropriate for the world of games and gave it to Willis Reed. Lawrence had worked on several television commercials with the Cap'n.

The Knicks came into possession of the piecegoods about the time DeBusschere was traded to the team. The coincidence of its arrival and the team's subsequent fortunes was not taken lightly. It became Whelan's responsibility to place the prop in eyeview for player egress from the room. Once, when it was inadvertently left behind, Knickerbocker management flew a man from New York out to Detroit with it.

THERE'S A LITTLE MEANNESS IN EVERYBODY.

The import of the message was not on the level of Spinoza but it was of sufficient relevance for the Knicks. Theirs was, after all, a game of explosive opportunism, of the sort that prompted a pioneer to blow a bird to the heavens. The idea was to find a *pigeon* in sneakers.

This was not a new approach to the game. Basketball had long been a game in which inferior personnel were isolated on the

79

wood and treated shabbily in public. Lacking inches or accelera-
tion or smarts, a man was targeted until he found resources to
cope or it dawned on him that he might be more fit for selling
insurance or supervising dodgeball games in playgrounds.

Exploitation was not limited to stiffs. Advantage was taken of
legitimate stars. When Boston used to play against seven-footer
Wilt Chamberlain, it abused his braking function by placing a
small man in his path just after a foul shot was made. Chamberlain would whirl and start upcourt and suddenly encounter a
Larry Siegfried or K. C. Jones; before he could collect his body in
one place he would bowl over the Celtic and be called for a foul.
If he detected the trap in time, he was then forced to tippytoe
around the man, while his Boston counterpart, Bill Russell, raced
down the floor undefended and free for the sucker pass.

There was considerable subtlety to this and other maneuvers
that exploited the moment or the man. Not so many years ago, it
was the habit of referees to view a jump shot from directly behind
rather than at an angle to the shooter, a position that obscured the
action. What happened was that the defender would raise one
hand quite visibly to harass the man and use the other to more
furtively brush his elbow and influence the shot.

Certain men were celebrated for their exploitative craft. The
most memorable was the NBA's answer to the Great Wall of
China, a 6–8, 255-pounder named Wayne Embry. Rookies with
legs like pogo sticks would go into the air for a rebound against
the terrestrial Embry but somehow not manage to get the ball. It
took a while to figure out that Embry allowed them to leap first
and then leaned on their floating bodies so that they drifted away
from the ball. By the time a rookie discovered he should delay his
jump, Embry might be holding his trunks.

It was the job of the referees to discourage hooliganisms. But
the contestants were adept at treading the thin line between infraction and shady legality; often the frequency with which they
performed a borderline act militated for interpretive reforms.
"There was a rule against face guarding," remembered referee
Richie Powers. "Face guarding was waving your hand constantly
in front of a man's face. But what the defenders would do instead
was to get the hand in front of his face, like a jab, so that the

shooter would either blink or pull back, he'd be intimidated. You're not hitting him but you're intimidating him. The trouble is that you don't know when a mistake can happen and have an eye popped out. So there were some officials, when we talked we'd say, 'We're not going to allow that, we're going to call a foul.' And it stopped it, there is none of that today."

Since con was limited only by its efficacy, some strange practices arose. The Syracuse star Dolph Schayes would emit a pained grunt on drives, whether or not illicit contact was made by the foe. When it drew sympathetic whistles from officials, other players began to emulate Schayes. And for a while the game sounded like the chimp house at the Bronx Zoo. Gradually, referees trained themselves to ignore spurious noises, so that the only extant grunter among NBA players was said to be a forward named Jerry Lucas, and he used it not so much to induce fouls as to persuade his legs to aspire greater heights.

What run and jump faculties could not accomplish, motherwit might. Players perpetually sought to disadvantage a foe on the sly. There was an element of the spirited dupery that a W. C. Fields or Harpo or Chico perpetrated on ingenuous souls but little of the mirth that the celluloid engagements provoked.

But whatever a player schemed for the opposition, it was small change in exploitative traffic compared to what such intent on the grand scale could effect. Bradley read a book called *Cat's Cradle* and asked, "What is the *wampeter* of this team?"—*wampeter* being a term the book's author, Kurt Vonnegut, had devised in his weirdo-real world for the animating force of a group. In the case of the Knicks it did not take a scholar to figure the answer: The *wampeter* of the Knicks was defense to the exploitative powers, defense many times over, SEE THE BALL DAMMIT, SEE THE BALL. Holzman, standing in the midst of a sloganistic Bethlehem dressing room, had pointed to a sign that said LET'S GO DEFENSE and nodded. The rest of the hoo-hah was baloney and bullcrap to him, his standard terms of disapprobation.

Defense was not a vision acquired at the deity's foothills. It was for most professional teams an avowal on the order of a New Year's resolve to quit smoking. Players were coaxed to the defense by tangible proofs of its merit, and for that a coach needed to be persuasive and a winner; nothing sustained defensive torpor as further defeats did. Holzman had in his favor a record of success; it made his authority a tool as functional in games as the double screen or reverse pivot. Players could not choose to ignore the coach when he ranted from the bench, GODDAMMIT, SEE IT, CAZZIE, SEE IT . . . COME ON WILLIE, GET BACK, GET BACK . . . CLYDE! CLYDE! PICK UP. Backsliders got it from him without fail, and he would as readily call out (and did call out) YOU FUCKING DUMMY to the cerebral Bradley as to anybody else.

The targets of the Knick defense, the so-called pigeons, were those ball handlers who strayed into the strategically unsound pieces of the floor or, on safer expanses, got inopportunely within pawswipe of a New Yorker. It was not by chance such bumbling occurred. There was to Knickerbocker defense a sinister logic that had for its foremost goal the creation of a moment come apart, an instant of court dislocation in which the unwitting dribbler found himself in the maw of a double-team maneuver, two Knicks thrusting and groping at him like slapstick buffoons, the purpose of their gymnastics to pry the ball from him or hasten a misguided pass. The way New York accomplished this was by channeling the dribbler to locations on the wood where he was most vulnerable to assaults on the ball. As the bullfight had a mathematics of terrain, so did basketball, and if a matador sought the more perilous stations of the grounds to enhance his show, a ball handler proceeded to these places for no such ennobling purposes; likely he was carried there by the drift of the game or the guile of Frazier and Barnett.

The riskiest spots on the floor were along the sidelines. The deeper into a corner the worse the peril. On the middle of the floor a ball handler whose dribble was terminated had outlets denied him on the sidelines. The Knicks deployed in such a way to ensure that a pass thrown in a territorial bind would end up a casualty. Two men applied pressure to the ball; the others edged toward the outlet men.

If such a procedure left a man ostensibly uncovered, the vacated man was farthest from the ball. To make a pass to him under the pressure of a double team was a feat akin to throwing accurately from the bottom of a well.

Even if the short pass were completed, the opposition remained in trouble. The bustle engendered in keeping ball possession destroyed what theoreticians called *court balance,* a reference to spacious intervals between men. The result of doubling was to compress the action and force men less accustomed to handling the ball to work under pressure: it became an exercise in movable pigeons.

The instigator of New York's doubling was usually Frazier. To give him more range for troublemaking, he was matched against teams' weaker guards. Only against certain teams or for brief snatches of games did he cover the best in the league. One such team was Baltimore, whose Earl (the Pearl) Monroe referred to the moves he made from whirling starts and fits as *la-la.* The Pearl's *la-la* was as slick and eyepleasing as any in basketball. *Yeah, I can get up for him, no trouble,* said Frazier. *But that's because he tries to show on you. He tries to star, do all kinds of funny things with the ball. So it's either me or him, you know. I don't want to be embarrassed.*

When finally it was for reee-ul, Frazier did the embarrassing. Striking out for the ball in the new season, he forced turnovers by himself or with teammates. On October 14, opening night of 1969–70, he got the player-coach of the Seattle Supersonics, Lenny Wilkens, so distracted that Wilkens did not see Barnett obstruct his lane, and charged into the veteran for a personal foul. Later, Supersonic Art Harris got a step head start to the basket when Frazier tried to poke the ball from behind. Frazier did not get it but Harris was so harried that he proceeded blindly toward Barnett, who stole the ball. Harris had justifiable concern, earlier Frazier had given him a one-step advantage and converted it to his own when he deflected the ball from the rear. There was lightning in Clyde's limbs, and Harris did not want to be struck twice.

A few evenings later, a Los Angeles rookie, Willie McCarter, went to fetch the ball from the team's star, Jerry West, and when Laker coach Joe Mullaney saw him bring Frazier to the ball, he envisioned trouble: GET AWAY, WILLIE. It took no savant to share his premonition and, sure enough, Frazier lashed at the ball, it came loose from West, another steal.

In his own way, Frazier, like Bill Russell before him, was a defensive omniscience. His presence on a court was like that of the most striking woman at a party; if the mood of the room changed and there was eyeball telepathy everywhere when she came in, so the game was on a different frequency when Frazier was in it—it became charged with gratifying possibilities; the musk of encounter was in the air.

Frazier was lit up by defensive prowl, he got his kicks going after the ball: *I'm sort of like a dope addict, if I can't get through to the ball, really I'm floundering around, I can't stay away from the ball.* To make a steal was for him no robot function; it agitated his metabolism: *After I've made one steal, I'm really keyed up. Like, for three or four minutes I might just go wild, in spurts. I like to hear the cheer of the crowds, it really psychs me up, and I think my steals help psych the Garden up too.*

There were nights, however, when he came into the game with the sort of neutral blood he had in offhours, when he'd lie like Oblomov on the twenty-ninth floor of the New Yorker. These were games that were for *ree-ul* but against the tapped-out franchises like Chicago and San Diego and Boston, teams without flash in the backcourt. It sometimes took embarrassments by their journeyman pros to godspeed the adrenalin. One night Chicago's Bob Weiss hit a succession of shots against Frazier and suddenly he was roused: *He really got me pissed off, like the baskets he was making over me, that's why I made so many on him. You know, like I hate the guy to score on me. Somehow if I don't feel like playing and the guy makes a basket on me I get mentally mad. I get mad as hell and I'm ready to play.*

Frazier had come to his defense the way the neighborhood shut-in arrives at his piano or palette, for lack of alternatives. Declared scholastically ineligible for intercollegiate ball at the end of his sophomore year at Southern Illinois, Frazier's only choice was to be a defensive scrub against the regulars the next year, a role he played with a vengeance. "Since we did scrimmage the varsity team, you know, like we tried to humiliate them, which we did. A

lot of days they couldn't do anything against us. So this would piss
the coach off and then in this I found satisfaction. Like he'd tell us
to stop fouling so much, he'd get upset because they couldn't run
their plays. I wouldn't say anything 'cause I knew I was getting to
him, but I knew I wasn't fouling. He had to take me out sometimes so that they could run their plays, take me out of the defense. I didn't have a grudge against him except that he wouldn't
let me play offense. I thought that was pretty cruel."

That servitude and bodily assets helped make Frazier a superb
defender. Much ado was made of the speed of his hands. There
was one widely circulated exchange in homage:

GUY: Bet my hands are as quick as yours. I can catch a fly in
midair.
FRAZIER: I can catch two flies at a time.
GUY: Yeah, but Bob Cousy was so quick he could catch three of
'em at a time.
FRAZIER: Not bad. My trouble is that the flies have heard about
me. They don't come 'round anymore.

For all the fanciful repartee the sporting journals propagated,
Frazier did, in fact, have remarkable handspeed. He could recall
the retrieve he made in a bar one night of a glass that was sliding
off the counter, and other saves he'd made in the john of his New
Yorker residence. But the hands worked in the service of an unconventional methodology. Frazier was the maverick talent Mu-
hammad Ali had been in the prizefight arena; as the champion
created heretic art so did Clyde.

In the classic man-to-man situation, Frazier resisted the ortho-
doxy of touch. Where other defenders constantly fingered opposition jerseys while on the move, Clyde did not; he required no
palpable assurances of control. In this he was like the defensive
revolutionary, Bill Russell. Russell laid off the shooter. A big man
would get the ball in the pivot and not know precisely where Russell was; it made him more dubious about his shot. So the persua-
siveness of Russell's flights and swoops was abetted by their un-
predictability. The shooter played a hunch game against him.

Russell varied the distance and pressure to further the confusion and camouflage his formidable means.

Frazier confused people by the distance he kept. That distance was created by a one-step retreat and then a glide that made him appear to be miming the dribbler; the two moved stride for stride like men swept along the street by a backing wind, their motion locked together by its irresistible force. Riordan's footwork was more frenzied. His sneakers moved together and apart like shuttles of a loom; he worked stiff as an Irish jig dancer. Barnett's locomotion was a rag doll's; he always appeared on the verge of tipping over; his rump was set low, and when he was forced to change direction, his arms flailed out like a melodramatic actor prolonging his battlefield death. Riordan and Barnett were perpetually just out of synch; they could not get inside the rhythms of the dribblers the way Frazier could. *Barnett and Riordan,* Frazier said, *they aren't as relaxed on defense. See, when a man get a step on them, they like panic, they got to bump into them and try to slow them down, whereas I try to beat him to where he's going.*

Frazier worked a dribbler the way a clever prizefighter does his foe, suggesting pieces of moves that were intended to lull a foe's senses so that when he struck for keeps he caught his man unawares. Frazier caught them, he made no distinction among pigeons. He could feint and a rookie like Jo Jo White of Boston would reel as if he'd contracted palsy, or he could thrust and a veteran like Wilkens of Seattle would lose the ball to him.

Clyde had evolved to that point where instincts empowered him to improvise wonderful things. Against Seattle, Frazier chased a long pass that the Supersonics lofted downcourt and caught it without ever looking at the ball; he allowed the eyes of the intended receiver to direct him, and when he reached over his shoulders like a split end on a fly pattern, the ball stuck to his hands. In a game against San Diego, Frazier's assigned man, Stu Lantz, passed to rookie Bernie Williams and then started down the foul lane to clear out for Williams. Frazier took several tentative steps after Lantz and, anticipating that Williams would be moving directly into the vacated area, whipped around, went for and got the ball.

He made art out of routine situations. Holzman would order a give-one foul and, to expedite it, Frazier would shout PRESS, causing the man to pause and ponder. Only when Frazier "gave one" did the man realize the press was nonexistent. Other times Frazier might catch the foe offguard on an inbounds pass. "A lot of big guys get careless on that pass," he said. "And sometimes they'll get mad because their man just scored a basket. So my theory is just like in football when you go for the bomb after an interception. You catch them when they're still unsettled. It's all in figuring how you would feel in that position, you'd feel the same way."

Other Knickerbockers did not have the innovative flair of Frazier on the defense, but professionalism did not suffer by their work. Barnett shuffled about as if he came to the job in bedroom slippers, but the flatfooted manner did not hinder his coverage of the game's best shooters. When a Robertson or West tried to back into the basket, the veteran was a master of *bellying* technique—curving his body like a parenthesis and resisting their encroachments with an assertion of stomach. Riordan worked on his toes and with so much intensity that sometimes he was ordered off the bench and told to curb a hot shooter and the hell with SEE THE BALL.

DeBusschere had no distinguishing motor traits as a defender. His game was understated. *Guy like DeBusschere,* said May, *for six, seven, eight minutes of a game you don't even see the man he's guarding. He cuts him off from the ball, takes him right out of the game.* DeBusschere had the big-shouldered manly look of a Marlboro Country stud, but it was not a blacksmith's body. His musculature was supple enough to cope with rough stuff or acrobatics; DeBusschere could belt or finesse. Bradley was not as well endowed—in Knickerbocker parlance his body was not as *togethuh* for defense as DeBusschere's. His upper torso was that of a long-distance runner, his rump was a linebacker's, there were limits to his strength and spring. Nevertheless, Bradley drew for assignments Tom Meschery of Seattle (6–6, 230), Paul Silas of Phoenix (6–7, 220), Mel Counts of Los Angeles (7–0, 230); these were the secondary forwards of their teams and Bradley, at 6 feet 5 inches, 205 pounds, was considerably dwarfed by them. But the problem posed by the disparity in size was not so insoluble as it appeared. "Red," said Bradley, "was one of the first coaches to see that when a big guy takes a smaller man into the pivot, it's not necessarily an advantage. Other teams see it as a mismatch, but if the forward is not the big scorer, sometimes this just disrupts the offense."

The way teams tried to exploit such matchups was by looping a pass over Bradley to the taller man, a strategy eventually abandoned. Whether it was Seattle with the league's only published poet, Meschery, or Boston with the rubbery-limbed Tom Sanders, clubs found passes went caroming off rims and boards, or were intercepted by the sloughing Knicks. So the outsized forwards swung to the corners where Bradley could use his agility to prevent a man's getting the ball, or his handspeed to confound the dribble, and even occasionally come off with a basketball.

Reed was the Knicks' last recourse for containing a shot and, unlike Bellamy, he had no aversion to moving off his station and blocking the thing. Reed would rise in stiffened arc and unwind the instant the shot ascended; these strikes from a body of his topheavy dimensions had uncommon grace.

In Holzman's defense, Reed's function was not limited to face-saving deflections. His central location gave him the traffic cop's vantage for anticipating the flow to the middle. The dictum here was SHOW YOURSELF. Teams like Philadelphia, Chicago, Boston moved their shooters off a big pivot stationed at the foul line and hoped that the defender might be stayed by their monumental screens. At such times Reed was to step out, SHOW YOURSELF, so that the dribbler was persuaded to bypass the shot. If the Cap'n had a flaw on defense, Frazier felt it was in these situations. *Like a guy like* [Boston's 7-foot Henry] *Finkel,* Clyde said, *as bad as he is, you know, he does that good. We can't run that play on them because he steps up and if he comes at you he comes all the way out and you can't even pass the ball, you know. He really smothers the guard.* The feeling was that Reed was too wishy-washy at shutting off the play.

Closer to the backboards, there was nothing unsubstantial about Reed's play. The little meanness purported to be in everybody was in greater supply for Reed, a gentleman off the court. The nature of the game transfigured men. Braun remembered that in at least a dozen games, he and Boston's Bill Sharman had come to blows, and yet afterwards had enjoyed beers together. *I'm sure,* said Braun, *people sitting in the bar who might have seen us fight at the game had to think what a great act this was, you know. They'll never know if I could have hit him I would have knocked his head right in.*

When Braun played, the violence was more calculated than it was these days. The custom was for teams to carry a burly provocateur who drew wages for his ability to unsettle the superior talents of the opposition with the kind of tricks wrestlers like Dick the Bruiser and Bruno Sammartino use nightly. Not all teams contracted for "hatchet men," but those clubs that didn't were obliged to allocate policing duties to a legitimate player whose physical stature would give bullyboys concern for their own welfare.

Things were now more subtle, but teams still required a man to keep the opposition civil. For the Knicks, Reed filled the role with considerable figure. In his second year in the league, the Cap'n had acquired the kind of notoriety that thereafter made men mind themselves when he was around. That repute came in a game against a Los Angeles Laker forward, Rudy LaRusso, a player he came to face after the Knicks got Bellamy for the pivot and shifted Reed to forward.

"Rudy had been around quite a while," Reed remembered. "He had a reputation as a hardnosed player. That night he was doing a lot of pushing, shoving, climbing my back to get the ball. The referees weren't calling it. I told an official, I said, 'Watch the guy, he's pushing.' The official looked at me as if I was crazy. I told the ref, 'If you don't take care of it, I will.'

"I remember after a basket, elbows were exchanged and he took a wild swing. I was angry. You go out and play ball and play ball and here's a guy who just because he's a veteran is trying to misuse me. I'm just as much a man, and if I have to pay a fine for my pride, I'll do it. Sometimes a man has to establish himself as a man."

For certification, Reed hit LaRusso two punches on the mouth. In the confusion that ensued he knocked down Darrall Imhoff and broke reserve John Block's nose, escalating violence prompted by attempts to restrain him. "When a fight starts," Reed explained, "you don't hold anybody. I tell the guys on my team not to hold me, I'll deck 'em."

The Cap'n had come to this policy in his college career. "We were playing ball down in South America," he said, "and my own teammate, he, uh—I don't know, something about the ball game or something. Anyway he got upset and we started to have a fight. So the guys ran over and they grabbed me. And, uh, in the meantime, as they was holding me, the other kid, got a bottle and . . . I think I still got the scar on my head somewhere."

It was motion and not violence that gave basketball its aesthetic, but muscle could arrest and cow it. What the New York defense did to the Wilkenses and McCarters and Harrises was repeated game after game to the point of exasperation. The defense that helped New York win 7 of its first 8 games led the opposition to consider malevolent strategies. On October 28 Atlanta was the first club to try.

The Hawks wisely averted Reed, but still had their bluff called early. Remembered DeBusschere: "[Atlanta's] Bill Bridges said to me: 'The next time you put your hands on me I'm going to take a swing at you.' I got very surprised because I never heard him talk like this. I put my hand down, well, he swung his elbow at me. I said, 'What are we going to do, Bill? Is this going to be a one-way street? I'm not going to back off from you, we might as well get it over with here, let's start.' That's when we started to move, but nothing much came of it.

"I think the Atlanta coach, Richie Guerin, said he should do this, I really do, because I think there was a couple other times in the game—once when Frazier got a little excited and very rarely do you see Frazier get excited, but [Walt] Hazzard kept hitting him. I saw Don Ohl and Dick Barnett yelling at each other, and there's two guys—I played with Don Ohl and now with Dick Barnett. I think they're probably two of the quietest individuals, and I've never seen them say boo about anything, and they were yelling at each other. So I think there might have been a little something—they were under orders to antagonize or provoke us."

Atlanta's aggression did not disturb the Knick defense. New York won that night, and nights after, and what nastiness there was was limited to the backboards where Reed instructed the rogues. One such edification occurred November 1 when the Milwaukee rookie Lew Alcindor, 7 feet 1 inch tall, got his baptismal psych. The summer preceding the season, Alcindor had quieted doubts about his combativeness in a *pickup* game when he shattered the jaw of a professional from the rival American Basketball Association for tactics he deemed abusive. Reed allowed less margin for bravado, and when he felt provocation the Cap'n whirled and let fly an elbow in a looping arc. The air turned combustible in that moment, as it does on Garden prizefight nights. *What happened,* said Reed, *was that when I got the ball, Lew wound up with his back to me. There were a lot of bodies around. In the process he came back with an elbow and that was enough. What happened to him was an automatic response. What happened to me was an automatic response.*

Rookies brought out the reflex responses in a pro. A big man's trade was as much toughness as agility and, over the years, veteran pivotmen had laid blows on newcomers for psychological purposes, *When you're a rookie,* remembered Bowman, *uh . . . older guys, like the veterans, they're kinda hard on you, . . . they'll try to scare you.* A caste system prevalent in the NBA permitted these liberties. Referees were said to promote the welfare of the game's celebrities. *A lot of times,* said Bowman, *I mean, like, I can be out there playing Wilt sometime and, and [referee] Mendy Rudolph can be right in the middle of us, y'know, and he'll see Wilt push me and just do everything, and Rudolph'll just look at it, y'know, look at me like I'm crazy.* A veteran protected his prerogatives the way a looney hermit guards against trespass of his woodsy shelter, particularly since the system worked to an incumbent's benefit. *And I say to Rudolph,* said Bowman, *'man, look at the man pushin' me,' and he says, 'Ah, play ball' and any time I brush up against him, he's blowing a foul on me, man. I guess the referees are just so used to them doing things, they just don't blow on them.*

THERE'S A LITTLE MEANNESS IN EVERYBODY.

"Look at it, here's a man," said Reed, "and you're assuming here's a bird that he wants to eat. Rather than him reaching out for it with his hand he's gonna pull the trigger. Well, in this game you're out there for the kill, the objective is to win. There's a lot of methods to get that bird, his is the most crude. A lot of things that are obvious on the surface, it's not the way the situation turns out."

Professionals of all sizes were accustomed to spirited play. A so-called small man like the 6–4 Riordan had, in his collegiate days at Providence, engaged teammate Jimmy Walker in one-on-one workouts at nearby Brown University that were heated enough so that a coach there inquired whether the two were feuding. They were just routinely pugnacious, a trait that was schoolyard herit-age for Riordan. In the playing grounds on Long Island, contact was taken for granted, outsiders who wandered in and lamented push 'n' shove were laughed out of the place. The games were sufficiently rugged to bring offseason football professionals to the courts. On one occasion a New York Giant linebacker, Tom Cos-tello, and NBA player Neil Johnson had a go, *head to head,* said Riordan, *nobody moved, just the sound of it, flesh being banged all over. The word of that fight got around and unless a guy could take care of himself he didn't come down there anymore.*

Riordan's travels through the schoolyards of metropolitan New York, where the mores varied with the neighborhood, gave him a resourcefulness for changeable scenes. Once he and his cronies played in an all-black recreation facility run by former Knick Em-mette Bryant, where the score was kept by voice, "White 5, Black 5." Other times he went down to Long Beach.

"That was a funny place," he said. "A guy named Moe was king of the outdoor courts then and, from what I hear, he still is. He used to be a big star in college. Down at Long Beach—I mean, it's his rules, his ball, he organizes sides. He was great at arguing calls. He'd psych guys out. Say its an eight-point game, you have to win by two. Okay, it's seven to six, Moe's losing and he's guard-ing a young kid who's six-four, heavier and stronger. The kid takes him low. Moe fronts him so that he can't get the ball. But that leaves the kid in good position for the rebound. The kid gets the ball on the rebound. All of a sudden, Moe raises his hand and says, 'Nope, nope, you're pushing off.' And he's got the peanut gallery—all these guys who come to watch, and love him—he's got them hollering for him. For five minutes, the peanut gallery and everybody are arguing. Finally, Moe will relent 'for the sake of the game.' What he's done is saved the game, and made it look like he's doing all of us a favor when he's not.

"Down there, Moe always had his scapegoat. He always picked one scapegoat. If things were going bad he blamed him, threw him out of the game, bring somebody else in. Say he's down five to nothing in a seven-point game and it looks like they're going to get blown out of the court, so he stops in the middle of the game. This guy named Red—Red something or other, he played for CCNY or something and he was a pretty successful businessman apparently—and Moe threw his hands in the air and said something to the effect of, 'Red, do you agree when it comes to business you're great but you don't know a damn thing about basketball. Go over and sit down.' The guy just shrugged and argued with him and sat down. And Moe would bring in somebody that he thought could shoot or whatever he needed."

Pros used schoolyard bluff in dealing with NBA officials, particularly newer ones who were entranced by players they had once admired. Established players sought to legitimize their borderline habits with rookie referees. DeBusschere, for instance, gave a man little leeway for moving straightahead without the ball, a legal ploy to limit his access to the ball. But to a referee whose vision of the game was founded on more sanitary collegiate methods, the bumping and jostling such crowding occasioned smacked of the illicit.

GIVE HIM ROOM, a rookie official named Jerry Loeber told DeBusschere.

GIVE HIM ROOM, HELL. MAKE HIM GO AROUND ME, DeBusschere replied.

DeBusschere was no backboard sneak—next to an Embry he was an Arthurian knight—but to deprive him of the game's contact was to render him less effective, a reduction he would not abide. Where a collegian sought a favorable site from which to leap for the defensive rebound, a pro eyed the foe and dug his rump into him before going for the ball. The move was made to stun the opposition to a moment's immobility, time enough for a man like DeBusschere to surge to the basket and wrench a ball from the air. The contact beneath both boards had its costs; the pain was particularly keen for a rebounder trying to follow his

team's shot. Big men used their elbows like construction picks to
ward off offensive pursuit of the ball, and the blows landed on
unpadded parts of the torso, the chest and arms. *At times,* said
DeBusschere, *my arms in particular are really black and blue, and
usually after every Baltimore game I come out of that scratched
somehow because Gus Johnson is quite a physical specimen. Their
whole team is very physical. Atlanta is that way, too.*

DeBusschere had no corner on pain; such discomfort was considered routine. Monroe of Baltimore had played at one time with
trainer Skip Feldman's battery-operated kneepads that gave him
therapeutic heat. Others made do with cortisone shots or more
spiritual resources, and not a few were spooked by the whole injury business. San Francisco's Nate Thurmond, a shot-blocking
facsimile of Bill Russell, incurred broken bones the way ordinary
citizens do the common cold. He came to brood about it like a
Dostoyevskian hero and, for fear of tempting the game's presid-
ing Furies, refused to touch a ball in the offseason, choosing to be
under contract at the next betrayal of his flesh.

That pain which did not require bedcare was accepted with
stoic resignation by the pros. And if from time to time DeBusschere violated that spirit by confessing ache to an understudy
like Hosket, he transcended hypochondria by going onto the court
those nights and performing with the peppy abandon of Jack La
Lanne. On a team not overstocked with rebounding muscle, De-
Busschere and Reed were expected to react to mortal pain with
the indifference that turbaned yogis were credited with in the
block drawings of Mr. Ripley.

Reed had had experience in this occult art not in faraway Tibet
or Nepal but in downhome Grambling, where he had once carried
on in a shoulder harness. *Everybody knew he was hurt,* said
Grambling College coach Fred Hobdy, . . . *but he told me, said,
'Coach, I'm gonna play if I play with one arm.' He got 35 points
that night and 27 rebounds.* In his career, Reed had been damaged from head to toe, from an oft-broken nose to a bone spur on
his foot. The Cap'n was a walking seminar on injuries. His recall
of a new season's affliction had the tone of a pedagogic recitation:
*First of all, I had a dislocation in training camp in my left pinky, I
still wear tape. And then I had the second finger to the pinky on*

the right hand jammed, and then I had the thumb, the bone right on the left thumb jammed. You get a lot of these from around the basket, y'know, from hitting the backboard and so on.

Nothing hurt the Knick defense. Its advantage in the early season was that of an entrenched army waiting the foe's landing; offenses that encountered New York were not yet locked into their collective genius. There was feeling here that Holzman had had a notion of the creaking hinges the offenses would have at the outset of a season and so had driven his defense in preseason.

In their first 11 games, the Knicks allowed opponents only 101.3 points a game, less than any other team in the league. Over the same period, New York won games by a margin of 16.1 points a game. Milwaukee was next best with a 4.9 points a game edge. The variance between New York and other NBA franchises was so marked as to suggest that the old scout was, once again, stealing a little.

There was a degree of larcenous acquisition to the offense, too; its plays were snatched outright from professional and college teams alike. A play called *Philly*, for instance, was based on a 76er maneuver in which a forward started up from the corner to the ball and then suddenly spun to the basket; executed properly this so-called *back-door* ploy caught the defender leaning the wrong way and yielded an easy lay-up. Another Knick play was a Bradley contribution whose origin was said to be Princetonian; players confessed that *Tiger*, as it was known, was so intricate as to be practically useless.

Neither *Philadelphia* nor *Tiger* was at the core of the offense, but the calculated patterns to create clear shots were. And if all this had a spontaneous look that could lead a national newsweekly magazine to misrepresent the Knick offense as *freelance*, it was a deception perpetrated by the ease with which the team swung from preordained play to the various options afforded it when the flow was thwarted. The Knicks themselves viewed with amusement the outsider's attempt to decipher the controlled flux; the same journal that had taken New York's offense for freeform showed a diagram purporting to be a play the team used but which was nothing more than authoritative bluff—*a ghastly fabrication,* Hosket called it.

Not all teams used plays with the frequency that New York did. Clubs like Baltimore, Phoenix, Detroit, Los Angeles, San Diego ran an offense on open throttle and boardinghouse reach. New York's preference for classical patterns did not confer on it a superior character; it was a matter of means. The Knicks were loaded with spot shooters whose accuracy was better served by formal setups. The same system that could have been chafing for a team as mobile and spirited as Baltimore was right for New York.

This reliance on plays did not make the Knick attack any less visual. The New Yorkers could put a twist on a move as readily as other pros. Frazier would tantalize a defender on the fast break by showing him the ball and then turning serpentine ways to goad him into a fouling grab. Barnett went driving through lanes with the syncopation of a Slinky toy and released a ball over soaring defenders that would bank off the backboard with the authority of a well-stroked billiard shot. Stallworth's writhing reverse lay-ups took their instructions from the trampoline. Russell's dashes upcourt had the power and pounce of a sleek cat. Whatever discipline the Knicks required on the attack, it did not dull their instincts. In moments of necessary deviations or in freewheeling interludes, the players could trot out jive aesthetics. They were not embarrassed for lack of *la-la*.

But the "moves" that were to scorers what the "walk" is to sex queens did not make the Knicks go; it was the plays that did. And if they seemed to the uninitiated like the secret ingredients of bathroom products, illusory and cryptic, *Barry, Trap, D, X, 22-C, 19-F, Third Man, New York* were no more foreign to Knickerbockers than *Gardol* was to the chief chemist at Colgate.

Familiarity, however, could breed contempt for the small motions that gave plays their precision. If shoddiness here was not rued to the extent it might be in close-order drill or choreography, Holzman still did not disregard it. *These plays,* he would say in practices, *aren't worth a shit if you don't make your moves good.* The moves to which Holzman referred were those performed in mime, without the ball, aimed at filling a defender with false rhythms and rhymes. *Say he's playing me tight,* said Bradley, *I move, and fake catching a ball, then maybe I smile. It's not to psych him. He reacts and realizes I'm playing with him. But the next time it might not be a decoy, it might be the real thing.* Deceits were tailored to the man. The bard from Seattle, big Meschery, fancied poetic feet in motion more than his own, so Bradley ran on and on in epic fashion and gave Meschery to plead, *Why don't you stop?*

What made Bradley run was the sad state of his dribble, it was not, at season's outset, the madly dancing dot that Frazier's or Barnett's was. Clyde could shuttle it from one hand to another behind his back and cause enough turbulence in a defender's shoes to have the man recline like the tower at Pisa. Barnett accompanied the ball like a man negotiating the downward side of a slope, and if his lurching rides unsettled the foe, they did not perturb his high dribble. Footwork did for Bradley what ball handling did for Frazier and Barnett.

Plays for Bradley or anybody else were initiated by word, hand gesture or, when Russell was in the contest, by Riordan's imitation of a crow. This sound of nature was said to closely resemble Bowman's laugh and, for Riordan and Russell at least, served to designate the *Barry* play.

The *Barry* play was named after a former San Francisco forward, Rick Barry, and the success that New York had with it, particularly against San Francisco, caused the Warrior coach, George Lee, to examine it in slow motion on the videotape machine in his team's locker room and afterward proclaim it a dandy enough play to borrow from New York.

In its execution, Frazier drove down the side of the court, while Bradley vacated his corner spot and moved along the baseline toward the other edge of the court. Midway there, he would jam the instep of the sneaker to the floor, turn and loop back to take the ball from behind Frazier. Clyde squared his body so that the discommoded defender could not come straightaway at Bradley but had to sidestep the Frazier screen. Dollar Bill, as his teammates called him, leaned slightly forward from the waist so that his rear end jutted, and then flicked the shot to the basket.

Trap got him the same shot by having him run off a double screen that Reed and DeBusschere formed at the bottom of the foul lane. Bradley made the move quicker along the baseline on this play, and before he swung up to the screen, he suggested a directional change with some shoulder business that froze the foe to the spot for the instant Dollar Bill needed to get clear, and left neither the angle nor the time for the defense to recover. Frazier or Barnett, crossing to Bradley's side of the floor, gave him the ball as soon as he rounded the screen.

The precision with which Bradley maneuvered on *Trap* prompted the Knicks to write into their repertoire a play for last-second contingencies, the *2-3-F* (or 10-second play). The *2-3-F* was *Trap* with movable parts. DeBusschere swept into the lane to screen for Bradley, and Reed remained where he had been on *Trap*, at the bottom end of the foul lane. Bradley was expected to lose his man in this staggered interference and emerge free for the quick shot from the side of the court.

The shots that Bradley got from the corners were within De-Busschere's shooting range, but he was not as nifty at the soft-shoe that Bradley did to station himself. So the Knicks more often ran the *D* play for him. Frazier passed the ball to DeBusschere deep at the side of the court and opposite the foul line, and came around to retrieve the ball from him. On Clyde's approach, Reed ambled up from a low pivot site to one just outside the foul line and near the two men. After DeBusschere returned the basketball to Frazier, Dave idled toward Reed as if to screen for him. But instead he veered away from Reed to a location at the side of the key or back of the foul line, and left the foe to slide around Willis, no easy task when Reed spread himself like the marshal of Dodge City at shootout hour—in basketball terminology, he "set wide." The shot was taken from behind Reed.

Reed was as fine an obstacle in pro basketball as anybody since Embry. The sight of him gingerly settling near a dribbler suggested that a piece of action was about to move off either side of the Cap'n's haunches. But in no way did a man find this fore-glimpse reassuring; navigation about Reed was as treacherous for the defender as the Cape Horn route was to a medieval mariner, there was no saying what might fall upon him. When Reed rooted himself in harm's way of a defenseman not his own, he called attention to his part of the boardwalk so that if the ball was moved abruptly to the other side of the floor, as it was in the play called *New York*, the defense might not be committed to that area in sufficient measure.

On *New York*, it was Barnett who usually worked with Reed. Other occasions he used the Cap'n's screens at the side of the court for virtuoso drive and jump moves. He would dribble one way and the other until he eased by the screen, then into the air he would go, legs tucked under him, and off his agonized release, came the ball, Barnett's hand flicking out convulsively. The sight of it suggested he had suffered a seizure in midflight. But nearly as often as not, the ball fell cleanly through the basket.

For *New York*, though, Barnett did not shoot. When he and Reed set up, the forward on whose side the play started, say, Cazzie Russell, moved across the baseline and up to the head of the key where Frazier and DeBusschere drifted together to form a double screen. Barnett would steer wide of Reed and give the ball to his roommate. Cazzie's low-trajectory shot was deadly from there.

Not all Knickerbocker plays were studiously rehearsed configurations. Bradley and Frazier arrived more spontaneously at *X*, a play with the cut-and-pass science that Holzman had learned under Nat Holman at City College of New York. *If you get movies of the 1955 Knickerbockers,* said Bradley, *you'll see Dick McGuire did fifteen different variations of this move. . . . Someone's implied that there's spiritual magic to it, that Clyde and I have a special communion. It's nothing special, it's a simple play.*

X came out of the practice hall. In scrimmages, Bradley dribbled down the left side of the floor, Frazier moved from the foul line up to the head of the key and then reversed, hastening down the lane a scant beat ahead of the defender to take a bounce pass that Bradley would make off the dribble, and go in for the lay-up. The pass came right off the man's fugitive heels and made Holzman warn the wretched fellow, SEE THE BALL, as Clyde teased, CHUMP! Such a pass lit up a defensive oversight as clearly as a flare does a battleground.

It also made it plain enough to Frazier that the play could work in game conditions. "Clyde got to the point where he believed in it," said Bradley. "Sometimes guys wouldn't go back-door because they thought it meant giving up a chance to score, but that's not the case." When Frazier sensed that his defender could be had, he would call X, or cross his index fingers in that alphabetical designation; occasionally the play came off without forethought. Clyde did not always give an elaborate fake; he might just fidget in place and then cut for the basket, or gain his step by first giving a devious push. The pass always came from Bradley.

Circumstances dictated what plays were used. Against those teams whose forwards indulged in shadow games on the defense, *Barry, Trap, D* and *New York* worked; the forwards of San Diego, San Francisco and Detroit wandered on the defense like tourists in a strange land. Not all plays sprang from the other man's weaknesses. New York used *22-C* for Reed against Thurmond, the close-guarding pivotman from San Francisco. *22-C* was a big man's version of the *Barry* play: Reed came along the baseline to get the ball and shoot it behind DeBusschere; it helped the Cap'n to be in motion against Thurmond, and that motion created distance he could use to shoot over the San Franciscan's long arms.

Knick plays were not so often prescriptive as *22-C* was for Reed. The attack sought to abuse; whether on offense or defense, a pigeon got the same abrupt disposition as the fine-feathered thing atop the rifle barrel. The standard means of disposal was an isolation play signaled by calling a Knickerbocker's jersey number; on *22* a side of the court would become clear for DeBusschere, on *33* for Russell, on *10* for Frazier and so on. In this fashion did the defense's overreactors (Hawkins of Phoenix), underachievers (Dischinger of Detroit), unconcerned (Hetzel of Philadelphia), unknown (rookies like Foster of Cincinnati) and unlikely (the smallish Adelman of San Diego) become exposed.

To keep its own plays from being exposed, New York used alternate names. On *Barry*, the call could be *Frisco* for Rick Barry's old team, or *Washington, Capitol,* or *D.C.* for his new ABA team, the Washington Caps. *D* was, on occasion, *Dog. New York* was *Bailey Howell.* A raised fist indicated a play in which the guard came off the forward for a side jump shot. From time to time play calls had riders attached. Clyde would say, DOG, AND GO THROUGH, GOT IT? signaling DeBusschere not to stop for his shot but continue down the lane for an arcing pass from Frazier.

Or Bradley, hearing D.C., THE NEW WAY, would let the defender overplay his baseline route and thereby facilitate his detour to an alternate position higher on the foul lane.

Reed did not require the contrivances his teammates did. If 22-C gave him some distance against the super-pituitaries like Thurmond, Chamberlain and Alcindor, and 19 gave him an isolated strip of court, neither was imperative for his shot. Reed was used to maneuvering in the kind of spaces that accommodate the pay booths of Bell Telephone. What made him able to work those close quarters was the knack he had for levitating very big men; he jabbed the ball into the air as if it were a dog's biscuit, and the Boerwinkles and Unselds and Imhoffs would snap to it like old Fido, the takes varying with the man. Elvin Hayes' infatuation for the blocked shot caused him to soar like Captain Marvel at a sweeping all-out fake. Thurmond was not so impetuous, but a workmanlike tick or two would hold him so that Reed could retreat a step and shoot. The business he did with the ball steadied the Cap'n's bulk when he whirled into spaces, gaining for him the body control he undid in others. Moreover, Reed's left-handedness confused a defender's switchboard the way driving a vehicle in Britain does for a Yank, and so the ease with which Reed jocked the brutes owed something to congenital blessings.

Reed's shooting touch was, in a man his size, just as divine an appointment, and if it thrived on its own, it was no knock on the system. Reed was, after all, a short enough distance from the basket to make plays superfluous. What Reed and/or Frazier did when the Knicks went impromptu was to diversify the attack. The Cap'n's jump shots and Clyde's driving solos to the baskets were diverting acts that served the plays for the attentions they diffused. The swirl of possibilities that Frazier set off when he moved toward the basket and the threat Reed posed when he had the ball were entertainments that kept a foe in flux and New York's plays from calcifying in his mind. And so too did the Knick defense distract, no more allowing a man to ponder the incidence of *Barry, Trap* or *D* than a pack of hounds permits the fugitive to speculate on rent money. The attack was never better than when the team went on its first extended road trip in November with a record of 10 wins in 11 games.

The road this time did not lead to the dim provinces of preseason and so travels bore stranger fruits. The days again swept on top each other but not with the bland insistence they had in the chastelands. The change, though, was not so evident from the manner in which the Knicks occupied these cities. They drifted through hotel lobbies with indifferent slouch, as if the movable 'scape was of no consequence to them. Even Hosket affected the abstracted air, having gained that bearing at some loss to his farmboy gait, an oafishness intermittently recreated by one or another Knick in corridors of airplane terminals and inevitably accompanied by the delighted yowl of WIL-MUH, for Wilmer, Hosket's proper name.

It was fitting that a man's carriage was a matter of some regard. Hosket's evolution had gotten its impetus from his teammates, and suggested the detached figure that players held up for ideal, a standard not arrived at randomly—the cool with which a man carried on in games being much esteemed by pros. The player considered his response to pressure in something of the vain way Lotharios do their profile. A man's failure was met with coy disdain by mates; late-game miscues by Frazier might prompt Reed to say, LOOKS LIKE WE GONNA HAVE TO GIVE THE BALL TO RICH [Barnett] FROM NOW ON, HE GOT THE ICE IN HIS VEINS.

That emphasis on "cool" carried over to the interaction among the players. Two Knicks might slap palms or lay fist on fist at articulated hilarities one moment and pass by one another like strangers the next.

Time in strange places did not alter those circumstances but rather left each man to his own diversions. Barnett's was chess. He would clip theoretical problems that were printed in the daily news sheets and, with his immeasurable calm, figure the solutions on the miniature board he carried with him. In absence of such recreations he evidenced no metabolic changes; his walk caused his teammates to speculate on his waking condition. The ponderous solitude that Barnett's manner conveyed likely was no accident; he had had the loner's habit since a boy in Gary, Indiana. In those days he sat in movie houses and practiced on outdoor baskets alone. *I never really had anybody,* he said, *like . . . that you call close friends, guys that come over to your house and talk with you or stay all night over at your house. It was never like that with me.*

DeBusschere did not share Barnett's implacable acceptance of road life; he had a fair aversion for it, remarkable progress for the roustabout he had been as a professional baseball pitcher in his younger bachelor days. In a town like Vancouver, British Columbia, he and a couple of ex-marines, Bill Fischer and Warren Hacker, would drink until the bars closed at 2:00 A.M. and then would drive forty miles to Horseshoe Bay, where they would rent a motorboat to fish for salmon until noon. Returning to their hotel, they would sleep three or four hours and then have the chef at the hotel cook their salmon for dinner before proceeding to the ball park. Basketball travel by contrast did not have the leisure of baseball schedules; it was a procession of one-night stands whose dreariness got to DeBusschere. "I'm bored to death with it because I'm sick and tired of it," he said. "I just hope there's a cowboy movie on TV. That always kills a couple of hours, maybe it starts me dreaming or something, I don't know what."

Another diversion for DeBusschere was answering the many calls that roommate Bradley got. *I don't know who the hell it's from and I don't really pay any attention . . . ,* DeBusschere said, *but it's just ringing itself off the hook.* The calls rarely caught Bradley in. He kept busy on the road with constructive programs that were legacy for him, his mother once being quoted as saying, "I wanted a Christian upright citizen, and I thought the best way to begin was by promoting things that would interest a little boy." In his youth Bradley had taken instruction in golf, tennis, swimming, piano, French, trumpet, and dancing, and gained a feeling for the use of time that did not cease as a pro athlete.

"The problem," he said, "is the multiple fracture of an athlete's day. It gets a bit irritating, just because I think I play better when I do other things. On days I've had eleven hours' sleep, taken the proper number of limbering steps, eaten the right food, I don't think there's an *obvious* improvement. Some of the best games, I've had no sleep, five appointments, worked in an office all day, walked around the city too much.

"What I'm trying to do is to establish a certain discipline in other areas of my life, because that's always been there . . . provided by school. So I look at time as time to be used in that respect. Depending on where you are, there is always time to do something enjoyable and/or productive and, at times, that which is productive is enjoyable. Obviously you can't read economic theory on a plane or write poetry in first class. You become self-conscious, there are a lot of people looking. But you can read novels or reports, or when you're alone, you can do other stuff that requires more time and thought."

Bradley's literary tastes were diverse, a trip's reading might include *The Iceman Cometh* (O'Neill), *God Bless You, Mr. Rosewater* (Vonnegut), *Exile and Kingdom* (Camus), an anthology of poetry, periodicals, newspapers. Writing was what he called one of the "intensities that are constantly in flux [in my life]."

"I've written," he said. "Not much fiction, mostly essay stuff. I try to record feelings, try to express things clearly. Most of the fiction is autobiographical. It deals with some of the things that happened in my life, impressions of moments that are very strong. Sometimes sport, or social or family things. My stories are fairly naturalistic, sometimes too sentimental. I'll finish one and put it down and say, 'What is this?' I end up putting them away, filing them."

Riordan did not take such tweedy leisure on the road or at home; his habits struck teammates as more eccentric. "Mike and I ride into the city on the train sometimes," said Phil Jackson. "I like to sit and talk, he buys papers and papers. He'll buy a *Times* coming in, a *Post* while he's in the city and the *Daily News* going home from the game. He reads four papers a day—he gets the Long Island paper delivered to his house. So he's constantly busy with it, himself. And it's funny, it's very funny. He's always on planes with two, three papers or books; it's like he doesn't ever sit back and think to himself and close his eyes and relax, you know. He'll sit at the bar and talk to you, but he's always fidgety."

"My mind has to be busy," said Riordan. "If my mind is not

busy, my body has to be busy. When I say busy, I mean active, not just wondering to yourself or thinking about possibilities, this and that. . . . I just can't sit in a room and dawdle, and look out the window, that sort of thing, I get very restless. Planes, something like that, sometimes I get claustrophobia on planes, even on buses from airport to the hotel. I have to have a book in my hand. I just can't keep looking out the window to look at the scenery, I get restless."

"He thinks," said roommate Hosket, "just because I like to sit down and eat a meal like DeBusschere or Bradley or anybody— any normal individual like yourself—he thinks that I'm lazy and fat, calls me Burly Bear because I like to sit down and wait on food. He's probably the most impatient person I ever met. He can't sit down and relax, the guy absolutely cannot relax. Restless or high-strung, whatever you want to call it. This room temperature thing. Like he waits till I fall asleep and then he opens up the door—yeah the door, it's like camping out. When I'm sleeping I like the room real hot and he likes it real cold, that's what I'm talking about."

The compatibility that odd couple Riordan and Hosket lacked, Bowman and Stallworth had. The two had known each other as schoolboy athletes in Texas and as roommates at Wichita State. Bowman recalled an incident just after Stallworth was released from the hospital for the diagnosed heart condition.

Q: So you met him at his hotel?

BOWMAN: I called him, and I came by, y'know.

Q: What was said? Do you remember?

BOWMAN: Uh . . . yeah, he said he had a gift for me, y'know. He had a Christmas present for me. He got me a watch.

Q: What did you say to him?

BOWMAN: It really threw me off because he had never given me a present before, and I couldn't understand why he was doing it this time, y'know.

Q: Did he explain himself?

BOWMAN: No, I didn't ask him to, I just accepted it, and thanked him for it.

Q: Were you moved by it?
BOWMAN: Yeah, I was.

Past times for Bowman and Stallworth were more noteworthy
for mischief than pathos. "Nate had a habit of crushing every center that came into practice with us," said Stallworth, "like fellows
from the freshman team, fellows from the second team. Every
time one of these fellows came in here, Nate would physically
wipe these guys out, it was really funny. But on one particular
day, this fellow named Jerry Davis said, 'Well, I'm going to my
bag of tricks.' So the man, the coach, put Jerry against Nate. Jerry
was a freshman, Nate was an upperclassman. Jerry went up for a
shot and Nate slapped it down and he hit Jerry in the throat and
Nate said, 'Get on back, chump, I'm gonna kill you,' this type of
thing. Jerry said, 'Now, if you keep this up, Nate, I'm going to
take you outside and kill *you*,' shoot on the outside, and Nate said,
'All right, all right, you do that, I'll break every bone in your
body.' So like Jerry moved to the corner and got the ball. He
made a move, faked once, faked twice and stopped. Then he
screamed, just screamed. And Nate damned near touched the ceiling of the gym."

"One time," recalled Bowman, "we were playing in Oklahoma
City in the Oklahoma City tournament and, uh, Dave and I were
roommates, so . . . uh . . . there are always broads around,
even now, but then there were quite a few around too. So this was
the night before our final game, our championship game and, uh,
like this girl had come up to see Dave, y'know, to the room, and
she was in there for about ten minutes and, uh, she said, OK I'm
gonna split and let you guys get some rest, so we say OK, we'll see
you after the game. So she split . . . and about a minute later,
just as she walked out the door, I'll bet it wasn't two minutes,
man, our coach runs in the room, he goes, 'Where is she? Where is
she?' 'Where is who, man?' I'm talking on the phone to one of the
other guys on the team, y'know. 'Where is she? I heard you had
that girl in here. Where is she?' And Dave was laying over there in
the bed, playing like he was asleep, y'know, I'm still talking on the
phone. And the coach is looking all around in the closet and he
looked in the bathroom and he's looking under the bed and he

says, 'Where is she? Where's that girl?' Said, 'Man, there ain't no girl in here.' He said, 'You keeping this boy up, keeping this boy from getting his rest.' And the girl had come to see Dave, man, and he jumped on me. 'You keeping this boy from getting his rest.' "

The road was anointed with night lights and laughing ladies, not a few of the women who waited in hotel lobbies or in arena corridors were camp followers. *So after a couple of us had been with this girl,* one Knick recalled, *she said, "Don't tell so and so of the Celtics." She was something of a namedropper. She took three of us on one night. I think she was a little sick.* The affliction was for celebrity sex, and if it took a girl to request a moment at the crucifix . . . *Look here,* said Barnett, *most of the things that happen when you're a ballplayer, you really can't tell about because most of it has to do with broads and chicks and most of it isn't . . . if you really want the best seller in the world, if you really ran it down like that, you'd have a hell of a story.*

Romance apparently was not part of the game. *It's just a relationship,* said Stallworth, *where when I'm here I'm yours, this type of thing and this is it, like no strings or anything like that.* And so players rode the waves of chance meetings, and if sometimes they took a ludicrous turn, so it went.

"This girl called me," said Bowman, "and said, like, 'Hey Nate.' I said, 'Hey, who is this?' She told me her name, y'know. I can't recall the name and, um, she said, 'Well I'd like to come up and see you.' And I said, 'Well, I don't remember you.' She said, 'Well, I remember *you* and when you see me, you'll remember me.' So I said, 'OK, well come on up,' and, uh, she took a little while, y'know, so when she got there, I was in the bed, y'know. I got up, went to the door. She said, she said, 'Who are you?' I said, 'I'm Nate.' She said, 'No, you're not. You're not Nate Thurmond.' "

Often names did not matter so much as the uniform. In one celebrated case a girl romped about a room with nothing but a Knick jersey on. "Well, in the locker room talk," said Frazier, "the guys are always talking, most of the time it's the same girl. They swap all week. Yeah. Like, if you're a Knick you can get this chick. Like, really, I've gotten out of that bag. Just having a girl just for the sake of . . . like now it's not a challenge to get a girl.

So I set my sights on something different. Maybe she's really beautiful, maybe she can help me in some kind of way, you know, rather than just getting laid, just to be getting it, that's no trouble."

Sugar 'n' spice . . . were not necessarily what the girls were made of. *Like, you might see a guy go out with a girl,* said DeBusschere, *who goes out with every rookie who comes in.* For Knicks who purred GOTTA HAVE IT, GOT TO HAVE SOME in postgame locker rooms, there were ladies in number plotting to give them what they purported to have to have. Some were amenable for all seasons. *In Chicago,* said a Knick, *there was a girl who worked sports all year round, and one time she came into this room a bunch of baseball guys were sitting in and playing cards. She got undressed and sat on the floor and nobody paid any attention—she'd been around too much. So she's sitting there, naked, and begging guys to take her on, trying to make deals. She'd do this and that to them if they just ball her. But no deal anywhere.*

"I've had some call me on the phone," said Frazier, "and say, 'Thank you for coming over to me in the lobby, like I didn't think you'd really remember me.' And so I said, I said, 'Yeah, I still remember you.' I might not even know her but I don't like to make anybody feel bad. Most of the time those chicks are ugly. Every chick I've talked to on the phone—this week I've had about three or four that came to the door—I got sick they were so ugly. I say, I could just tell them, 'What the hell would I want with you? What have you got to offer?' But they seem to be the ones that are always coming after you."

Celebrity romp was not just a road game. Hosket drolly remarked, "New York is a big bad world. This is one thing in college I didn't get too often. Here you'll have Danny Whelan getting notes down on the bench from women in the stands or something. I think some of us who don't get in might do better because our hair keeps nice on the bench or something, maybe the guys get hot and sweaty don't look so good."

The correspondence from women admirers did not have the bleakness of the lonelyhearts columnist's but the mail did bring some weird pieces. Bowman had received several letters from an admirer at Monmouth State College who worked her way up to requesting a photo of him. When Nate later asked that she send him a picture, it was the last he heard of her. Reed heard from a teen-age blonde who wrote voluminous letters that were composed over the course of several days and proclaimed him her flame. Bradley was used to such stuff even as a collegian: at Princeton, mail call invariably brought cookies and cakes sent him by female admirers, and an occasional social proposal. He recalled a discussion he and his secretary had had on whether or not he should escort a corresponding high school girl to her senior prom. The secretary pleaded the girl's case to no avail.

The mail was not limited to bachelor Knicks. "There's this girl," recalled Hosket, "and she used to play around Columbus [Ohio] according to her letter and was an Ohio State fan and now she's playing out on the coast in a girls' league. She wrote me a four-page letter and sent me her statistics—and not her figure either. They were her basketball stats. My wife Patty read it and laughed."

Not all wives were so goodnatured. "I got a letter from a girl this season," said Riordan, "who was in journalism and she wanted to interview me. She went to Fairleigh Dickinson, and wanted to meet me and interview me, any time or place. She had been a debutante. She had modeled for *Vogue* or *Seventeen* and she said I had met her in an East Side pub somewhere last year after the game. I had walked into a place and knew somebody sitting at her table, and she said I didn't take my eyes off her and all throughout the night I kept looking at her. So I left the phone number and everything, put it in with the fan mail. I didn't know what the hell I was going to do with it, and my wife read it before I had a chance to show it to her. She wanted to know what the hell this was all about, who was this girl you couldn't take your eyes off last year, and I pretended like I was going to follow through, it was a very sincere effort on her part to get into journalism. I said, 'Listen she needs a break and I'll give her a break,' and my wife said, 'I'll give you a break.'"

DeBusschere had had at Detroit less calculating admirers who remained dedicated to him even with his departure to Manhattan. "I remember in Detroit," he said, "they would wait there every single game regardless how late you came out, and they'd give me

a card every time, a little card, it was two girls, I don't know who
the hell they were, and [on the card] it could be anything, a cute
little joke, *sink the ball,* some kind of damn thing. And one time I
had a cold and it was put in the paper and I had a get-well card,
at Christmas I got a card, I got a Valentine card, and they waited
every game, sixteen, seventeen years old they were. What brought
it to my attention was last time we were in Detroit, they were
there again. No, I never talked to them outside of they'd hand me
a card, HERE DAVE, and I'd say thank you and keep walking. I
never bothered to spend any time."

The Knicks spent time with each other on the road that they
did not at home. Back in New York, men arrived in the carpeted
well-lit locker room at staggered moments and left for aftergame
pleasures on their own. Coexistence was limited to those short
hours whose focus was the game. Circumstances changed on the
move. The team traveled together, exceptions being made only on
Holzman's approval. On all trips of more than two hours' duration, NBA clubs went first class. Airline policy was to board the
team and its accompanying journalists before other passengers.

Mixups were common for touring teams. Changes in weather
conditions might send Blauschild and Whelan to terminal counters to rearrange itineraries or unravel baggage confusion, the
classic accident in this respect occurring when Bradley's gear was
rerouted to Munich. The confusion that attended road trips did
not cause undue concern among players; they appeared to be
above such petty business. It was all the same for them.

Meal money was sixteen dollars a day. Tastes in cuisine varied.
Russell was conscious of a balanced diet. Riordan espoused the
roast beef sandwich and special dressing produced in mass at
Arby's roadside stands. Bradley sluiced wines in his mouth for
heightened taste. Holzman ate lightly before a game, took his big
meal after the game. He had acquired in his travels as a scout the
repute of Hines or Claiborne; Chicago Bull scout Krause remembered how basketball men always deferred to Holzman in the
choice of restaurants; Whelan called him the daVinci of the dining table.

Lodgings generally were made at short distance from the arena
in which the game was scheduled. Blauschild, Whelan, Holzman

and the writers took single rooms, the players doubles. On those occasions that the hotel was not near the playing house it was apt to be near the local racetrack, the horses being a particular passion of the coach and his retinue, a group that included Blauschild, Whelan and the writers.

The locker room on the road was a more casual place. The team was not so beleaguered by the New York press, whose epicurean leisure in pregame dinners profitted team privacy, working most conspicuously to free the Knicks' foremost raconteur and jive-talker, Barnett, of inhibitions.

"A reporter," recalled Hosket, "says something like, 'Dick, this feeling the fans have, you know, this great throbbing, the way they're getting up for these ball games and the way they roar to the last instant and how they want the team to keep the other guys under a hundred points and the great roar you got tonight, does this have a real tendency to fire you up?' And Dick looks around and says, 'No.' Just like he was asleep or something and the guy was expecting, like, a five-minute quote. He asked Barnett a series of seven, eight questions, you know, and Dick would just say, 'No, a crowd's a crowd, man. I've been playing too long,' he just refuses to talk to them. Like last year, Dick got thirty-two [points] one night and the news guy says—you know, he hit about like fourteen for seventeen from the floor and it was unbelievable—and the guy says, 'Dick, this thirty-two is the most you scored in thirty-five ball games, how do you feel?' and all this. And Dick says, 'It's sure great to win,' and looks down and starts untying his shoes and the guy says, 'Well, do you feel like the moves you were making . . . you always seem to be taking Loughery one-on-one tonight, is there any particular reason?' 'No,' Dick would say, 'it's just the flow of the game,' or something like that, real quiet. And then the press left, and Dick jumped up and yelled, 'GodDAMN, I was a monster out there tonight,' and he just starts talking about this move and that move and how he was doooo-in' it tonight. He's always talking about doooo-in' it tonight."

Barnett had a flair for taking words to rarefied dictionary heights. The standard derisive *boo* was transformed to BOO-AAAY by him and used as the ultimate locker room squelch. *This is when a fellow has been trapped into something,* said Stallworth. *Like, if you make a mistake, say something wrong, get caught in a lie or something, then it's BOO-AAAAY BOO-AAAY-AAY-AAY.* The wonders of hipped tongue did not cease for him. *Like, when you need your hair combed or something like that,* said Stallworth, *he might say, "Your afro ain't togafro," stuff like this. Nobody knows how Dick come by any of that stuff. He just comes up with it. Like, sometimes I think the fellow dreams about these things, I really do.*

The reconstruction of the language was for Barnett a minor amusement, what gave him eminence on the team were the outlandish tales he told. Literal facts were said to be sacrificed for comedic effects to such an extent that once when Barnett's account of undergraduate days at Tennessee State were overheard and printed, the authorities there marked him down for slanderer. Whether or not this experience taught him public caution is nowhere recorded, but in attitude toward a stranger like Sly he remained circumspect enough to give for his residence a fashionable address on the East Side rather than the room number at the Hotel New Yorker where he lived. Only the trust that time brings made him change his cover.

The stories that Barnett recounted were not, to his thinking, society's possessions. *I call what I got inside humor,* he said. *Some of it is for the ballplayers and nobody else to hear, put it like that.* Nor was he a source for the personality cultists. *Like, what the writers do is get all these anecdotes about you, most of them boolshit, so that you come out like one big anecdote, like a clown.* He maintained in locker rooms the inscrutable front of a sphinx save for those moments when the doors were barred to outsiders. Then the tales came.

"All the time, all the time," said Russell. "He talks about guys in his neighborhood, they used to get involved in mischievous things. One guy had a bad leg and they were chasing him, the cops were chasing him and the guy was hollering that he couldn't run because he had one leg longer than the other, so he got up on the side of the curb and he evened himself up."

"He'd tell you stories," said Hosket, "like one night they're playing an exhibition game in a high school gym or something and there was this guy Madman McMillan—he's always talking about this guy—and they'd taken all the basketballs in after the teams warmed up, which is standard procedure in a lot of places, and so Madman McMillan fouled out and had a tantrum right out on the floor. And he left the floor with the game ball and went and locked himself in the locker room and the janitor had gone home and locked up the other balls and they didn't have a ball to play with. So Barnett said they're going up to the locker door one at a time trying to find out who Madman's best friend was, to have him give up the ball."

Always he harked back to Tennessee State, particularly the unpredictable things that could occur on the road, such as the foul lines at Jackson State, where a free throw was a long lay-up at one end and a considerable set shot at the other. "We were playing Arkansas A and M," Barnett would say, "and they had a one-arm official and they had really been cheating. It was tough to win on the road and, at this particular time, a guy named John Barnhill stole the ball with about five, six seconds left and the score tied. Barnhill stole the ball, he was running in for a lay-up and I was watching this guy, this one-arm official, I was watching him 'pecifically to see what he was going to try to do to nullify this play. I knew he was going to try. Barnhill was going in for the lay-up, so the ref tried to reach for his whistle, but he reached for it with the short arm and he couldn't get it, he couldn't get the whistle into his mouth. By the time he reached there with the other arm, Barnhill had made the basket and the buzzer had gone off but otherwise he probably would have called traveling or something.

"And then there was the time we were playing at a college called Philander Smith in Arkansas. And, like, first of all we shouldn't have had a problem beating this team. I think when we played them at Tennessee State, we beat them like 130 to 40, and then when we got down there, the score at the end of regulation time was about 70–70. So we won it in overtime but now we were on our way back to Tennessee State the next day and we read in the paper where we had got beaten in double overtime, that after we left the floor the ref called a technical on the coach and the guy made the two free throws and they beat us. In that same game they had no net on one basket, so I think I made about five baskets that—like, if the ball comes straight at the basket and you're behind the play, you can't tell if the ball went in or if it dropped short, so the referee was calling it short all the time. But I exposed the sucker, I started banking it."

For the Knicks, time came undone on the road. *Tell about the same food, the same hotels, the same stewardess minds,* said Bradley, *and how you lose track of the days.* There was a strangeness on those days, a netherworld quality heightened by the similarity of mechanisms in each city. The feeling of dislocation from their surroundings made Knicks resort to devices that brought them a sense of their customary days' rhythms. For some it was through music: their "sounds" created familiarity within alien spaces. The television served the same purpose: many players tuned in first thing upon entering a room and sometimes left it playing without bothering to look at it. Once or twice in interviews with Sly, a Knick would silence the voice but leave the picture, and never bother to eye the screen during the session. For Frazier, the telephone was his pacifier: on the road, he would run up substantial long-distance bills. Others found their comfort at the dining table, taking meals or snacks on the slightest pretext; in their rooms were Fritos and apples and candy bars and sodas and other morsels for the compulsive eater. In all these rituals was the numbed traveler's search for place. Holzman once remarked on posttime at the local racetrack, only to be informed that he was not in the city he suspected but in some other instead.

For most Knicks, the games regulated their comings and goings; until they departed for the arena, most players did not want to be bothered. *Somebody called,* said Riordan, *and rang thirty-seven times. I counted them. Well, I figured if he was stubborn enough to let it ring that many times, I was stubborn enough not to pick it up.* Sly got a feeling for the dreary waiting around, and the restlessness that drove players to dining counters at any hour of the day. In informal ways, he also got a sense of the players. Bradley, rushing off to practice from a coffee shop, forgot his bill and left Sly to cover. Bowman, noting Sly's seatmate on a flight, winked authoritatively and afterward inquired about her friends. When Sly, sporting a mustache and long hair at the time, was mistaken at an airport for a member of the Grateful Dead, a rock group,

May found it mildly amusing. A stewardess doubting Sly's credentials for early boarding of a flight led Barnett to say in his dead-
pan way, "They don't think you got the Knick-a-bocker image."

And so it went. Road life was ritualistic stop and go. Whisper
jets. Marquees saying, WELCOME NY KNICKS. Room service.
Ringaling ringaling, SAY, LOOK HERE MAN, NO CALLS FOR
THE REST OF THE AFTERNOON. BARNETT, ROOM 642.
Afternoons were spent in sanitarized odorized notarized hotels
and motels where jockstraps and jerseys were strewn on carpeted
floors, and players read SKIDDING ROCKETS FACE KNICKS
TONIGHT. When it was finally time to come together, sneakers
and gear were packed in Adidas bags. There were words laughter
BOO-AY. Holzman would say CLYDE, CLYDE. WHERE'S
THE CAP'N? And off they'd go

to

these

places

MILWAUKEE
where a sign on the Bucks' dressing room wall read: "They said it
couldn't be done but the Jets did it. They said it couldn't be done
but the Mets did it. They say it can't be done but the Bucks will
do it."

Milwaukee had a pep song, too, and a dixieland band to play it.
Alcindor was more meditative. He paced up and down the side-
line before the game.

Referee Manny Sokol (Asofsky knew him in the Brooklyn
YMHA leagues as Sokolofsky) got it from the wunderfans in Mil-
waukee. HOPE YOU CAN SLEEP TONIGHT, YOU HEBE,
which caused Bradley to remark afterward, "They're very
efficient people, you know."

Riordan got it from Alcindor, an elbow in the face after a stra-
tegic foul. Riordan smiled, patted him on the rump and told him
the Cap'n would fix his ass.

In the game, DeBusschere pulled a move not unlike the quar-
terback bootleg. He faked a handoff to Bradley at the foul line

*and went the other direction, by Greg Smith. The Knicks won,
109–93.*

On the way to

PHOENIX

*the stewardess announced it was 81 degrees there the day before,
prompting Blauschild to say, "When it reaches 84, I sell."*

A near sellout was assured in that city through a tie-in arrangement with the state fair on the premises adjacent to the Veterans
Memorial Coliseum.

Phoenix was Goldwater country. On the fairgrounds were
booths for Operation Crime Stop, the Citizens Committee for Respect for Authority, hymn singing. From a local paper: "A hearing was set yesterday for November 13 to determine if a controversial Swedish picture now playing in Phoenix is obscene. The
film, I Am Curious (Yellow) . . ."

A man introduced as Arizona's own cowboy, Rex Allen, asked
the crowd to kindly join him in the singing of one of his favorite
songs and, so saying, launched into the anthem.

Shortly after, debris came down on the court in, lawd, an unorderly fashion when officials' calls contradicted public opinion in
Phoenix. Fried chicken, corn cobs, paper cups littered the floor. In
the stands, a female partisan called referee Ed Rush a popular
compound obscenity. None of it helped the local team. New York
won, 116–99.

In Phoenix, Cazzie Russell was sidelined with an aching back
for which he had slept on the floor of his room in Milwaukee,
without even a mattress. Russell's affliction gave Reed occasion to
debunk the wonder wheel as a crippler and in

SAN DIEGO

to remark, "What the cat say? Cazzie the most perfectly developed humpback in existence."

BOOO-AY.

The San Diego team was having troubles, its 1–8 record led
Knicks to visualize trades. WSHOO, WSHOOO, Riordan blew
into Hosket's ear and announced, "Hear the trade winds, Hos?
You and a hairpiece for Toby Kimball."

In San Diego, Sly joined a private workout of several Knicks, *and came away surprised by the rigorous screens that were set. His own game was pronounced impressive enough—for a writer. Stallworth, seeing him sink 15-foot jumpers later in the year, would chant, "Sly-yyy, Sly-yyyy. All right."*

There were offdays in San Diego. Stallworth used them to visit an old friend. Pinky was now living in the San Diego area and doing creditably in schoolboy sports there. Other Knicks piled into a rented car and, with Sly at the wheel, went to Tijuana. Directed to a night spot there by a local cabbie, the group executed a smart fastbreak when the place was discovered for a mangy brothel. At a bar later that night, Frazier said, "Chick that latched on to me was old enough to be my grandmother."

In the locker room before the Rocket game, old pro Barnett squeezed a rubber ball and announced, "Trying to get myself like Cazzie." DeBusschere filed a callus on his foot. Frazier lay on his back reading the Sporting News.

The game was not close. New York won, 129–111.

Afterward, the injured Russell performed a Ray Charles concert. He used a Falstaff beer bottle for his microphone and his imagination to conjure up a piano. As he mimed some fancy keyboard work, Whelan said, "He's playing that piano for his bad back." Cazzie was oblivious to remarks. Signing off after a fine rendition of "Georgia," he said, "That's jazzie Cazzie you're listening to, and he'll be back tomorrow night."

On the bus to the airport, Barnett commented on Whelan. "Seen in a wheelchair with varicose veins in his eyes . . ." And the scotch-drinking trainer smiled all the way to

LOS ANGELES
where the arena was a version of the ancient Colosseum.

The pressroom there had a miniature hockey game over which Augie Borgi of the Bergen Record *and Tom Rogers of* The New York Times *bent in competition.*

The Lakers were playing without Wilt Chamberlain, who was hospitalized with a ruptured tendon high in the right kneecap. His replacement, rookie Rick Roberson, was not in shape for Reed. The Cap'n had him shooting shots off the side of the backboard and got him so enraged that Roberson threw a fist at a loose ball one time. Unfortunately, his aim was poor: he hit DeBusschere in the nose and broke it.

Whelan offered to straighten the nose, but DeBusschere recommended a hospital.

The Knicks won, 112–102, and had fried chicken in the locker-room afterward, compliments of Laker forward, Elkin Baylor, a vice-president of a local quick eats organization.

In

SAN FRANCISCO

Hosket called Sly a ballhog when he wouldn't pass him the ball in an informal two-on-two workout. Sly contended that Hosket should work his defender, John Warren, near the boards rather than from the corners of the floor. Pursuant to this conviction, he put the freeze on Hosket.

In the prelim to the night's game, there was women's basketball.

"It's a strange game," said Bob Macaluso, one of the coaches of the women's teams. "I'm used to coaching high school boys and sometimes by reflex you go to pat 'em on the rear end, you got to be extremely careful."

Women reacted to the game as men did. Missed shots drew muttered obscenities and one player, Dana Klein, raised her arm every time she scored, as Dolph Schayes used to.

Walking through a special chandeliered section for season ticket holders was a cantilevered cocktail waitress. The way the Warriors were playing, a belt or two helped.

That night, Reed acquired a puffed lip which Bowman said made him resemble Moms Mabley, and DeBusschere played with an aluminum and foam contrivance over his nose. Riordan was sent into the game to check San Francisco's Jeff Mullins, who'd scored 24 points in the first half. He limited him to six points the rest of the game. WAY TO CLEAN UP THE COAST, KNICKS, said Psychedelic Sid after the 116–103 win, New York's ninth in a row and 15th in 16 games.

The success did not spoil the Knicks but created a few waves in their environs. In the Knickerbocker office on the fourth floor of 4

Pennsylvania Plaza, telephones rang incessantly, and once when Blauschild required a line to the outside world, the team's gracious secretary, Joanne Dinoia, was forced to obtain it in another office.

The cause of most of the commotion was the urgency for tickets that people felt, a situation that made ticket scalpers ecstatic; moving furtively through pregame crowds on the Seventh Avenue side of the Garden they flashed their overpriced pasteboards like dealers in French postcards, carrying on with an eye to the roving copper. Business was good, a man could turn a $20 profit on a ticket and even after a game started could make a $5 margin on a $7 loge seat. A New Jersey housewife paid $12 so that she could keep an eye on her two sons in seats also acquired that night through a scalper.

Nowhere was the madness for tickets more evident than in the team's Penn Plaza office. Each day there were on the jingling phones people seeking tickets who claimed to be blood kin to Reed, Frazier, DeBusschere, maybe even Irving Mitchell Felt. Miss Dinoia jotted the names down on the chance that one of them really might have a claim to lineage.

Another approach was more direct. Adults who needed tickets would phone the Knick office and offer everything from hot plates to all-expenses-paid vacations in Atlantic City. "One man worked for a furniture company," said Joanne Dinoia, "and he told me if I got him two tickets to one of the games, he would give me free furniture for my bedroom and things like that. He'd been trying all year to get the tickets, and he said last year at the beginning of the season he didn't have any trouble and now the box office wasn't able to give him anything. He'd tried theater agencies, and he said if I could get him these two tickets, he'd be glad to give me any furniture that I would need."

People went to even greater lengths for tickets at the time of the Knick winning streak. A member of the team's official scorers' crew, Al Martell, one night discovered that tickets left each game in his name at a lobby window had been claimed by another party. Subsequent investigation found a tenant from his apartment building occupying one of the seats.

Some tickets were, of course, available. Blauschild and his as-

sistant, Jimmy Wergeles, had for each game complimentaries that
were dispatched to a privileged few. In the gratis courtside seats
directly behind the press table and teams' benches sat, on occa-
sion, former Knick coaches and players like Braun, Levane, Joe
Lapchick; columnists Larry Merchant and Milton Gross; Holzman's wife Selma and daughter Gail; comedian Phil Foster; New
York Mets Art Shamsky and Ken Boswell; Phil Jackson and Milt
Williams; NBA commissioner Kennedy and his assistant Carl
Scheer, novelist-screenwriter (*Butch Cassidy* . . .) William
Goldman, Garden executives and assorted acquaintances of the
Knickerbocker organization. Family and friends of the players
and opposition sat there, too, each Knick being entitled to three
complimentaries, the foe two.

The furor about the Knickerbockers at this time was fueled by
the media. Representatives of radio, TV, newspapers, magazines
crowded into the New York locker room after each game in dizzying numbers. Hosket, at midway station between Frazier's and
Barnett's dressing cubicles, feared being trampled by them and
flippantly considered asking Holzman for permission to shower
early before the games were finished. DeBusschere and Riordan
took to slugging their postgame beers in the sanctity of Whelan's
training room.

Holzman had a dim view of media business. He regarded it the
way young lads do ballroom dancing, as a social obligation that
affronted hairy-chested dignity. The verities for him were sweat,
sirloin and SEE THE BALL. He might mock a writer not part of
his drinking clique by suggesting notescribbling as a sissifying
process—LOOKIT YOU WITH THAT DAMNED NOTEPAD—
and, failing to embarrass Sly into acquiescence, thereafter ignored
him.

It was tougher for Holzman to ignore the mob that accompanied the streak. Not only did he consider what they did as *bullcrap*, but also he feared the effect it could have on his team. *All
the time, he keeps emphasizing*, said Riordan, *the only reason
they want to interview you, the only reason you get a commercial
is the fact that you're ready to win, ready to come out and play
ball every night. So he emphasizes that a lot, he tries to tone
things down.*

The attentions that Knicks got did not distract the players; most of them had no idea of the cumulation of victories. "You know what?" said Barnett. "I wasn't even aware that we had a streak until we got to about fifteen. I very seldom read the New York sports pages and I don't even keep up with it, you know, because it's like I said, it's so much boolshit in there that I don't even like to read it. Most of them are half-truths if not outright lies. So I don't even go into it. When I really became aware of it, when we were coming out on the floor in Atlanta and the guy announced, you know, sixteen straight."

"Like, we didn't have that many nerveracking games," said Frazier. "We were winning by twenty points or more, so this made it a lot easier, I guess, than if we were just squeaking by, the pressure would begin to mount. But the way we were winning, like, it was no big thing."

Knickerbockers were as much pressured by friends as by the opposition. The search for the elusive ticket kept their phones ringing. Riordan would go to a family affair and relatives would pester him for tickets. DeBusschere would get a call on the road from a man alleging to be a very close friend of his father, and DeBusschere would inform the man that his father had been dead many years now, and no ticket.

Players developed routines to handle such requests. At home their wives might screen phone calls or, in the case of others, the receiver would come off the hook at strategic rest hours. "I don't have that pressure," said Barnett, "because when I get home I put a 'no disturb' on my phone, and I don't be bothered with anybody, I don't get any calls. I don't receive no calls from the time I'm there [at the Hotel New Yorker] to the time I leave. The majority of people don't even know I'm there, but the people that do know—and the majority of 'em I don't want to be bothered with—I just cut off. No phone calls, and that's it."

There were so many phone calls at the Knick office that management eventually installed an intercom system, hired another secretary, Gwinne Bloomfield, and added one more phone to increase their outside lines from four to eleven. "We had to have these extra lines," said secretary Dinoia. "As soon as we put down the phone, another one rings. And, you see, the switchboard operators automatically throw a call on to our line, so that one day we could not get in touch with people."

The pressures sometimes got to people who worked in the office. One night in the Garden pressroom, Wergeles lost his cool when a writer from Newspaper Enterprise Association, Lee Mueller, asked him for an authenticating press badge. Wergeles first suggested that Mueller was in possession of it and, when the writer asserted he was not, the Knickerbocker publicist threw the badge off a wall so that it landed near Mueller, who looked down at it and walked away.

The Knicks were not so affected by the streak. The nerve that was touched in their case was situated in the funnybone, the laughter the hearty asskicker's sort. BOO-AAAY-AAAY, *My man* [Jim] *Fox go into the closet tonight,* Barnett proclaimed after Reed manhandled the Phoenix pivot. *My man Bernie* [Williams] *trying to get on the books* [i.e. score], *the mutha almost broke the backboard,* said Cazzie Russell. Reed teased Bradley about his late-game baskets: *Good thing you got the last three baskets or your scoring average in trouble, way to keep up the pressure, Dollah Bill.* Bradley might hear as well the remark of a frustrated fan, *Go back to Rhodes.*

The professional consecutive victory record of 17 was first set by the 1946 Washington Capitols and equaled by the 1959 Boston Celtics, and when the Knicks tied it against Atlanta on November 26, they did it in the uncompromising fashion of the bird-shattering pioneer. New York led only 68–61 when the third quarter started but in short order the Knicks ran through Atlanta with a thoroughness not witnessed in those parts since Sherman.

DeBusschere made the first of many interceptions and turned it upcourt to Frazier, who drew the ball back like Sagittarius on a jumper, and was fouled. Clyde hit both shots: 74–66. Moments later, an inbounds pass by the Hawks' Jim Davis exceeded its receiver, Barnett picked it up and dribbled in his flatfooted way downcourt for the basket. The Hawks came apart. Atlanta's Lou Hudson drove down the right side where Bradley took the ball from his hands before he could spring from the floor, and passed it to Frazier for the basket. When Hazzard tried to drive the middle, Bradley again pried the ball away and gave Frazier another lay-up, 90–69.

Then Clyde, the portrait of the artist as a young ballsnitch, performed glide and thrust assassinations on Atlanta guard Walt Hazzard. The first time Frazier got the ball he eased ahead of the dribbler on the right sideline, crouched and then poked the ball away. Shortly after, he caught Hazzard on the left sideline calling a play and in this slack movement he again turned on the ball. The third steal and basket came when he put the stroke on Hazzard from behind.

Somewhere in here the scorers lost track of a Knick basket and referee Jack Madden had to consult Knick TV announcer Bob Wolff for the proper count. Mercifully for the Hawks, the quarter ended soon thereafter, the Knicks having scored 38 points to Atlanta's 12, assuring New York of its 17th consecutive victory, 138–108.

The game for the record was two days later in the Cleveland Arena against Cincinnati. The Royals' coach, Bob Cousy, had been a member of the 1959 Celtics team that had won 17 in a row and, in his day, was a nonpareil at what journalists called legerdemain, and fans more commonly knew as *hip-pah dip-pah*. To rouse public interest for basketball spectacles in Cincinnati, Cousy had the week before returned to active playing status at age forty-one, seven years after he had announced his retirement in 1962–63.

The locker rooms in Cleveland to which Cousy and the rest repaired were small and low-ceilinged and had an exposure of radiators and pipework, places more suited to the American Hockey League players that dressed there than the rangier basketball sorts. (On a towel-dispensing machine: HAVE YOU EVER SEEN THE [Cleveland hockey] BARONS PLAY? and this scratched in response: OUI OUI.)

Before the game a young fan who said he had come from Buffalo, New York, to see the game, asked Cazzie Russell for his autograph, and was refused when he mistook him for Willis Reed. Later, when Russell signed for those who had no confusion about his name, the lad returned.

"Are you Willis Reed?" he asked, whiningly. "I came all the way from Buffalo."

"What I say, man? I'm not Reed."

When the identity crisis finally was resolved, the fan swearing his faith in the Knicks and Russell, and offering once again for proof the commendable trip from Buffalo, he got his autograph and Cazzie got some peace.

There was no mistaking Russell for any other dribbleball specimen on one of his characteristic scoring tears. If most other players affected petrified boredom at their own inspired deeds, Cazzie did not; in a league of Buster Keatons he was Cantinflas. At work, Russell's devices were a spare jump shot in which he rocked back and let the ball go on a tight trajectory (he did not require Barnett's tortured elevator or Frazier's calibrating sling) and driving moves he made with arms akimbo and shoulders rolling, as if he were wired to a Tito Puentes LP. When Russell's game was on, the magic adrenal ingredient sporting titans are said to possess was roused, and he and the body rhythms to which he referred in sacrosanct tones became the lovely fusion one sees in the whirl of prizefight knockouts. Cazzie seemed to savor how *to-gethuh* sinew and step were; the artful gestures that attended his baskets became more pronounced, from the thumb-raised melody of arms to a held followthrough that gave him the aspect of an artist admiring his brushwork. The pleasure he had at those moments put galleries in raptures. Russell's emotive quirks were for them the semaphores that cunning winks can be, and what the crowds gave back to him was a collective ooomph that swelled to orgiastic rah for baskets, or expired in literal moans when he did not shoot the ball, which, in either case, agitated Cazzie as much as he did the house.

That night in Cleveland Russell got the Knicks going. At 8:16 of the second quarter he hit a 20-foot jump shot and before the period ended he had made 6 of 7 field goals and 2 of 2 free throws to turn a 30–23 first-quarter deficit to a 55–52 halftime advantage for New York. New York could not maintain the momentum that Russell gave it, and the game settled into what broadcasters refer to as a "seesaw" contest. Cincinnati led 101–98 with a minute and

49 seconds left when its star, Oscar Robertson, was expelled from the game for his sixth personal foul of the evening, the legal limit. At Robertson's banishment, Cincinnati coach Cousy inserted himself into the lineup rather than risk using a rookie, Herman Gilliam, or a so-so ballhandler Adrian Smith. Cousy was now graying in the scalp, and the one-hander he loosed from a grounded stance was a relic like Packards and penny loafers. The sight of his thin slope-shouldered body amongst the sleekly wrought younger men struck the eye for time's mismatch the way Joe Louis' had next to Marciano's prime beef. Next to these springy studs, Cousy resembled a gym teacher and not the man whose court trickery once inspired more hyperbole per column of newsprint than any other pro.

In his first moments into the game, Cousy renewed his legend by throwing a crosscourt hook pass to a rookie guard, Norm Van Lier, for an open jump shot, and by coolly sinking two free throws to give Cincinnati a 105–100 lead with 26 seconds remaining in the game.

Only then was Cousy, to use a term of Barnett's, "exposed," the Knickerbocker guard himself getting by Cousy with a stutter dribble to create defensive swarm that left Reed open near the basket. The Cap'n got the ball and, in crowded quarters, barreled from a standstill but missed the shot. Reed recovered the errant ball and was fouled on the follow shot by Cincinnati's Tom Van Arsdale.

Now Riordan came into the game for Barnett, and he and Frazier rather than New York's forwards lined up on the foul lane, making plain the club's intention to deploy in a full-court press after Reed's free throws. In the bonus situation afforded him by Cincinnati's surfeit of team fouls for the quarter, Reed made two of three shots and narrowed the score to 105–102.

On the inbounds play, Van Lier was unable to work free of Bradley's coverage, and Cousy was forced to call the Royals' last time-out, which gave Cincinnati the ball at half-court. Cousy managed to get the ball into play this time but with regrettable consequence. DeBusschere beat Van Arsdale to the pass and continued to the basket where he flicked the ball downward with an uncharacteristic dunking flourish. *I didn't want to take any chances*, he said. *A guy like Johnny Green is liable to come from the side door and put it in seventh heaven.*

Cincinnati still led, 105–104, when Cousy made the pass in after the basket. Van Arsdale dribbled up the right sideline against De-Busschere. SEE THE BALL, DAMMIT, SEE THE BALL! Riordan saw the ball and went for it, forcing Van Arsdale to change direction but not dribbling hand, a technical omission that made it easier for the onrushing Reed to deflect the ball as Van Arsdale tried to pass it.

The ball bounced into the air, Frazier got it and started to the basket. Just beyond the keyhole he spied DeBusschere open, *you know, for a lay-up, but I knew there was only a short amount of time.* Instead Frazier bounded into the air like a broad jumper and let the ball go in midflight. It missed but came directly back to him: *see, my momentum kept me going to the basket so as it came back I tried to shoot it on the way down. And Van Arsdale fouled. I was wishing like hell that it had gone in. I didn't want to go to the line like that.*

The foul line on occasion was troublesome for Frazier; in an earlier game against Philadelphia he had missed three free throws in the last minute. *At times*, he said, *I stand on the line like I'm standing in mud. My feet, no matter how I put them, don't feel comfortable.* Clyde did not rattle now. The first foul shot was, as he put it, all bottoms, it went through cleanly. *I was confident then*, he said. *If I had missed the first one I would have been a little uptight. When I made the first I knew it was over.* The second shot won the game, 106–105.

POP! POP!

Flashbulbs went off. Barnett obliged a photographer with an open-mouthed look of ecstasy. Clyde held a bottle of Black Label and stared at the floor. Bradley wandered around the room, grinning. FAR BE IT FROM ME TO BOAST, shouted Russell, BUT WE DUNNNNNN-NIT. Hands clapped, feet stomped. Holzman and Frazier stood for a photo. YOU KNOW WHO THE BEST-LOOKING GUY IN THIS PHOTO'LL BE, Clyde said. Falsetto voices. A shower hissed. Newsmen scribbled on pads, the electronic media pushed their mikes at people. WE DUNNNNNNNN-

NIT. . . . THE KNICKS, said Cazzie Russell, HAVE ESTAB-
LISHED A NEW RECORD . . . they laughed all the way to the
taverns . . . some of it BOO-AAAY . . . *Cincinnati's dressing
room,* remembered Riordan, *was right next to ours . . . and a lot
of guys just forgot about the fact that they were next door . . .*
BOOOO-AAAY . . . COUSY . . . CHUMP . . . BOO-AAAY-
AAAAY. It was a night for BOO-AAY, one of the last for a while.
The streak was to finish right there in Cleveland and the times be
less rollicking a while. But for now there were smiles.

An unsmiling Cousy came back to the Holiday Inn, at which
both teams were in residence. He had the aggrieved expression of
a mourner. The sight of it so disheartened Knick telecaster Wolff
that he chose not to get on the same elevator with him. *I've
known Cousy for a long time,* he said, *and just felt funny about
his embarrassment.*

Cousy had problems more permanent than a lone game's bungling. Like many other NBA coaches, he had to contend with the
friction that assailed a team not so advantaged as the Knicks,
in particular that of his superstar, Oscar Robertson. Robertson
had most prepossessing talents for the game but an autocratic
tendency in regard to the ball. On Cincinnati teams Robertson
had controlled the ball the way the Vatican does blessings and
dispensed passes only to those who observed the dogma of cut 'n'
shoot. Should a man prefer that the ball and not the player be the
source of an attack's motion, likely as not he would wait for
Godot.

That is what often happened to the team's best forward, Jerry
Lucas. In his rookie year, he returned to a Royal huddle and alluded that the ball was scarce for him. Robertson told him to get
it off the backboard if he wanted it. Such strictures did not promote harmonic function. Lucas developed a waspish attitude
about ball deprivation. "There was a situation in Cleveland," recalled a former Royal, Harold (Happy) Hairston, "that arose one
night where Jerry Lucas and I got in an argument over whether I
should or should not have passed the ball. And he yelled at me
and I yelled back at him—this is on the court, and it sort of proceeded to the locker room."

Some felt the source of team discord was Robertson. "Jerry,"

said Hairston, "stated a lot of times he should have gotten the ball
more, but there'd be nights where he wouldn't. He'd get about
three, four shots. Oscar would never really say anything about it.
If he said anything it would probably be to himself or to his
friends. . . . [John] Tresvant got traded for the same reason
Fred Hetzel [did]. They said that, well, you know, Oscar controlled the ball too much."

Those not *simpático* to Robertson's ways who remained on the
team might be ignored by him. Said a writer traveling with Oscar:
"Like every time you see a team in the locker there's always some
noise between the guys on the team, 'Let's go out there and give
them a game,' and this and that, just something that shows the
guys know each other but between Lucas and Oscar there was
none."

At San Diego, five Rockets could not make do with one basketball, the most notable malcontent being the team's leading scorer,
Elvin Hayes. There were historic antecedents for the tumult here.
Newsman Marty Ralbovsky recalled a Rocket game in Cleveland
the previous season in which Hayes had berated his teammates on
the court for not getting the ball to him. San Diego writer Bud
Maloney charted Hayes' avarice occasionally that year and, in one
game, found he shot the ball 28 of 29 times he handled it.
"Hayes," said Maloney, "is interested only in himself. He doesn't
pass, he doesn't screen and he's answerable to no one but the
owner."

Ralbovsky recalled, "The night I saw San Diego in Cleveland,
there was a pretty good indication of trouble there. After the
game the black players tossed on their sweat suits and overcoats
and, without showering, walked across the street to the Holiday
Inn. When I checked things out with different players, I found
that what I'd seen that night was not an isolated instance. Just to
check it out further, I called Phil Norman of the *San Diego Union*.
He said, 'Oh sure, that's common knowledge out here.' Two hours
later, I got a call from the Rockets' publicity guy. He said, 'We're
gonna deny it. If it's slanderous, we'll sue.'

"An hour later, I got a call from the player who'd been my main
source, a guy I knew from high school. He said, 'What I told you,

I told you as a friend.' Later he called again and said that management had called all the ballplayers in and asked who'd spoken to Ralbovsky? The guy admitted he had, and they made him make the call in their office. They threatened to trade him if he didn't."

The advent of Connie Hawkins, a new superplayer at Phoenix, altered the situation of the team's incumbent star, Gale Goodrich, requiring him to accommodate Hawkins by delivering the ball to him from his backcourt position. Whether or not he did it at a frequency commensurate to Hawkins' talent is a cloudy question; suffice it to say there was a disagreement among the players that was divisive for the team. The situation depreciated under coach John Kerr whose predicament resembled that of the gentlemanly Dick McGuire. "What happened," said an observer there, "was that a guy like Hawkins might be late fifteen minutes, couple of other times he was late, he was always late. He was continuously testing Kerr and he'd come up with some really bullshit story, why he was late and stuff like this, and then everybody else started in. Then Goodrich was late, then other people were late. He gave Jerry Chambers a week to lose, I think it was, ten pounds, and it would cost Jerry two hundred dollars if he didn't lose it, and Jerry didn't even try. And then John forgot about it, you know, that was it.

"And there was malice. Just kind of mimicking things that Kerr does, the way he would talk, the way he would phrase, you know, in pantomime and stuff like that. In other words, he told you to go out there and do something and then guys would go out there and fuck around and run all over the place and never even try to do it and there wasn't any discipline there. He wouldn't take a guy out of the game or anything like that. Then in a game going down to the final minutes where a lot of games are decided, the team wasn't prepared at all, it didn't have any special things. All he could say was, 'Give the ball to Hawkins or give the ball to Goodrich.' "

At Baltimore, the problem was again of shot equality. Backcourtmen Monroe and Loughery were contortionists at getting a ball into the air, and when a toothpick-chewing rookie guard named Mike Davis proved nearly as unconscionable a gunner, Bullet forward Gus Johnson remarked every so often about the neglect of a fine broth of a lad like himself.

Dereliction was, for Johnson, habitual in the organization at Baltimore. Recalled an NBA man: "Last year Gus gets hurt. Gus gets his knee cut on . . . it's really bad. Now he's doped up and lying in the hospital in Baltimore for six days and [former Baltimore general manager Buddy] Jeannette is up there—Buddy is no longer associated with the team, he's been fired—he's up there four days out of those six days, just sitting with him, no word from [Baltimore coach Gene] Shue. Mr. Shue hasn't been up there, Mr. Shue hasn't said boo to Gus Johnson. About the seventh day, the sixth or seventh day, Gus is finally over being doped up, he's sitting in the room and Gene calls and Gene says, 'Gus, you think you'll be ready for the playoffs?' just like that, and Gus says to him, 'For seven days I've been laying up here and my ex-boss Mr. Jeannette has been here and he's been sitting with me and I haven't heard hide nor hair from you or anybody else on that damn ballclub.' He says, 'I'll be ready next October. The hell with you and the playoffs.' "

The uneasiness between Johnson and Shue originated in earlier days when front-office politics led to Jeannette's dismissal, a loss Johnson apparently regarded as Shue's doing. Whether or not that embittered Johnson is not acknowledged by either party, but a former Bullet remembered: "In the beginning, Gus didn't want to play for him. He resented him." The feeling may have been mutual. Late in the 1969–70 season, Baltimore arranged to trade Johnson to Cincinnati for Oscar Robertson, a deal voided when Robertson asserted his contractual right to nullify such business.

There was no tradition like Detroit's for petty madness, a condition aggravated by the perpetual turnover in players and coaches. The only constant at Detroit seemed to be the eccentric nature of the pivotmen who passed through. When DeBusschere was coach, the position was manned by Reggie Harding, who when not being arrested, had a corrupt regard for the amenities of time and place. "I had the trainer call him one night at seven thirty, the game's at eight, and he's still at home," recalled DeBusschere. " 'Oh, we play tonight?' "

Harding's successor at center was Joe Strawder, a man whose saturnine disposition required that a coach have the sensitivity of an Esalen graduate. Strawder announced a premature retirement from the game in 1967.

Bellamy carried on Detroit's pivotal tradition. In a preseason game, van Breda Kolff asked him to join the team in its huddle. Bellamy neither acknowledged nor moved for him, and only after van Breda Kolff sent in Otto Moore to replace him did the Bells participate in the huddle. His attitude did not get any better in the season. At one point an uncommonly spirited performance by Bellamy led a teammate of his to say afterward, "Gee, Walt, I thought you'd retired."

The spiritual state of the club was no better amongst its other players. The team was said to be divided into cliques. "It was a big clannish thing," recalled Happy Hairston, after he was traded from Detroit to Los Angeles. Divisions served to insulate players from each other. "Like at Detroit," said DeBusschere, "you try and kid a guy about his shooting and, you know [gruffly] 'What do you mean?' Like that. I'd say, 'I'm just kidding you.' Stuff like that. 'Alright, forget it, I won't say anymore.' The guy's real touchy and that's all it takes is a few guys like that and then if the general attitude of the team becomes that way, then it's not a healthy situation. You have to be able to kid one another because, God, it's a long season if you can't get a laugh out of a guy here and there."

With a 23–1 record New York was not yet troubled. Holzman's biggest problem was the deployment of his personnel and the Knick bench made this a felicitous chore. The reserves, particularly Riordan, Russell and Stallworth, had a desperado flair. Theirs was a vertiginous and spontaneous game. Riordan, for instance, drove to the basket in a kamikaze way, and, at such times, no configuration of Xs and Os on locker room blackboards could be instructive. So were set patterns superfluous for Russell's shot, when by swerve and dribble he could make the space happen. Space served Stallworth for motion; in setup situations his dribble was not the catapult for floating devilment that go-man-go was. Together, these Knick reserves gave the game a kind of sock the chase scenes did in a Mack Sennett comedy, and left tutored nuances to the starters.

What it left to the subs was the problem of acquiring instant getup. Ex-player Schayes recalled that a Syracuse substitute named Togo Palazzi sat in pregame dressing rooms with his feet raised up against the wall to reverse the blood flow and soothe his legs. Palazzi came to the frigid gyms that were prevalent then looking like Nanook of the North with gloves on and a towel around his neck. Riordan and Russell had their rituals, too, most notably workouts before each game. Riordan took his in the afternoons to burn off fevers that might make him reckless in a game. If a gym was unavailable he was content to throw a football about with Sly and expound on the pass-catching patterns the football pros ran; the intricacies of post, fly, buttonhook intrigued him.

On game evenings, Riordan left the locker room early for more warm-up. Sometimes he, May and Hosket played a rotating competition called three-o'-cat. The winner of the contest was proclaimed the three-o'-cat champion of the city in which the team was playing. Win or lose, Riordan returned to the dressing room and, shortly before each game, showered; he was the only Knick who had that habit.

Russell's habit of perpetual physicality gave Reed and general manager Donovan occasion to speculate on the dangers of excess, but Cazzie was not deterred. On offdays he might practice mornings with the team at Lost Battalion Armory in Rego Park, Long Island, and evenings on his own at the 92nd Street YMHA in Manhattan, where he would confer with Asofsky afterward. The workouts taken game days he deemed "priceless"; a particular fan of his, he said, could state whether he'd had one of these sessions of inestimable worth merely by looking him over in the team's warm-ups. Before each game at the Garden, he would undress and walk to the scale in Whelan's training room and weigh himself, as if to certify his body's fitness another day. To maintain it, he required certain food supplements and juices and vitamins at appointed hours of the day.

"I don't look for anyone to give me a lollypop for doing these

things," he said. "It's just something to get me ready. Why do I do
it? Because it's the way I enjoy playing the game and, who knows,
it may put two, three years of life on. It's not just for basketball.
One, your clothes look better. Two, it helps you resist sickness.
Three, it's good for your complexion. And four, it can't hurt for
later on in life."

Russell's devotion to body culture sometimes amused teammates. "Like when they had him riding the [stationary] bicycle,
strengthening his ankle up," said Bowman. "He said he rode
the bike about thirty miles and, you know, he didn't know that
the mileage would be recorded on there. Danny Whelan looked
at the bike after he finished, and there was about half a mile on
there. He was telling everybody about it, we really cracked up."

Bowman's roommate, Stallworth, did not have the compulsions
for pregame rites that Riordan and Russell did, being more tran-
quil than either of them. He was not, be sure, so placid that the
events of a comeback year did not move him; in particular he
remembered opening night at the Garden and the standing ovation he got. "You feel like doing something other than standing
there," he said, "but also you feel that anything you do, it might
be out of place. I felt like screaming, I really did, I felt like
screaming, just screaming along with them, I really felt that good.
I could feel my insides turning, and just felt like letting it out."

The presence of Bowman gave Stallworth's return a sense of
continuity. There were times when Nate remained as unpredictable as he'd been at Wichita State, where once he and Stallworth
had gone around with shaved heads. "In Milwaukee," Stallworth
recalled, "some people in the hotel were having a party, but it
costs three-fifty or four dollars. So we checked into our rooms. I'm
completely undressed and Nate's gone out, I'm laying there,
checking the TV. It wasn't that late, about ten o'clock. Anyway, a
knock on the door. I said, 'Who is it?' Five, six girls at the door.
'Well,' one says, 'I talked to a tall guy, Nate, I believe that's the
name. He said there would be an after-the-party.' I said, this must
be Nate's game, I'm gonna follow through. I said, 'Yeah, but it
will be about an hour before we get set up.' So they said, 'We'll be
back.' Well, this went on for about the next thirty minutes, nothing but girls knocking on the door. And they were very attractive

134 MIRACLE ON 33RD STREET

girls in Milwaukee. And I keep saying, 'Man, this beats me.' So I put on my clothes, they come, I let them in. I'm sitting up there, there was approximately fifteen, twenty girls and one other fellow. Then Nate called. This is the happiest thing in the world for him to do at this time. I said, 'Say, man, did you tell these people to come on up here?' He said, 'What people, man?' I said, 'There's about fifteen, twenty girls said you told 'em there's an afterparty.' He said, 'Oh, man, I was just joking. . . . How many girls you say were up there?' He said, 'Look here, hold them there, I'll be there.' "

Bowman was capable of strange things wherever he happened to be, even seated on the bench during a game. "There's a bunch of fans that sit behind the visitors' bench in Baltimore," recalled a player, "and we were down there for the playoffs last year and this guy is yelling at Nate in time-outs all evening long. He's sitting right behind the bench and he's a very well dressed man, about five foot three or something like this, and the woman he's with is about five-eleven, all kind of makeup and jewelry, the full works. Yeah, and Nate's getting on him and telling him to shut the hell up. Once this guy yelled at Nate, and Nate said, 'Oh, shut the hell up,' and waved his hand on him. And so he comes over to the bench. Got out of his seat and walked up during a time-out and Nate was facing him, you know, as we stand up, the starters are sitting down, Red's talking to the starters. This guy says, 'Bowman, I'm tired of your language, I can't stand to hear that. I've got my wife with me, we got friends, we got mixed couples, we're here for an evening.' So Nate's looking right at the guy and he says, 'Well fuck you.' Everyone around laughs and giggles except the guy's wife and the couples they're with. They're abhorred by this, so the guy says, 'Bowman, I can't believe you're real,' or something like this. 'I can't believe what kind of person you are.' And Nate never took his eyes off the guy and says, 'Fuck your mother,' real plain, you know. Nate kinda talks with a Wichita Negro drawl, a kinda cross between the two, and now he's talking this perfect English at the man. So Red says, 'Nate, get back here,' and some of them, even the starters, a couple of them were kind of laughing because we're playing well, we're up about ten, a couple of minutes to go. Red can't stand this guy either, and then the guy gets on Red for having a guy like Nate on his team, and Red wheels to the guy at the end of time-out and says, 'Hey, fellow, just go sit down and be a good boy and after the game you can come in and watch the guys take a shower.' And he said it real loud, the first couple rows heard. The guy was really embarrassed. The rest of the playoff games down there he never said a word. He was sitting back there but he never said a word either way."

Reformation did not come to Bowman in the new season. When fans at Baltimore took to wearing buttons saying, KICK THE KNICKS, he acquired one for his own warm-up jersey. What he did not get was a renovated shooting touch—shots continued to escape from his bedeviled hands like epileptic birds. "The thing that really hurts my shot," he said, "is . . . my fingers are, I don't know, they're kind of screwed up, y'know, 'cause they're not normal fingers. Like, my fingers at the ends they curl up, y'know, like they can't lay flat on the table. So I have to palm it. I mean, the way my hands are made, I can't shoot it like a normal person would."

Nor could he station himself for the shot in a routine way. His body swayed, and had ever since his first pro year at Cincinnati. "Oscar [Robertson] used to tell me if I just go and shoot it and leave all that weaving, moving stuff out, I'd have a better shot. But this is just part of my game. Maybe it would be better for me to stop doing it, I don't know. But I don't think my shooting has been that bad."

No muses of the offense whispered sweet strategies to Bowman so that by artful deceits he could accomplish what bob 'n' weave could not. The improvisational eluded him so thoroughly that the Knick offense was hobbled with him, and was further impaired by Nate's fitful recollection of plays, a habit he shared with roommate Stallworth. Once when Barnett was on the floor with Stallworth and Bowman, Holzman shouted for him to run the plays. Up and down the court the teams went and no plays developed. Again Holzman shouted for a play. This time Barnett looked over to the bench and said, "Mother-fuckers don't know no plays."

If Stallworth at least could relocate into the flow, Bowman could not. On the attack he had the look of a commuter trying to board a moving train. The Knicks coexisted with Nate's mnemonic

flaw by restricting plays for him to *New York* and, more often, the
2-1-F. On the *2-1-F,* Bowman came from the low post to the foul
line, received the ball from a guard and turned to pass it to either
forward moving off guards' screens.

These liabilities did not disaffect Garden crowds. If they relished the order the Knicks imposed on a universe, they did not
disavow the chaos that Bowman provided. His comic frustrations
more nearly resembled theirs and, in boom times, they suffered
him gladly. The rare nights Bowman did succeed, he lifted audiences to the heights of ecstasy; those evenings had redemptive
substance, for when Bowman coped with the giants there were
echoes for every beleaguered soul in the place.

Such nights were improbable enough so that their celebration
was festive. The first time Bowman engaged Alcindor and confounded purists by outplaying him, the cheers that descended on
him had the raucous pitch heard at the bullfight when an inept
man becomes intrepid. That night against Milwaukee the Garden
crowd gave Bowman a standing ovation of such clamor that had
Nate been a matador it would have won him, at the least, two ears
and the tail.

The competence of Stallworth was not so startling to Garden
patrons once they got used to the spills his frisky game occasioned. The first few times the Rave went down in transit to the
basket, it precipitated fearful murmurs among the witnesses. But
the pratfall was inevitable, the full throttle of Stallworth's game
considered. And nights when a contest turned reckless, he ran the
ball down the foe's craw. In one game against Phoenix, he was to
hit 9 of 10 shots coming off the bench.

Stallworth had not lost the primal kicks for sport that had made
him bound from boyhood bed and meet the summonses of his
peers for wee hour footraces. Even now the more intricate maneuvers that he performed inspired self-congratulatory jigs.

What Stallworth lacked was the enlightened consistency that
DeBusschere brought to the forward position, and the brawn and
reflection needed to defense physical cornermen like Baylor and
Bridges and Gus Johnson. To his credit he had an instinct for
motion that extenuated his shaky coexistence with plays and often
got him baskets on busted plays.

Riordan got his scores on no-nonsense bursts to the basket, and a jump shot that finished with the hand thrust forward from the wrist in the Evil Eye Fleagle manner. The coiled nerve that agitated his game, and the quick first step that delivered sprung energy, were more operative in the wide-open games in which Stallworth thrived. Restrictive tempos cramped the high-speed dribble and exposed its lack of unbalancing rhymes.

The rise of Riordan from comic give-one executioner to legitimate Knickerbocker was a triumph of metabolic power. *I can't remember ever a day going by,* said Jackson, *where he had an opportunity to work out that he didn't do it. He's a very intelligent kid, Mike is, but without basketball he'd be crazy.* And it had especial relevance for Riordan's having been a follower of the team for years.

The boundless energy of Cazzie Russell was muzzled by Holzman's spare use of him, but it did not crimp his spirits. He remained fastidious about his workouts and quirky in his habits—"his" ball was still his ball. That Russell could remain buoyant in what was an unenviable situation bespoke of uncommon resiliency. *At times,* said Hosket, *I admire the guy because I know for him not to start is the biggest crush.* Hosket was well advised of the ruin that crushed prospects could give a man. When, on the second day of training camp, Holzman had ordered him aside for Stallworth in a group photo, Hosket had commenced an eating binge that fattened him sufficiently to merit the name of Wally Walrus that Riordan gave him.

The faith Russell kept was not blind, particularly to the notion that Holzman had of his usefulness. "We beat Philadelphia once, before I got hurt, on my jump shot with three seconds to go, and then he took me out. He called time out and put Phil Jackson in. I guess it was a defensive measure. I asked him about it, and he said he had a chance to put Phil in. I said, 'Man, I don't want to be no one-sided ballplayer.'"

When the subject was defense, Russell remained sensitive in 1969–70. He recalled a game against Seattle when John Tresvant beat him to the rebound more than once and hastened his return to the bench that night. "I said to Red, 'Tresvant got two three rebounds and you snatch me out right away. Bob Love got two three offensive rebounds [for Chicago] off Bradley, you didn't snatch him out.'" When, in the course of a game against San Francisco, Russell picked up Jeff Mullins, he heard Holzman's urgent cry for Riordan to switch to Mullins. Later he spoke to the coach about it. "I said, 'You don't have any confidence in me?' Then he started B-S'ing because he really had no answer. A guy don't have to try to bullshit me, man, to make me think . . . That's when I told him I didn't think I fitted in his plans for his ballclub. He looked very startled."

A sedentary plight was no more tolerable for Hosket and May on that far flank of the bench they referred to as the *Gatorade end* than it was for others. For relief they fell to a peculiar rite. "Hos," said May, "started this thing called 'I wonder.' We're on the bench and he'll say, I wonder what airline we'll be taking, or I wonder what I'll have to eat afterwards, I wonder what kind of beer I'll drink. We should be talking about the game and he's talking about good malts and sundaes. In the pregame, I wonder how many plays Nate will forget today? Or, I wonder whether I ought to have an orange drink now or later?' We do it to keep our spirits going. It's something to laugh at."

The humor found in a benchwarmer's predicament was no sanction of it. Where Hosket could blithely fantasize authorship of a season's chronicle he proposed to entitle *A Foot from the Floor*, and May could immerse himself in a shower even while Holzman delivered his postgame critique, neither of them fancied the wood. It was the aversion to it that led May to devise a ruse to get playing time. He did it one night as Holzman sought to reinsert Bradley into the lineup: when the coach beckoned Dollar Bill, May sprang up instead. On subsequent clarification May took on the wounded expression that he later perfected as the badly groomed knave in a Vitalis commercial; for now it won Holzman's sympathy and May a cameo role in the game.

There were limits, of course, to artifice, and no few moments of plundered time could requite a scrub's predicament. "I remember Donnie and myself in LA came out of the locker room," said Hosket, "and we'd beaten LA out there and Donnie had played, I think, two minutes. I don't think he touched the ball but two or three times and I hadn't played at all, and some people asked us for our autographs. We gave them to these boys, and as they were walking away one said to the other one, 'Man we really got all of the big autographs tonight.'

"Then you'll sit through a night when you don't get in at all and the team wins by twenty-five. I'll be getting on a train or something and I'll hear someone yell, 'Hey, Hosket, you're all washed up!' I think that being a little embarrassed about not getting in in a twenty-five-point victory, I think you might have more rabbit ears for something like this than you would at other times."

For both, it was an abrupt change in public regard. At Dayton University, May had had privileged status in barber shops, restaurants and among the traffic police of the city. Hosket fared just as well at Ohio State. "I've had a couple of speaking engagements since I've been with the Knicks," said Hosket, "and I have a question-and-answer period at the end and some little kid will look up at you and ask, 'What do you average a game?' Now, what are you going to say? You know, three points a game, it just doesn't carry any emphasis with a crowd. Or, one night I was leaving and a little kid asked me how come the Knicks sent me and not Willis Reed. You expect some of this, but it bothers you. Even a kid that's eight or nine years old knows the Knicks' averages from top to bottom. They pay more for the seats than what they pay to see any other games or any other type of entertainment, so they feel like they know what's happening and they know where you stand in relation to the ball club and they let you know it definitely."

There were other unaccustomed embarrassments. "Once in a while," said Hosket, "I'll get a phone call from somebody back home saying, 'Hey, you hurt your knee again?' I'll say, 'No, I just haven't played in the last five games,' 'cause the only thing people have to go on is the box score, and if you don't get your name in it, they're concerned. So you say, I just didn't get in, and then there's that dead silence over the phone and you start talking about how his wife is or how he's feeling or something. It's hard for these people to believe after watching you play four years in college."

Life at the Gatorade end of the bench wore on morale. If Hosket was by nature gregarious, May was not, and as the season progressed, he insulated himself to that point where teammates referred to him as the Phantom. *You'll be talking to him one minute*, said Riordan, *turn around and he's gone.*

"Sometimes I'll be really friendly with Mike and Hos," said May, "then the next moment I'll just quit socializing with them and it's just a period that I go through, I don't want to talk to anybody. Like they might do something that irks me and I just don't want to mess with them and the best thing to do is rather than try and bullshit with them and all that, just to leave them alone."

Seclusion was not new for May. "It goes in streaks," said Hosket. "In high school, he could play well and he would be a hell of a guy for a month and then he'd go through weeks and he wouldn't say anything. Like, I can remember last year, Red would come up to me and say, 'Hey, what's the deal with Donnie?' 'Cause they all knew that I knew Donnie better than anyone. I said, 'That's the way Donnie is.' But, like, in high school it was a big deal—Donnie May is moody and let's pamper Donnie—but here, what the hell, you get moody, who gives a damn?"

To May, it appeared nobody did, not even Holzman, whose infrequent communications were viewed as token courtesy. *He can't very well pass by me without saying something*, May said. *So he'll ask, 'How's Dayton?' or, 'How's [my wife] Brenda? Otherwise, I feel he doesn't give a damn.* May stated it not as an accusation but as a fact whose apparently irreparable state was what groused him, a not particularly startling turn. Bradley, for instance, had withdrawn when he did not succeed in the beginning. *I felt then I didn't deserve to be part of the group*, Bill said, *or didn't deserve to be a teammate.* He would avoid other Knicks by reading incessantly or, after games, by hurrying back to his room.

May did not have the academician's pretext and, in some quarters, his detachment was construed as apathy. "Last year," he said, "Lewin wrote after I'd scored twenty-one points one game . . . he was trying to point out that in the past I'd been collecting my money without offering anything, because I wasn't very emotional, I wasn't a crazy hopped-up mutha like Cazzie. I asked him about it and he said, 'You give the impression you don't care.' "

Withdrawal was not especially unique. Reserves from Russell to rookie Warren had their own escapist diversions. Cazzie's were rhetorical, Warren's simply hallucinatory. "Yeah," Warren said, "like last night, for example, I was lying here and I saw myself blocking Jerry West's shot. Like, I never saw anybody block his shot, but I saw myself blocking West's shot, and I stole the ball from West a couple of times, it was outasight."

Of all the benchmen Warren appeared least perturbed about woodburn. At least, he said, he had good seats for the games. The progress he had made in practices confirmed for both teammates and himself that he was worth the substantial money management had paid him and gave some conviction to his fantasies. *The dreams are never two-sided,* he conceded, *I just see myself doing everything right.*

A setback Warren did suffer was instigated by his roommate, the Cap'n. "This was in Baltimore," said Reed. "They've got this rooftop restaurant that revolves. And we're sitting up there, there's two pieces of metal on where it's revolving. And so, I was talking with John and I said, 'John, check those two pieces of metal.' So John sticks his hand on it and he got a shock. All night long he's trying to trick me into putting my hand down there without success."

Success did not spoil Red Holzman, it hardly touched him. He resisted the sporting page's romance with footwork that would have dazzled both houses of Congress. The fences he straddled to elude apotheosis would have given a lesser man a hernia; at times his knack for it bordered on clairvoyant. One night telecaster Wolff referred to the man's genius and, when the camera panned to Holzman, he was busy at his nose. Red's idea of a fit reward was to have his name appear in the crossword puzzle of the Sunday *New York Times.* He conferred with that paper's basketball reporter, Tom Rogers, to see if he could accomplish it.

The image Holzman preferred was the prince of the pastrami prerogative. When an usher took him for a gatecrasher and prohibited his accompanying the team onto the floor it was a fine moment. Of course, Holzman was not the benign chap he was cracked up to be; on the bench he fumed and raged at ref, player and fan alike. "The year I played in the Eastern League, I came down to see a game at the Garden," said Riordan. "This particular game, [Dick] Van Arsdale was on the bench for New York. And a fan kept yelling at Red to put him in. Pretty soon the guy got profane. About the third quarter, Red called time out. The guy got on him again. Red turned around and said, 'He's sick, you stupid shmuck.'"

Holzman had coached before. From 1954 to 1957 he was boss of the Hawk franchise that existed first in Milwaukee and then in St. Louis. In those days he would show his players a photo of his young daughter Gail and suggest what might befall her should the team falter. Apparently the Hawks were not moved: in 203 games in Milwaukee and St. Louis, the club won 83 times. Holzman was fired. That experience impressed upon him the tenuous nature of the profession and caused him to view romanticizing of it with fishy eye.

Untoward things had happened in his regime there. "We had Frank Selvy then," remembered Marty Blake, the Hawks' general manager, "and he was like a country boy. One time we're losing the ball on the boards and Frank is half asleep in the locker, so Red looks over and says, 'Frank, Frank, wake up.' Red says, 'Where are we losing the game?' Selvy says, 'Well, Red, we're losing the game right here in Milwaukee.'"

Holzman's successor with the Hawks did no better. "We made Slater Martin our player-coach," said Blake, "and Slater couldn't stand the job. He didn't want all the headaches. Coaching was so bad for him that he actually couldn't remember the plays when he was in the games."

Holzman's problems when he relieved McGuire were not so comical, and required a resolute approach. "Well, I guess when he first came in," said Bowman, "—first came into bein' a coach, he had to, right off the bat the first day, he had to fine a couple of guys, y'know, 'cause they were late for the meeting. About ten, fifteen dollars something like that. Van Arsdale, Bellamy and Komives. Under McGuire, if something like that happened, uh, you probably wouldn't get a fine behind it. 'Cause he might be late hisself. But Red, he's the kind of guy if he's late, he'll fine hisself, y'know, because he's very punctual."

He also changed the locker room atmosphere. Remembered Russell: "He said, 'Listen, there's not going to be any hot dogs,

we're going to cut all that bullcrap out, no hot dogs at half time.'
Now guys are in the locker room earlier. Like, if the game's at
eight o'clock we're there at six thirty. McGuire himself would be
late, he would rush in and shave before the game. And borrow a
razor blade and borrow some shaving cream. Oh, man, McGuire
was too much."

Unlike his predecessor, Holzman did not mind personalizing
losing for his players. "Like, I remember when we had Bellamy
with us," said Bowman. "He had his own room until the time
when we started losing a lot of games. And Red told him, he said,
'Well, you don't get any special privileges, 'cause you're not doing
anything special.' So he took the room away from him."

If Holzman required discipline he did not pursue it to the ends
that, say, Charley Wolf did. "Wolf used to wake you up," DeBusschere said, "make sure you went to church on Sunday. He'd call
your room. 'Now there's church at such and such.' And guys
would go 'cause they might not get to play, they would actually
go to church so that they would see some playing time. Except for
Reggie Harding. He didn't mess with Reggie. Because Reggie
would say, 'Oh, yeah, okay, fine, I'll meet you there in five
minutes.' You'll see Reggie the next day sometime. No, he didn't
mess with Reggie."

The Piston coach was so steadfast a moralist that only threats to
his person kept him from informing wives of their spouses' road
debauches. "Can't drink, smoke, swear," remembered DeBusschere. "A guy would swear and he'd say afterwards, 'I think
that's uncalled for because there's a lot of children, wives and
ladies and you're representing . . .' and go into a long spiel.
Charley, on the other hand, instead of yelling at the refs, he'd go,
'You haven't any intestinal fortitude!' Guys would stand there and
look back and say, 'Christ, the refs don't understand that. Call
them something else.'"

Holzman did not have so sacred a regard for the moral fiber of
his charges. To get what he wanted he regimented their professional lives only. Repetition was a device he used (SEE THE
BALL, SEE THE BALL) for results; on the practice floor or in
the pregame dressing room the message did not change nor the
attitude vary.

Repetition made sense; in the absence of such entreaties players might grow sloppy. Stallworth had, in his leave, coached a high-level amateur team whose guards he constantly warned of the territorial perils of a zone press, in particular the restrictive corners of the floor. So it was with considerable horror he watched a player of his dribble four straight times to the corner against a zone press employed by another team. "I called a time-out and just looked at him," he remembered.

Holzman was convinced that laughter was a prescriptive element for a team and, when the scumbag tradition paled, he suggested it be revived. It was not, but every night he came into the room he consciously sought to resurrect its spirit. *Definitely he has particular guys,* said Phil Jackson, *and it's never with a white ballplayer. It's always with colored ballplayers, not that I know it makes any difference.* Holzman wandered about the room, throwing scraps of tape at players and kibitzing, CLYDE, CLYDE, COME ON NOW, GET READY. He treated Frazier the cozy way fathers do their youngest. DAVE THE RAVE, DAVE THE RAVE. Stallworth would smile and expose a gold star on his front tooth; blood relatives of his had hearts, quarter moons, stars in clusters on their dental-work. NATE, NATE, SHEEE-IT. Clyde, the Rave, the Cap'n, Nate. His highest-salaried player he called Bradley.

Not all coaches were so concerned about pregame effects. "Back at Detroit," recalled DeBusschere, "Paul Seymour—you never knew what the hell was going to happen with him. He'd just come in and start ripping everybody, you didn't know whether he was kidding or not. Every game the same thing. He used to knife into Otto Moore, he'd get on him, kid him about his girl friends and all that BS. Like, her legs were so thin if she didn't have feet they'd stick in the ground. . . . I don't understand this kind of thing. . . . Some of the guys didn't pay attention to him. Like [Jimmy] Walker didn't like him at all. Seymour was constantly on him. 'Are you moping tonight, Jimmy? Oooh, how's the little girl?' And Jimmy resents it, Jimmy is the type of personality he needs a lot of attention, backslapping, babying and so on."

Holzman was more predictable. DAVE THE RAVE . . .

CLYDE, CLYDE . . . THE CAP'N GOT HIS HOT STUFF?
"Then he'll start pacing a lot," said Jackson. "He'll walk in from
the training room through the little corridor seeing that everybody
is sitting down. He wants everybody to be sitting there, ready.
He's got a few pages of notes. Then he talks. He just goes over the
offense and goes over the defense and he says the same thing
eighty-two games out of the year."

Holzman steered away from emotionalism in his talks. "Charley
Wolf," said DeBusschere, "talked above the guys half the time.
Butcher would scream and pound, he'd get a little excited. Well,
Red is very sober, very businesslike. I would say Red's speeches
tend to be generally along the same line, rather on the boring side
because you know what to expect before you go in there. . . . I
know myself, my mind wanders at times, because after your first
time around the league you're listening to the same thing. After
the fourth time you play Milwaukee you get a pretty good idea
how to play Len Chappell."

The calm with which players and coach reacted to the streak
was deceptive. As Bowman said, *Everything is groovy as long as
you're winning but when you're not it can be bad.* There was the
hint of stifled friction. When the Knicks commenced to lose more
regularly, there were portents of trouble. One afternoon Holzman
became querulous with some gentlemen of the press with whom
he did not drink. "*Look* and *Jock* magazine, "recalled Riordan,
"had a big squabble about who should have had what . . . and
we just wanted to get the hell out of there, but these guys wanted
a couple of more minutes here and a couple there, and they want
Bradley and DeBusschere to lay on the ground. Holzman said,
'Let's get a couple of broads if you want that, these guys are basketball players. They're not laying down on the ground. Get out
of here if you want that sort of scene.'"

That was mere smokescreen for internal trouble brewing.

Q: Have there been flareups between players and coach?
FRAZIER: Yeah, I've had run-ins with him . . . Bradley has . . .
    Willis too.
Q: Can you particularize them at all?

FRAZIER: Oh, he was telling me that . . . something about getting up on the defense, you know, and I thought the other guys weren't really helping me out, so—

Q: What game is this?

FRAZIER: I don't remember specific games. So he would always keep calling me. It got to a point where I told him, "Fine me or something or even take me out if I'm not doin' what you want. It's like I get tired of you always calling me, like I'm always screwing up the defense." But that's only the time I—

Q: How did he react?

FRAZIER: Well, he got heated too, you know, told me to shut up, stuff like that.

That was only part of the trouble that arose in Chicago on December 19, the unexpurgated version of which was related by another player:

"Bill [Bradley] and Barnett got confused as to whether they were going to stay with their men or switch on this one play that Chicago was running for Bob Love. So Love hit three straight field goals and Red yanks Bill and gives him some crap about his defense. This is the only thing to me that Red really coaches, you know. Most of our offense is from DeBusschere; he put in all the good plays and everything. We didn't have any of this stuff we have until he came last year. To get back, Red really knows defense, I give him credit for being really a good team defensive coach, so he felt he had a right to say something. Bill wheeled on him with a comment, said, 'Bullshit,' and sat down on the bench at the time. Yeah, then Red spent the whole time-out screaming at Bradley. You know, he forgets where he is at times and he doesn't use very good judgment. Red spent the full minute screaming his ass off at Bill, about I don't give a fuck who you are and I don't care how smart you are—all these things he'd never mentioned, you know, it just came to the top and he lost himself and he couldn't keep his cool. He just yelled and Bill just hung his head—like I'm the player and you're the coach, Bill didn't say a word.

"In the fourth quarter in the same ball game, Clyde got yelled at about three times and Clyde is a lot like Cazzie in this respect, he doesn't take coaching too well. He reads the paper a lot how good they are and they don't want to hear it, so . . . it was a simple thing about . . . his man drifting out to the corner and Clyde not covering him and they were hitting him and the Chicago guy scored a couple of buckets. So Red got on him and Clyde kind of popped off and made an excuse the first time-out. When he said something about it, Red said bullshit this and that, Clyde, I don't want you to do it. And they went back on the floor and there were like two minutes left in the game, we're fifteen up and it happened again. So Red called a time-out and got after Clyde about this thing; like, Clyde was feeling that he's a hell of a ballplayer and the game's won and let's forget about it, and let's just talk about it after the game or something. So I saw Clyde eye the bench right before the time-out, as if, 'What the hell, he's called a time-out just to holler at me about this, what is this shit?" And he came over and that's what happened. Red exploded at him and Clyde yelled back at him, and Red said to shut up and Clyde said, 'Go ahead and fine me if you want,' and gave him some excuses and they talked. Well, then he put Clyde back in, Clyde finished the game, didn't do anything more in like a minute and a half.

"I think we won the ball game by ten or so points [108–99] and I was walking down to the dressing room and I said to Barnett, I said, 'I think we better get some earplugs.' There was just a little tension during the streak, a lot of things were being said and, I mean, I can't give you any specific things. It was just a feeling that we all had that it was due to bust out, guys were complaining about this guy holding the ball, it was everybody. 'They're not running the plays.' 'I'm not getting enough playing time.' Just tension. I could tell how a team builds up a feeling about something before it comes out in the open. Barnett said, 'You think this is the night, huh?' So I could tell the way Barnett said it to me, I could tell that he felt the same thing.

"So we got into the locker room. I was hoping that Red would either discuss it calmly or talk to the two of them after the game, but it was so obvious that it was going to happen that we beat him to the locker room and Nate starts clapping his hands, 'Hell of a win, hell of a win.' So we all picked it up right away, although it was a bullshit victory, a game that we should have won by

thirty-five. So everybody was acting like, well, the night we set the
streak. I think this was the loudest our locker room had been, and
we knew we were doing it just kind of to pimp Red when he came
in, trying to say that we're together on this thing.

"Red came in and said, 'Alright alright alright,' and then he
said, 'This is bullshit.' He said, 'This is great alright, we won the
ball game but this is bullshit. Why don't everybody just sit down.'
Then he pointed a finger at Walt and he started hollering, said,
'Clyde the reason you're fucking up is because nobody can talk
to you anymore.' It was obvious that he was feeling his power and
loving it, and we were reading too much in the papers how good
we were and we were uncoachable and we were getting cocky.

"True, Bill shouldn't have said bullshit and Clyde should have
kept his mouth shut, but at the same time Red's attitude toward
the thing was, he's not going to give the ballplayer an inch, you
know. Then he wheeled around and said, 'The same goes for you,
Bradley,' and he wheeled around and pointed to one of the other
guys, Bradley was like a few stalls over. And the guy just looked
at Red like what the fuck. And then Red had to kind of get his
balance and go on. 'Not you,' he said. 'You,' and he pointed at
Bill.

"It was coming to a head, it didn't surprise me. Because we
were talking in practice, he'd say come on you guys, get serious
now, and they'd keep yelling and screwing around; he would act
disgusted at times. We had the string, we had done it and we
were just kind of cocky and somebody had to knock us down a
little bit, but the way he knocked us down, it was the kind of
things he said that made it like it was more personal with him. It's
almost like this David Frye thing, 'I am the President, make no
mistake about it.' A couple of nights, Red will say, 'I'm coach of
this fuckin' team. No one else will tell me what to do.' I think he
felt he was losing control of the team, that the guys were just
playing basketball and then getting all this press and everything
and kind of leaving him out, like he was the unknown thing except for, let's say, Leonard Lewin of the *New York Post* constantly
calling him the genius. I don't know if you fully understand this.
Like, when the reporters all leave the room, he'll say, 'Hey, you
know this is all bullshit,' or something, and then he'll walk away."

The Chicago incident suggested the delicate "ego-librium" involved in the game, and the fragile nature of its participants. For Holzman and his players it was an irreversible event, the charade between them was blown. *Like two nights later,* said a player, *Red tried to come back with the old stuff, CLYDE, YOU'RE MY MAIN MAN, and throw a piece of tape at him, and then Red went into the other room and Clyde just shook his head like who is this goofy bastard trying to fool?*

The chemistry that all teams sought was forever under siege because of the assorted egos that had to co-exist.

"I'd be curious to see what would happen with team therapy," said Phil Jackson. "It could do something like what Lombardi did at Green Bay. There it was done in a dictatorial way; everybody subjugated his ego for the team, almost like mass hypnotism. This is the other side. A football team is a machine. Basketball is not like that. You can't have a dictatorship. It's a uniting of people. You saw it last year. Because basketball is a very individual sport. Therapy would be an ego-building thing.

"I think athletes kind of consider themselves manly, insensitive, without personal hurts or feelings, or their personalities are so strong they can't be hurt, and I think this is incorrect. The biggest thing would be to try and make ballplayers realize that these are sensitive humans that they're working with. Now, there's some ballplayers—and I don't care what team you have—that can never do wrong. They can't admit wrong because they can always blame it off on somebody else. I've seen it on this team, ballplayers who won't take the blame and will end up arguing. This is something that is childish, naive and can be avoided. Like, DeBusschere makes a mistake, first one to admit it: 'I made a mistake, I'm sorry.' And the guys really really like that. And I think there's a lot of ballplayers that through honesty, you know, could become better ballplayers, could make a better team.

"When I was in college, you know, I was the star of the ball club and everything else, and I argued with my coach and he wouldn't take that, so one night I had to run like three or four miles around the field and that was to bust my ego, to take me down. It's good in a way as long as you can replace it, as long as you're not tearing it down to the point where you completely humiliate the ballplayer, and I've seen that happen. If ballplayers are honest with one another in every way, I think it'll develop a unity where other ballplayers will care about somebody else, and if somebody makes a mistake they won't say, 'Come on now, what did you do that for?'

"I can remember one of the ballplayers at practice one time was going to give four guys a ride home, you know, guys riding back and forth from the city, and it so happened he locked his keys in the car. Well, you know, no one stayed around to help him. They just jumped in a car with somebody else and he had to stand out there and try to get his keys out for half an hour. . . . And it seemed like the kind of thing where, you know, somebody is using somebody else. Eventually maybe we can get beyond this, can get to where guys will be able to trust each other with their feelings. This is a very basic thing, even in America."

Whatever rapport the team had was manufactured for the marketplace; rarely did players sustain it beyond the court and then only in a fragmented way. Too often chill winds blew through the house. *Like Donnie May last year at the Hotel New Yorker*, said Hosket. *I think he was the only one of the white guys that lived in the hotel and he would always say, like, they'd meet one another and all ride to practice in one of the cars and he'd have to catch the subway, you know. They would never be there when they said they were going to be there, 'til finally he just gave up on it and started traveling alone.*

Professional harmony was structured to last the working hours, and consciously so. "Like, most guys don't believe I'm a loner," said Barnett, "because in the locker room I boolshit and everything. But that's in the locker room. And it seems like that relationship that I have with my teammates in the locker room, that's for my teammates. That's why I don't like to get into a discussion with sportswriters because I really don't boolshit that much with sportswriters at all. I mean, I have a different personality. I more or less carouse with the team because this is a part of playing basketball. You see what I'm saying?"

Where Barnett gave the team laughs, Reed and DeBusschere

gave it a sense of its own sturdy structure; both were rooted in the world of responsibilities. Reed had built rebounding muscle in the Louisiana farmlands where he hauled hay for $4/day and picked cotton at $3.50/100 pounds. *I wasn't a very good cotton picker, no. If I could get around 200 pounds a day, I was doing pretty good.* At Grambling he had been the team captain, and Coach Hobdy remembered the time he walked into the locker room with Grambling losing to find Reed giving the half-time peptalk he'd intended. DeBusschere had the same sense of commitment; at twenty-four he became the youngest coach in NBA history with Detroit and, later in New York, he helped change the toxic atmosphere.

"I can remember talking one night," said Hosket, "I was popping off, coming back from somewhere, about I just can't stand it anymore, I'm not playing and it was driving me crazy. So I'm saying I'm going to talk to the coach about this or that, but Dave says, 'Hey now, listen, Hos, I've been at this thing a long time and I've never won a championship, never been on a championship team and I don't want anything to mess it up.' And to me, just like automatic, I came to my senses, I realized what the guy was trying to tell me. Here's a guy, he busts his gut out there thirty-five or forty minutes a night. Like me getting in for three minutes and scoring four points doesn't mean very much in the long run."

As captain of the Knicks Reed was the liaison between coach and team, a position that put him on stickier grounds as the season progressed. *We found out after the Chicago thing,* said a player, *that Red went up and asked Willis whether these guys should be fined or not, and this pissed off Willis because he thought that Red hadn't shown any judgment, he thought he could have gotten them both aside later, one at a time, and talked it over.*

When the Knicks tailed off, Reed was playing with an injured toe and a hyperacid stomach, infirmities that reduced his effectiveness and contributed to the 10–8 record New York compiled after the streak and prior to a road trip early in January. Whatever the reason, organic flaw or inevitable letdown, New York played the worst ball it was to play until the very end of the regular season. Reed's concern for the team at this time prompted him to make suggestions to Holzman in half-time locker rooms, but on more than one occasion the coach cut him off. The captaincy did not always privilege him with Holzman. Once Red remarked, "I get the first and last words, and all the words between."

The players again viewed Holzman's assertiveness as bad form; the feeling was that the Cap'n deserved better. Whether Holzman consciously sought to disaffect the team, as Lombardi had done at Green Bay, only Red could say. And lucid speech was not his habit. Such incidents did not change the Cap'n's role; by word or gesture he showed his concern for each player and remained the responsible party of the Knick team; his intention was to keep the team going.

Bradley's approach to team communion was as much personal as pragmatic. When teammates called him "Bradley" he reminded them of his Christian name. On previewing a magazine story about the team he asked the writer if he would mind changing "Frazier" to "Clyde" in a quote attributed to him. To an author whose researches required multiple interviews, Bradley politely suggested he give the rookie, John Warren, attention.

The paradox of Bradley was that his own emotional restraint limited the intimacy that he could envision in an ideal sense; introspection oppressed spontaneity for him, so that when he tried to authenticate himself for teammates in excursions that some Knicks affectionately referred to as "binges," he might come off wooden or vague.

REED: Bradley tells Hosket, says, "Be a man, be a man, pull my shirt pocket off."

Q: What?

REED: Says, "Be a man, be a man, pull my shirt pocket off." Hosket grabs his shirt and tries to pull his pocket off, and ripped the whole shirt, y'know, like the shirt came right across and made a big *L*.

Q: What did Bradley want him to rip the pocket off for?

REED: I don't know. You know how Bradley is . . . he's so funny.

Q: What prompted him to do that?

REED: I don't know, you know how Dollar . . . he's . . . he do those kind of things sometimes.

What perplexed the others about Bradley in those moments was the contrast to the reserved bearing he more regularly had. It was as if a satanic impulse sought to expel forbidden energies and then lie quiet again in him. The game that Bradley termed "sensuous" gave him a sanctioned outlet for wild blood; basketball's structure was not so forbidding as to disallow the demonic, and so on courts a perturbed Bradley shouted MOVE THE GODDAMN BALL and worse or, when miffed by a referee's decision, wandered downcourt like a sulky child in that peculiar stifflegged walk of his, muttering side-of-the-mouth words he would not have dared use in his scholarly dissertations.

PHIL JACKSON: I think he's strange.

Q: How so?

JACKSON: I really like him, I think he's really a nice . . . but he doesn't let himself ever really go.

Q: You mean in basketball?

JACKSON: No, I think he enjoys basketball, especially when he's winning. Bradley is the kind of guy, you sit down and talk to him and you ask him a question and he asks you why you ask the question, instead of answering it, instead of just being himself. But he's calculating and I think that's just about the way he is except when he gets on the basketball court. He runs with reckless abandon, you see that, don't you? He's a very reckless basketball player, his passes and everything. He's a completely different type.

Q: Can you expand on that?

JACKSON: You run into guys like that and . . . they just drive me nuts, man. You've met scholars like that, that want to give you that platonic kind of shit, and I get tired of it after a while, so I rarely discuss anything with him anymore. Because it's not going to be honest, it's not going to be personal, it's not going to be feeling that we both feel. But I don't blame him. Maybe he's trying to protect himself, maybe he's trying to drill himself in something, I don't know. Maybe he's got an ulterior motive. But for my own sake . . .

Q: What does he voluntarily talk about?

JACKSON: Last year we both worked for [Congressman] Allard Lowenstein at one time—not working but just went out to some kind of a deal—and he'd come up and talk to me about Lowenstein once in a while or ask me if I wanted to work for him again or something like that. And so we do talk about things, but very seldom do we ever come up and talk about an issue or talk about—

Q: What about the rhetorical tricks of his you mentioned?

JACKSON: He'll usually come back at you with the same shit, the same rhetorical kind of . . . "Well, why do you think I don't open up?" And then finally it gets . . . you know, I used to throw things at him. Listen, I used to throw things at him that are ridiculous. Ask him ridiculous questions like, "Do you believe in the birth-control pill?" Just something to see if he's really listening to me and he would answer back the same thing.

Q: What do you mean?

JACKSON: Well, just to see if he'd come back and ask me some rhetorical thing about the birth-control pill, just as if this damn tape recorder had something you pushed and it came back repeated to you in a different way, see what I mean? Once Bill sits down at a table and has a few beers, then he gets much better but he's still not . . . still can't quite enter into and be a real part, like a man's type of conversation, sitting at the bar . . . like a Jimmy Breslin type of conversation, you know what I mean?

Q: Why do you think he's that way?

JACKSON: He told me about Oxford, that he got a lot of that stuff at Oxford. I don't think that's what made him like that. I think he just doesn't like to commit himself on what he really thinks. He likes to be very sure of himself before he gives opinions. So if we're talking about something like a political move or something like that, I think he wants to be very careful, but I don't know why. It makes no difference to me . . . I'm not going to go back and blackmail him if he runs for Senator, but that's the way he is.

Q: Has he ever revealed something about himself that surprised you?

JACKSON: Not really. I used to kid him about his shoes. One time he said, "Well, I kind of have bad feet so I have my shoes made by this guy in St. Louis, by a shoe man." And I think that's the only thing like . . . that was kind of to say, "Well, I can take the kidding but that's why I haven't got new shoes." That's the only time I've heard him make an excuse for dressing or anything. I don't even know if this is an excuse or not. Maybe I led up to it, but he's just a nonrevealing type person. When he came to the team, I figured, wow, here's a guy I can probably really groove with and maybe I can grow a little bit intellectually with him, you know, if I can talk to him about school and everything else like that, you know . . . My parents love him because he's supposed to be a Christian, see.

Q: What do you mean a Christian?

JACKSON: Well, born again kind of fundamentalist type of experiences with Christ, you see. Can you dig any of this, am I too over your head?

Q: You mean—

JACKSON: You can dig it. And they throw him up a lot in my face, you know. Bill is a nice guy. But you don't know if he really likes you or not, he's that kind of guy. I mean I like people to come up and say, "You know, you're a good guy, I like you." Not to reassure me. I like to do that to people because I think it's just human to do it. But with Bill you don't know whether he likes you or not. For example, they had a testimonial in my hometown in Williston, North Dakota, and they said, "Can you get Bill Bradley?" I asked him and he said, "Well . . . yeah . . . maybe I'll do it." And so I said to the guy putting on the deal, "You approach him, I don't want to ask." So he approached him and Bill did it for nothing. They just flew him out. He's made . . . he must have made about two talks in all. He doesn't ever give any talks except to colleges, and I didn't know whether he did it for me, or whether he did it because he wanted to see North Dakota. It was just funny and I still don't know. I thanked him, I said it's a nice gesture.

Q: What about the—

JACKSON: I have to tell you about this. He was running around with reckless abandon on the floor recently, running into people, knocking people down, losing the ball, and he did it about three times in a row and Barnett said, "Hey, Bradley, what time is your appointment with your psychiatrist?" And it just cracked everyone up because it looked like he was a scatterbrain out there with the players.

Q: What was his reaction to that?

JACKSON: He was kind of embarrassed. He does funny things on the court—he's kind of like I am, looks kind of half-coordinated —but gets the job done very well. Anyhow, another time he was standing downcourt. Frazier threw a nice pass, all he had to do was react. Well, he saw it too late—he was standing all by himself—he saw it too late and he couldn't catch up to it. It went out of bounds. And Barnett turned and said, "Way to stand at the other end of the court and be daydreaming about something. You've *got* to go to your psychiatrist!" And that's the way Barnett is at almost every practice. But Bradley, he can be standing there daydreaming on the other end of the court . . . you know what he was doing? He was practicing his wrist action without the ball on the other end of the court. They're running the press and he's supposed to be downcourt. But he missed a shot so he's trying to get his wrist action better. He's like that. I suppose you heard the story in LA where he ran into the wall.

Q: Wall?

JACKSON: Well, he came in one time early, we came early to the game and he went out, he was working out, he came in to get his tickets, signed his tickets out to somebody and was joking and, with kind of reckless abandon, throwing up quick shots and jumping in the locker room pretending like he was shooting baskets.

Q: Without a ball?

JACKSON: Without a ball. He threw a hook shot and ran right into the wall and just knocked himself kind of silly. Once in a while he goes on these little crazy sprees. That's what the guys react to . . . like, this isn't the same guy once he's got his street clothes on.

In mufti, Bradley still was concerned for people. At the exhibition stop in Bethlehem, Pennsylvania, he prefaced his autograph to a ballboy with this note: "Thank you. You did a good job." Other Knicks just signed their names. His summers were spent working without pay in federal and municipal programs aimed at helping poor people. At the end of the 1969–70 season, he planned to travel through Asia to see conditions there.

Bradley was not as at ease when demands were directed at his emotional bank rather than his social conscience, the reticence with which he responded person to person acknowledged the complexities of his celebrity and identity, areas he feared people did not clearly distinguish.

The motives of others and his own introverted turn of mind inclined Bradley to work peripherally at communications, as if that tack would give him opportunity to sniff out foul or misdirected intentions. Sometimes what it did was lend magniloquence to trivia and cause journalists to disparage him in private for his solemnity. The comment was, "He takes himself too fucking seriously."

In the locker room Bradley's analytical bent and his indifference to the life's spoils made him a curio to certain players, and impenetrable to others, creating a strange case of muted affections on both ends, more intriguing for the paradox it presented: he who cared for camaraderie had less a gift for it than those for whom it lacked such import.

Barnett, for instance, could by the comic twist of a tale turn a room thermal, and not attach to it any particular significance: *Outwardly I'm laughing and grinning but I still don't have many friends. I got a lot of acquaintances in basketball but not too many I can talk to.* The needs of Bradley and Barnett were sunk in their beginnings. Bradley, the banker's son, was in society's swim in a way Barnett never was and perhaps never would be; the associations he had with teammates may have mollified whatever guilt he felt for his situation. Barnett's location on the fringes did not allow for such expansiveness; his life had been more a scuffle from which emerged the loner's detachment to the predicaments of others and an ironic feeling about his own.

Barnett began as what he called an alley ballplayer, a reference to the locale of his games, and did not touch a real basketball until he was twelve, an age at which Bradley took vacations in Palm Beach. The use of a Ping-Pong ball (and garbage lid) and, later, a volleyball (and three chairs) in those alleys required an unconventional sort of dexterity that suggested the origins of his peculiar locomotion.

The insularity of Barnett was not peculiar to Knickerbockers. Players were more like him than Bradley. In postgame locker room egos came down like curtains after the show, and Knicks eyed their favorite navel. Such focus was natural for the athlete, particularly so for Barnett.

"I've been introverted most of my life," Barnett said. "Now I think I can become, not an extrovert, but I can step out into different roles. But when I was in grade school especially, I was terrified of going before people and talking. I mean a whole lot of times that the teacher would call upon you and instead of getting up . . . I knew what the answers were but I was ashamed to get up in front of the class. Now whether this was due to my clothes . . . I didn't dress too well and a whole lot of people in class didn't dress well . . . but I was just horrified going before people and trying to explain myself.

"In high school, the coaches say every day, why don't you do this, why don't you do that? There's an opportunity to go to college and make something out of yourself. It was hard for me to relate college with myself, because, you know, no one in my family ever went to college, no uncle or aunties or anything. The image that I would see on TV, mostly . . . well, all of it was white and, like, it was kind of hard for me to picture. To show you how disconnected I was to this whole idea, upon my graduation from high school, they had a meeting where they had people from different fraternities to come over and talk to you, you know, what fraternity to join when you get on campus, this type of thing. This is after graduation, like, in June. College was in September. They would come in and tell you the benefits of joining a fraternity. Like, this is the first time in my life that I had ever heard of a fraternity and, you know, well, this idea didn't appeal to me because I had never belonged to any group in my life and I had no desire to. That doesn't appeal to me. I always want to try to stay independent. I can't belong to a group.

"Very seldom that a freshman ballplayer come down to Tennessee State in those days and made the first team and was number one scorer, so there had to be a little readjustment [to me]. Then, since really I didn't socialize with the players, this was like another thing they would try to hold against me. I guess this was a carryover from Gary, Indiana. I kept to myself. I studied by myself and everything. They tried to get you in certain fraternities, join certain groups on campus and, you know, just be another guy I imagine, which isn't bad. I don't hold anything against it, but that just wasn't my thing. I remember there was a panty raid one year that I was there. They had a blackout on campus and that was the panty raid. And now again I had to go to my television reference—I had never been in a panty raid and only heard of them. I didn't know what you were supposed to do on a panty raid. You know, this is like a new thing to me."

Frazier's isolation did not spring so organically from experience as Barnett's. It was just how Walt Frazier was. *Like, I could stay in this room a whole day*, he said, *and I'll never be bored.* He did not have the compulsion for organizing time as Bradley did. *Like, a lot of guys*, he said, *read books, but I can't see the need for it. Maybe if I was going to teach or something, otherwise why waste my time reading something that maybe I'll never use*, preferring diversions that were more passive . . . music, TV, bedrest . . . *I just stay in the room whereas a lot of guys, like Don May, he's restless, he has to keep moving. Like, he has to get up at eight or nine o'clock and eat breakfast. He just can't stay in bed like I can, because I'm not bored.* The pleasure of being Clyde was enough for Frazier.

He did not profess to strong social needs. *I don't like to talk, see*, he said, *and if you're with people most of the time you have to talk.* Nor did he have ties with teammates. *I don't hang out with anybody on the team.* In fact, what bickering there was among blacks and whites on the team, he remained aloof from. *I try to stay out of stuff like that. Maybe I see it. If I see that it's going on and some guys don't like each other, maybe they have a good reason, I don't know.* Frazier's kicks were localized. *He's pretty much Clyde's man,* said roommate May. *He's aware of himself. He likes to read about himself and maybe notice his quotes in the papers, magazines and such, how he did this, how he didn't do that or something. Usually it's something about himself. But rooming with him, he's easy to get along with, he doesn't say much, sleeps a lot.*

Frazier's interest in clothes dated back to boyhood. *I could remember when I was a kid,* he said, *I'd put on my father's shoes and try his shirts on—like, I'm eleven or twelve maybe—but they were all too big. I could remember watches and rings that he had and I couldn't wait 'til I got big enough to wear them.* That taste for dandyish appointments survived; there was in his room at the New Yorker a Robert Hall-like clothes rack on which hung fashions that his tailor, Lester, created for him, plaids and pinstripes, single- and double-breasted and three-pieced, ties of all cloths and dyes, including mod ones that Asofsky's friend, Fred Klein, gave him from the tie cache of his hobbyist father, and alligator and lizard shoes ordered directly from the Stetson factory in Massachusetts. Frazier also owned a tailor-made outfit of his design that was inspired by the movie westerns he had seen, a five-buttoned waistcoat with inverted pleat in the back, slanting pockets, peak lapels, trousers to match, pocket watch and string tie for accessories.

Frazier remained an unabashed pleasure seeker but his joy in it was private; he required no endorsements from peers. He was the unobtrusive hedonist. *Like, when I go out I don't like to take a chick,* he said. *I just like to go out and meet people, at random, just travel alone.* But even out socially, he kept his distance. *I just like to cool it. Like I go to parties with guys, right away I'll go sit down and I'll survey the premises and if I don't see nothing I like, I won't say anything, and if I see maybe a girl I like, then I'll rap to her. Otherwise I just fade in and get lost.*

Cazzie Russell did not have the habit of camouflage but rather a performer's need to be "on." In his workouts at the Ninety-second Street YMHA, he would have Asofsky throw him tricky passes to negotiate on the run. On a night Sly worked out with him, Cazzie wound up at a papaya juice stand on Eighty-sixth Street afterward to collect a foul-shooting wager, and while there quoted for Sly a saying the proprietor kept on his walls. "It is not how much we have," he recited, "but how much we enjoy that makes happiness." Later, driving downtown he launched into impromptu sportscasts, improvisations he performed with considerable skill. The Black Hawks, the Cubs, the Bears, all of Chicago's sporting teams were trotted forth by Russell, an aspirant for the broadcasting booth. Sometime later, he recalled the origins of it.

"I'd come on," he remembered of boyhood days, " 'Good afternoon, this is Cazzie Russell. We'll be back with our pregame show but first let's hear this message.' And if it was on radio, you'd pretend that you were pouring a cold glass of Pepsi-Cola . . . cla-cla-cla . . . and they [the listeners] would fall out, they would just die, you know. It would knock me out too. Sometimes I would say in between innings of my make-believe baseball game, I would say, 'You know, when you need ready cash for a long vacation, call this number: Hanover 5 . . . This was Household Finance, friendly Bob Adams.' They might not know what I was talking about, but they would fall out. This is something that I always wanted to do. Like, I'd be walking on the street on my way to school, announcing a baseball game, you know, like, 'A smash to so and so, second for one, to first for two, got it by an eyelash.' And guys would come up. 'Say, man, whatcha talking about?' 'I'm just recapping the game.' "

In Knick locker rooms, Cazzie remained on the airwaves. "Listen, I'd give an announcement," he said, "and I'd say, 'Well, we're going to be talking with Willis Reed, but first we got to pause and we'll be right back.' And then I'd put Willis on and if he said 'Duuuh,' I'd say, 'Oh, we're going to take a quick commercial,' and the guys would all start laughing. I kid Nate Bowman about using 'y'know y'know y'know.' I said, 'Well, why are you using the word "y'know"? If you take your time, you don't have to use "y'know y'know." You try it sometimes and then I'll put you on my program.' And I mean everybody just broke up. I told him, 'That's why you can't go to any banquets . . . y'know.' "

As Russell gave, so he got, but what ego accepted for approval, it did not suffer for criticism. "Well, I can recall an incident with Cazzie, y'know," said Bowman, "like . . . Cazzie like to dress real sharp and, I mean, when we were here in Milwaukee last year and, uh, y'know, Cazzie got on the bus and he had on his green suit and he had on some real loud green socks . . . real loud green socks, y'know. It was really funny, 'cause by the time he got on there, everybody noticed 'em, and he looked like a Puerto Rican, and everybody got on him as soon as he got on the bus. He said, 'Well man, these are outasight, these are new Supp Hose. Man, this is what's happening.' And everybody said, 'Naw, that ain't what's happening either.' So after the game I was no-ticin' him, I was sittin' over by my locker, and he went in his bag and got his black socks out and tried to sneak 'em on, and I caught him. And I says, 'Whatcha doin', Caz?' And everybody dug it, y'know, and . . . so he kinda felt a little embarrassed, and he never wore those socks again. He said, 'I'll wear 'em on the golf course, but I won't wear 'em around you guys anymore.'"

Russell's communications intimated sociability, but in the insa-tiate attentions demanded, what he did was to transform groups into audiences that were disposable for the next merry claque. The evangelical fervor of Russell turned experiences of his into affirmation of biblical faith; in interviews he could not sit but had to rise and wander about a room, gesturing with fists and spread arms. In his own way, Russell was a self-made loner.

"Because of the type of parents that I had," he said, "I did quite a bit of reading and I stayed up in the top ten of my class. And as I would think about it, it was as if I was a castoff because I did some studying. The background that I'm speaking of basically is that my mother . . . my parents taught me the ways of the Bible and I know when I say the ways of the Bible, people will say, 'Well, everybody has their own religion.' Well, I'm not going to go into all that. All I know is that I've been taught to live by the Bible, and I think that the way I've been taught has conditioned my life. With the guys compelling me to be a loner because I didn't drink or smoke or run with the in-crowd, I was sort of a castoff and considered a square.

"My father was a member of the Central Ivy Baptist Church. And my mother taught all of us how to play the piano. My sisters played the organ and the piano in the church. My mother was in the senior choir, and one of my sisters was in the gospel choir and, of course, another sister and myself were in the youth choir. I taught Sunday School in Baptists' Training Union and I knew the Bible quite well. I was satisfied with how my life was going. But I'd go to school and the guy would say, 'OK, he's a Sunday School man,' or 'Here's a guy that's getting better grades.'

"Before I got into high school I had one or two clashes. I didn't want to fight for this particular reason: I had run into one brawl when I was a sixth or seventh grader and knocked the guy over the desk and they thought the guy had a concussion. Well, you see what happened after that was, like, a chick tried to put lipstick on me, see. I was in the back—I sit in the back of the class—and I had finished my work and I turned it in, and I had got a hundred percent on it, see, and anybody that missed two problems had to do them over. Well, the little extra time that I took dividing the bottom number to the answer turned out that I was right. You see, it's not a matter of not knowing how to do it, it's a matter of making a silly mistake, writing the five and not carrying the three. So now they want to start a big ruckus, about why I was different, but I never said anything. That's what made them mad. I'd just sit there and look at them, and this gave me more joy out of just sitting there than anything.

"Okay, now here's a girl. She's going to crawl on the floor back to my seat to put lipstick on me, see. So I said, 'If you put that lipstick on me, I'm going to slap you, you know.' This is seventh grade, man. And I said, 'The devil doesn't like ugliness, and if you do that something terrible is going to happen to you.' Well, they already knew that I was reading the Bible in the back, and they would say, 'Hey, man, I caught him,' and I wouldn't say anything, I just put it in my briefcase and I'd try to remember what I was just reading. At that time I was in a program at church, learning the different scriptures of the Bible and trying to find books very fast. If a guy called out, "Find Matthew, second chapter, first verse,' I'd have to find it real fast. So it got to the point that the young ladies considered me as a castoff because they were going with some of the guys who were mad, who wanted to fight, and a couple of times I found myself running home because I was confused mentally you see. I didn't want to fight them over something stupid as a broad, so it finally got to the point where I got to playing basketball and all of a sudden these guys said, 'Gee, man, like we were wrong, we really mistreated this guy, because he's really not a bad guy.' Now my first reaction should have been, 'Listen, get away from me, I don't want anything to do with you,' but because of the way I was teaching young people and what I stood for, I accepted the apology but I became a loner.

"Anyway what happened was the girl tried to put lipstick on me and I pushed her hand away. Then I had to go into a long description to her boyfriend after school and I said, 'I don't have to talk to you,' I said, 'I'm sitting back there in the back of the class and she wants to put lipstick on me, fine. Now if you want to take me on, it's your prerogative . . . but over something as stupid as this?' I said, 'I'm not afraid of you. I just think it's a waste of time to be fighting on something as stupid, I don't want to.' Okay. Then the guy gets mad and it just so happened that a couple of guys said, 'Say, listen, why don't you leave the guy alone, the guy wasn't bothering your girl.' So I walk away and we start home.

"By the time I got to eighth grade, I started playing a little basketball, not much, and we won the eighth-grade championship. I scored thirteen points. And this instructor I had was a real neutralizer for me because most of my book reports were on biblical men, like Daniel in the lions' den, like David and Goliath, like Paul . . . great missionary, and great miracles that Christ performed. These were things that I knew about and I could write them in detail without looking at the Bible. So the instructor made the guys leave me alone. He said, 'You guys like him now because he played basketball for you, because you won the championship.'

"I really needed something to fall back on as a boy, I really needed something positive," he said. "In other words, I didn't want to go with the in-crowd, you see. I was continually going to church, not because I wanted God to see me, but because I believed in the Bible. And I believe basically today the reason that I'm as fortunate as I am is because I think the man upstairs has something to do with it. So I'm a believer in this respect: that I'll go out now to banquets and clinics and I'll talk to young people about my experiences and about what the Lord said in the Bible. I won't make up anything, I'll say just what it says in the Bible. If it's there, I believe it. If you show me something that's not there or tell me something that's not there, then I won't believe it. In college I was exposed to completely new things but I still became a member and started a program, or helped to start a program, called the FCA, the Fellowship of Christian Athletes, which I still receive magazines today, which Bradley, I think, is a member of. I still found a church to go to, sang in the choir and so on."

The zeal that Russell had was not exactly infectious on the Knicks. *We just call him Reverend Cazzie,* said Bowman, *because when he first came to the team, he used to kind of preach to us, y'know, about changing our ways and stuff like that.* Certain teammates thought him fraudulent. *He's just got the world bullshitted,* said one Knick. *He's a big showman, that's all he is, and, like, he'll talk to a reporter and his language will change and he'll pronounce every word distinctly like he's brilliant, and then he'll get with other guys and he's boo-aaying it.* The strength of such a reaction indicated the effect of prolonged association on diverse heads. As Bradley said: *I don't know if the team functions best when it's like a marriage of a family in a blood sense . . . because everyone knows everyone so well that minor irritations become major hindrances to team success.*

Familiarity led to problems even between kindred spirits. *Like when Nate sleeps, man,* Stallworth laughed, *his teeth will rub together in a crunching sound. I just have to beat this guy, make him put a pillow over his mouth or something, anything to keep him quiet.* The friendship that withstood Nate's nocturnal motor nevertheless recognized more glaring faults.

"Sometimes Nate had a tendency to be a little overbearing," Stallworth remarked. "I used to tell him he's overbearing and to be cool. Like, he'd make demands—I mean, he didn't ask for favors, he demanded favors—this type thing, and I wasn't going to buy it from Nate. And Nate was just this type fellow. Nate was arrogant. I'm going to do what I want to do when I want to do it, nobody is going to keep me from doing it, and if I want something from you, I'm going to get it. This type attitude he has, anything he might want. He might want money—like, Nate would do things like he would say, 'Lend me five dollars, man.' 'Well, Nate, I don't have the five dollars.' 'Oh, man, you lying, you got the money.' 'Well, I can't let you have it. Nate, man, I need this money.' 'All right, that's all right, you just forget it, you forget it, I'll catch you down, you just go ahead and forget it.' He practically would frighten a guy into giving him that money. He'll get a guy into thinking, well, maybe he might catch me down when I really need it. I call this overbearing. Look here, Nate does this sometimes *now*. I could be in here listening to my record player over there, he'll come in and change the record, right in the middle of the record. I'm not lying, he walk right through the door, walk straight to the box and change it. Everybody took Nate so seriously, there's a lot of people dislike him for that. Like, if you noticed—I want you to notice Nate on the trips. Nate is still like that in a lot of ways. He is a little bit more responsible but he still got the same type thing. He might stick his finger down your ear, things like this, grab your ear, grab you by the chin and say, 'Look at me,' this type thing, 'Look at me when you talk to me.' He hasn't changed too much but he's a little bit more responsible like I said. Overall, I think Nate is one of the greatest guys I ever ran into in my life."

The Gatorade guys and Riordan had their disillusioning moments, too. "Like, Hos and Mike talk a lot," said May, "and a lot of times I don't want to talk. They just like to talk a lot of times. Mike, if he wants to say something, he'll just interrupt you, more or less. He was reading a book, and I was saying something to him and he said, 'What?' and I repeated it, and he couldn't hear me. I said, 'What's the matter, can't you hear?' He said, 'Well, stop interrupting me while I'm reading,' like he had never done it before, and it was like I was really bothering him. He was reading that book, *The Rise and the Fall of the Third Reich,* which is like eight thousand pages and him missing one sentence to listen to me was really going to set him back some. So that kind of ticked me off and I guess, you know, I've been leaving him alone, so that's where he gets his Phantom stuff, he thinks I'm not really talking. It's kind of funny, like, when Hos wants to watch a [TV] show and Mike wants to watch a conflicting show, Mike's always got ten reasons why they should watch it, why Hos doesn't really want to watch the one he originally wanted to. Hos told me, he said once to Mike that he liked snow, that he thought it was pretty, and Mike right away jumped all over him and told him how messy it was and how bad it is to drive in and cold and just nasty and said, 'You don't like the snow, Hos, it's terrible.' "

As close as May and Hosket were, there was a fine edge of competition from schoolboy days that continued in the pros. Hosket, whose father had been an All-American pivotman at Ohio State, admitted he had been conceited then but thought it forgotten. "At least it was with me," he said. "When we came to the Knicks and we were out at my house Easter '69, Donnie and his fiancée came over and my mother was there and we got talking. I didn't think he was conscious of all this print that had gone on in high school. We kid about it once in a while, but not that much. Then, somebody had just had a birthday and my mother said, 'How old are you, Don?' I think he said twenty-three, and I said, 'Yeah, I wonder how it feels to be that old?' because I'm a year younger than Donnie. And he said, 'Yeah, remember EARLY START FAILS TO DETOUR HOSKET?' and he quoted an actual headline that was put in the paper when I was, like fifteen years old. He'd remembered it for, like eight years and my mother mentioned it after he left. Patty got out some scrapbooks we had and he had quoted it word for word. But even, like, I could sense it last year at times. One game he got in he got six points and there happened to be a writer from Dayton at the game, and Donnie came back telling me how they had written it up that he touched the ball three times and scored three baskets and, in the very end, the last line of the article said, 'Bill Hosket did not play.' He said that was the last line of the article and he just walked away . . . like finally . . . we got this damn thing settled now."

The differences that worked themselves out among fellows of the same flesh were not so easily resolved among blacks and whites together. The game had changed from the days when Holzman and his Rochester Royal teammates ate corned beef sandwiches with owner-coach Lester Harrison in the fraternal confines of one room. The pub travels and pool halls and all-night card games that Schayes and Braun and McGuire evoked with some feeling lasted only while the league's membership was slightly less restrictive than the neighborhood country club. The locker room, be sure, was now no fount of brotherly love. *When a*

guy sits down and starts telling me about the great relationships,
said Cazzie Russell, *I say, "Wait a minute, you go tell that bullcrap to the guy who just told you." I say, "Don't tell me about it,
because I know what's going on."*

The public image was of Knick harmony, but the reality was
far more complicated. *The feeling here,* said Russell, *is that other
than basketball, I don't particularly care about you, and I think
Red is probably the cause of some of it because that's basically how
he feels.* Disinterest in changes was not onesided. Knicks black
and white let it be. *It would be amazing,* said Dolph Schayes. *You
could find a black fellow on one team and there'd be a black fellow
on the other team; they had never met before in their lives but it
seemed just in a brief conversation that they were lifelong friends.*
So the traveling circles of black and white players overlapped
hardly at all. *You have to remember,* said Carl Braun, *the black
athlete is much more revered by his people that the white [ath-
letes] are, because again this is a man that's been able to get
ahead, he's making a few dollars, so there are many places where
he's welcomed like a king almost. Why go to a white man's place
where you're just going to be another guy in the door?*

Barnett did not find his situation so different from the black
masses. *After you leave that arena,* he said, *you just another
brother out there, just like anybody else.* Nor did it surprise him
that black and white players were not that chummy. "There are so
many forces," he said, "you have the environmental force, you
have the forces of culture, you know, you got so many things. Like
I want to see Sly and the Family Stone. Like, the white players,
they aren't hip to that, that's not in their world, you know, they're
apart from it. They might go see Johnny Cash, I can't dig him.
There are so many things. Like, most white players don't dance,
they don't know how to dance. In our world, they're considered
squares and maybe they'd feel inadequate in our world if they did
try to hang out with us, and maybe we would feel the same. They
just can't relate. We had a couple of dances where a couple of
[white] guys tried to dance. They just . . . they were out of their
class, let's put it like that. I mean, like, it's what do you have in
common except playing basketball?"

On the New York team, the marital situations of players appeared to provide a rationale for the prevailing social apartheid. (Bradley was the only white who was single, Barnett the only black who was married. Reed was divorced. Frazier's divorce proceedings were in the works.) But had all the Knicks been similarly situated it would not have narrowed the breach.

Blacks and whites went their own ways. The black way was more ritualized. Almost the moment they alighted from airport transport and set foot into hotel lobbies, the black players were in motion . . . TELEPHONE FOR MR. BOWMAN, TELEPHONE FOR NATE BOWMAN . . . the sweet buds in each city knew arrival times and worked on the early-bird premise . . . TELEPHONE FOR MR. FRAZIER, TELEPHONE FOR WALT FRAZIER . . . bids were put in for the two complimentary tickets that each visiting player was allowed, and for social privileges. Should the brethren disdain them for the prospect of crazier meats, they found no problem. Reciprocating arrangements among NBA blacks. LOOK HERE, BABY, MY MAN FROM THE KNICKS IS IN, WHYN'T YOU RUN OVER AND SAY HELLO provided suitable recreations. It was a network that functioned in pleasures. In Milwaukee, Bowman would ring up Flynn Robinson. In Boston, Stallworth called Emmette Bryant. The grapevine hummed with nice news of names, parties, numbers and places. In Los Angeles the football great Jim Brown was holding a party. In Detroit the Pistons were celebrating Eddie Miles' birthday, and so on and so forth.

Girls in these cities adopted favorites and wound up at the places to which the players repaired. The ballplayer for the lady from the black precincts was what the doc-tah was to the belle of Great Neck, and the same comedies ensued, touching pieces in which give 'n' get were balanced: LIKE I WAS RAPPING TO THIS CHICK AT ONE OF THESE PARTIES, recalled a black radio newsman, AND GETTING SOME GOOD FEEDBACK AND THEN SUDDENLY THE CHICK, LIKE, FROZE, AND SAW FRAZIER HAD JUST WALKED INTO THE ROOM, SO I GOT THE PICTURE.

The white athlete had neither the structured arrangement nor the professional fraternalism the blacks did. Road life was for the white more makeshift, dining and drinking and flickers and whatever folly that acquaintances in the cities might arrange. On the coast, Bradley and DeBusschere might have drinks with actor Robert Redford, a basketball fan whose plush mountain retreat they'd visit while in Salt Lake City. Riordan drank with relocated New York friends whose recollections of neighborhood con men were straight out of Damon Runyon or Breslin. Bradley's friends were a more cultured bunch; in Los Angeles he'd visit with writer Jeremy Larner; in other cities he would go off with international sorts, as Hosket said: *Any time there's a guy in an airport with a turban or something like that, Bill always ends up sitting next to him and talking.*

What black and whites did share was a simmering discontent for one another. In some cases it was a matter of discordant nerve ends. *One time,* said Don May, *we all got in one car to go to the hotel, it was about ten people and Nate had this soul music on up as loud as it could go, and Nate was, and everybody was, screaming and hollering. I was just sitting. I was, like, I was almost paralyzed. I felt like jumping out of the car. Geez, we finally pulled up. I got out of there as fast as I could and tried to relax a little bit.*

"A lot of times after we lose," said Riordan, "the locker room is almost like when we win—you know what I mean, the kind of feeling, people laughing and shouting and, like, there's no difference. [One time] I purposely went into the shower after a loss, I started to go into the shower as Red called everybody together again, he says, 'Hey, come on back here,' he says, 'you're not going anyplace anyway. What's the rush?' Later, I wanted him to call me over and say, 'Where the hell did you think you were going?' I was going to say to him, 'I wanted to get out of here before the celebration began.' He didn't give me a chance to, but that's the way I feel."

For some, the pregame locker room was just as disconcerting. "Cazzie," said May, "seems to instigate a lot of noise and yowling and screaming on the bus and everything because when he's not around it's not that way, it's more subdued, I don't know what it is. Cazzie especially, he'll be talking, he won't be talking, he just yells, he'll go *blooo-woo-ooo*, make all these noises and stuff, so

DeBusschere started mocking him, I mock him too. We walk around each other and go blooo-woo-ooo. It's just nonsense, that's what it is. Bradley? He usually doesn't say too much. He doesn't say anything. He sits there and laughs when they rib him. But he never comes back. Everything Cazzie does, he picks up from Barnett, that's where it originates, everything originates from Barnett, because he's funnier than hell. He's very quick, and Cazzie is so loud he tries to make everybody think that he's starting all this and he's really the center of attraction and originator and all this. I don't know how it got started. They just started making noises. Like, they'll be telling a story, they'll talk about some girl, they'll say, 'That girl you were with last night, she couldn't do it, booo-ay, blo-woo-ooo,' and start making all these noises to emphasize it or something and that's just the way it is every time. It's colorful except when they start screaming and all that. I can't understand why they have to be so loud and try to emphasize themselves. I mean, Barnett, he doesn't have to do that, because he's intelligent enough, he can speak plainly. Willis doesn't participate in all this. Nor John Warren. Clyde very rarely—he doesn't say much, he stays with himself. Barnett, he doesn't go for all that yelling. When he says something, he just says it, he doesn't turn and make everybody in the whole place hear it. It's like a big circus a lot of times. They laugh, they try to see who can laugh the loudest and the weirdest, just trying for attention apparently, I don't know [why], I'm not a psychologist.

"It's sickening for a while and then you just have to be tolerant like . . . DeBusschere is taking the attitude of making fun, poking fun at it, he just goes bloo-wooo-ooo right back to them. Maybe it makes them see how silly they are, but I doubt it. Like I say, it really irks you because you can't do anything else, all that noise going on. We just try our best to tune it out. I just try and go somewhere else, out of the room, anywhere."

The blacks, it can be noted, were not entirely thrilled with the whites.

RUSSELL: DeBusschere has pretty good rapport with Red. So the theory is there's something funny about DeBusschere. Now DeBusschere is a good ballplayer and he's a good defensive ball-

player and he rebounds and he hustles. This is fine. But De-
Busschere is very sneaky. He's sneaky in that he . . . will do
things to maybe let Red know that he won't want you to know
that he's doing them. He wants you to feel that he's, you know,
in there fighting—

Q: Can you specify what you mean?

RUSSELL: Can't do it. Because we already had one little incident
that we picked out.

Q: You and him?

RUSSELL: Some of the other guys picked it out. They happened to
see it and I happened to be aware of it.

Q: Is there anything—

RUSSELL: Like Mike [Riordan], I had to straighten him out. Several times in practice or in a game he has missed Stallworth or
Bowman cutting to the basket wide open. Now I had to make
sure that he wasn't doing this because they were black. But
then he turned right around and caught Hosket and May on the
same play going right up the middle in the same pattern, you
see. So what I was telling him is that if you're going to tell me
something about helping you out on certain plays while we're
playing, I would suggest that you make sure that I'm able to
communicate with you. Basically, you can't tell Mike anything.
It's as if he's in a daze or something. For example, we were
playing somebody, I think Baltimore, and one of their guys
pushed him or something, and I got in front of Mike and was
pushing him away, so he pushed *me* away and I said, "Don't
ever push me away again like that." I said, "Because I'm your
teammate," and I said, "I'm aware where the other player is but
I don't want you to get kicked out of the game." So he started
telling me shit about don't hold him. I said, "From now on,
when there's a ruckus I won't even be over there." See, if you
take an asinine attitude toward me and what you're basically
telling me is that you don't want to be bothered . . . Mike
seems basically like a good guy but when I get to talk to him, he
seems guilty. He usually gives me that impression . . . won't
look you straight in the face.

Q: What else?

RUSSELL: If Frazier missed Bradley on a cut or pass—I mean, Bradley goes into an uprage, man.

Q: Do you think that has racial overtones?

RUSSELL: I don't know what the hell it is. I don't think the guy has any intelligence in that.

Q: Why do you say that?

RUSSELL: Because he's missed guys on passes. I mean, he's missed an open guy, and there's no sense in making a big scene out of it out on the floor.

Q: What if, say, Riordan missed him on a pass, missed Bradley?

RUSSELL: He doesn't say anything, no reaction. That's all right, missed you this time. I don't think this is good for *you* because when you write the book I don't think you're going to be totally happy knowing there's not a rapport a lot of people think there is.

Q: What other—

RUSSELL: In other words, I'm not going to go up to a guy—I'm not going to go up to Donnie May and say I appreciate the way you've been acting, because I'd be lying, because I don't particularly appreciate the way he's been acting.

Q: How has he been acting?

RUSSELL: Like Donnie May, I don't basically have anything to say to Don. You see, for example, like in the warm-up line, he waits till I get right up on him and he drops the ball. Everybody else he passes and throws it up in the air. So I had to tell him, you know, I said just . . . I mean, you don't have to look at me, just pass the ball where I can catch it, you see. I don't care what color a guy is, when I'm out there playing basketball, if the guy is open he gets the ball. But it's funny to me, when you go to a gathering like the one DeBusschere had [at his home], how Don May can walk up and introduce me to his wife but still he has no rapport with me as a teammate. You understand what I'm saying? And the same principle with Hosket, you see. You introduce me to your wife, but yet still you don't want to communicate with me. What the hell is this? What kind of life is this, man? What is this, huh?

Q: Why do you think they regard you the way you say they do?

RUSSELL: I'm not at home listening in their bedroom, who knows? Listen, I'll bet you it's a great feeling to travel around the country not feeling there's any prejudice against you. It's got to be a good feeling for you. It really is not the same with blacks. I just do not like the feeling that a white will give you at times . . . like you dumb asinine nigger or something of this nature . . . you don't know anything. Just be glad you're here. When basically I have a degree from an institution that you have . . . but basically you feel that you're better than I am. OK, but see, in the Bible Christ . . . when he said, 'Thou shalt not kill,' he didn't mean just whites or he didn't mean just blacks. He didn't pick out any particular color. I don't have anything against blacks or whites. I don't have anything against whites 'cause I can't . . . because all my teaching over the last thirteen, fourteen years, gone for naught, you see. For example, I would take Mike Riordan and Hosket over to my house in Chicago just as sure as my name is Cazzie, sit them down and feed them and wouldn't think one minute that they were white, wouldn't think one minute, because I did it in college. . . . I just wish Christ was on earth today to sort of iron these problems out. . . . Like why would my teammate [Bradley] get mad at me because I'm coming in for him, when he knows the problem, when he's working in Harlem, when he knows what the problem is nowadays?

Q: Couldn't it be just a personality quirk of his?

RUSSELL: No, no. Not forty-five games.

Q: Couldn't it be just that you're coming in for him, and not have anything to do with race?

RUSSELL: It could be, it could be a number of other factors, but when DeBusschere comes in for him, I detect no reaction, none whatsoever. Why me? When I could really care less. You understand what I'm saying? Now, OK, so I get ready to come in for Bradley, he gives me this frown when he passes me. I go out on the floor and I happen to turn and I glance at him going to the bench and I see him muttering and all this, so he's not really mad at Red. So I asked him about it, so he says, "I'm sorry." I said, "Bill, don't give me a long song and a dance." I said, "You can continue to do it but I want you to know that I'm aware of it and I don't really care." I said, "And as far as I'm concerned with you working in Harlem, what have you, you seem to know the problem but yet still you do nothing about it. At least tell me who you're guarding and go to the bench and don't let me see you putting on a big front. When you come in for me, I don't have a thing to say. I just go and sit down and figure the man is tired of seeing me out on the floor. So I mean, why all the great facial expression, why the frowning, as far I'm concerned you could stay out there and play the whole game. I wish I didn't have to come in for you . . . period." That's my reaction. Now you ask him about it and see what type of reaction you get. Now he's smart enough to try to send you out on a long tree limb but you ask him about it, you ask him about it.

Bradley, regarded by blacks on the team as the white player most sensitive to them, acknowledged that he and Russell had discussed the problem; moreover Bradley thought it resolved. When informed of Cazzie's lingering doubts he shook his head repeatedly, pondering it, and asked for the account Russell had given. This brought more headwagging and frowns, and finally he said, "I imagine it's difficult for any black person in the racist society we live in to be sure of a white man's motives, whether he is for real or phony, whether he's sincere or deceiving. As a result specific unconscious actions on the part of whites are often interpreted as racial actions by blacks. Once you peel away all the layers of experience, that's what's there. I can't really believe that Cazzie thinks I'm anti-black or that I don't like him. I just think you got him at a bad personal moment."

The times were ripe for discontent. The record-breaking winning streak had faded into the past; success had worn thin. Suddenly the season was bereft of any real intrigue. The Riordans, Russells, Stallworths and Bowmans entered and left contests at predictable moments. Holzman ran the same show night after night. And the playoffs were too far in the distance to serve as a rainbow.

New York still led the league, but clearly it was not the team it had been earlier. The Knicks were losing for a variety of reasons. Reed's injuries hurt, particularly on the offense where the attack turned sluggish. The deference that other teams paid the defense deprived New York of the game stimulant of the stolen ball. The strain of NBA travel aggravated circumstances even more: on a Christmas week fling, the Knicks covered 7,172 miles in four nights, the itinerary read New York . . . Los Angeles . . . Vancouver . . . Phoenix . . . New York.

Theories for New York's failings abounded. So did culprits, each Knickerbocker casting aspersions on another. As Barnett said, "Even when we were winning there were still guys that don't like each other, I don't want to call any names, but like I was listening to Carl Eller the other day when the Minnesota Vikings won the championship, he was giving his boolshit about everybody loves each other. What did he say last year, you know, when they lost? When you're winning, everything is great, everybody loves each other and everybody is a great guy." The implication was clear enough. In slumping times, the rats came dashing out of the closet.

"You get tired of hearing it all the time," said May. "Hos and I don't go in the games but Mike gets in and he'll start criticizing all over again and he's not the only one that does it, everybody on the bench does it when they come out. Bradley, DeBusschere, other guys. Of course, they're always pulling for the team to win, but there's so much criticism, maybe I just can't understand why it is and that kind of irks me a bit, just makes me withdraw more or less. You wonder about, you know, if I get out there, they're going to be doing the same thing, because, you know, if they're talking about somebody else all the time, they're going to be talking about you. This makes me not want to do anything. It just makes me feel insecure.

"There's this one stretch I started riding both of them back and forth, Mike and Hos. And, like, Hos would say something to me about Mike and I'd say, 'Mike, I don't want to say anything, but Hos just said you are so and so and you do this,' and Mike will say 'He's a such and such.' And I'd say back to Hos, 'Mike said you were such and such.' Now I'm making fun of them. The whole thing, I'm not doing it behind their backs, I'm being between them, saying this."

New York was at its most dispirited on the road trip that ran from January 6 to 18. There was strife in the movable 'scape and not even victory was a mitigating circumstance. In San Francisco, for instance, New York won two games, but some players were more excited by the dressing quarters. These facilities were not one but two rooms, a setup that inspired euphoric visions of personalized locker rooms.

In the same city, Cazzie Russell blew his cool with Nate Bowman. "If I'm going to be a person that teaches the Bible and believes in the Bible, then I can't lead two lives," he said. "In other words, I left some tickets for a couple of ladies in the first row. They said they had met me but I didn't remember them, and at the game one looked like a roto-rooter and, when I walked out and saw her, I was really shocked and quite naturally I had never . . . as I recall I don't even remember her, but she really looked bad and I'm the type of guy, I'm not good-looking but I feel that I'm in a position where I can be discreet about the young ladies that I want to socialize with.

"Well, anyway, I told her I had to go in, because we have to get up early in the morning, and unfortunately she went to a party with some of the other Knicks and I didn't show up. So the guys in San Diego mentioned something about it. Nate Bowman got in the conversation somehow—and I don't particularly appreciate Nate Bowman or his attitudes because I've been the only guy that has tried to help him in practice—I mean, shooting, position, try to put some discipline ideas in his mind about shooting the same. He never shoots the same way. Like, the next night in San Diego, he looked pitiful, he's like out of it, man. So the next day he started telling me about . . . he and Willis were talking about how bad the broads were. I knew that. I said, 'Well, I left tickets for the broad but I didn't leave with her,' and actually I really didn't have to explain anything 'cause I wasn't going to be crucified or hung or put in the electric chair. But it's a matter of . . . I guess it's a matter of pride. So okay, I blew my cool and told the Bow where to go. And well what I'm saying is that anybody can lose their cool but I've been under more stress than that and so I think I should have just kept quiet. So now when I get a letter from a group that's talking about me coming to speak, then I don't think I'm worthy . . . I have to go by myself and sort of get my thoughts together and maybe not say anything in the locker room."

In San Diego, the next stop on the schedule, the laxity of the team's play offended Holzman and he did not hesitate to inform the Cap'n about it.

FRAZIER: Willis had stomach trouble or something, and they sort of, like, got into it.
Q: After the game?
FRAZIER: Half time.
Q: What was it about?
FRAZIER: Well, Red asked didn't he feel like playing, and he said yeah and Red asked why didn't he get back on defense. So the discussion . . . well, Willis said, then I don't feel like playing.
Q: He felt he was getting bumrapped?
FRAZIER: Yeah, that was it. So he didn't play. (New York lost, 123–115.)

Several days later the Knickerbockers were in Salt Lake City to play the Phoenix Suns. The sight of the Harlem Globetrotters in the night's prelim affronted DeBusschere's purist sentiment about the game, and rather than watch it he went off to the locker room to sit alone. *I'm not mad at the people for laughing. Just say I'm mad at being billed with the Trotters. Because I get sick and tired of the question—"Do you think if you guys played the Trotters that you could beat them?" Listen, David Lattin is playing and starring with them, for Christ sake, and he couldn't make Phoenix, which is an expansion club.* DeBusschere was already piqued by a remark a newsman had made earlier in the day suggesting that Connie Hawkins, the evening's opposition, was the better player. That night DeBusschere's face was uncharacteristically flushed and he played a strong-armed game. But his abuse of Hawkins helped New York win, 130–114.

The close circumstances travel imposed caused people to feel put-upon on the road where before they had not. Bowman became an irritant to some, particularly the white players, in moments when he was what Stallworth referred to as *overbearing.* "He's always got to be the first one everywhere," said May. "When he gets there, like on a plane, he's got to grab everything he sees;

in a restaurant he's like an octopus, just arms all over everything, and his attitude is he'll have this and this and right now." Russell agreed. "Bowman," he said, "has no concern for people at all. Whatsoever. That's probably why his relationship is bad between him and the whites." But however tempting it was to judge Bowman by his hangups, it remained for Bradley to suggest another dimension. "On the surface," he said, "Nate's a very abrasive kind of guy. But underneath he's a kind, basically gentle personality. He's one of the few guys who ever apologizes for things when he feels he's wrong in a personal situation. I think that says a lot about his reaction to the sensitivity of other human beings."

Such forbearance was at a premium toward the end of the trip. In Windsor, Ontario, where the team was lodged for its game against Detroit, players were suffering from road fatigue. Bradley ate eggs in an all-night diner in the Canadian town and wondered if it wasn't a little odd that he should be there to play a game for money and, self-mockingly, puzzled whether poet-laureate Meschery had had the same thoughts. Hosket sat in his room rather than attend a party DeBusschere was giving at his Detroit residence, professing that by now he would accept for company a mere prose writer like Sly over his teammates. Phantom May had wearied of wandering the streets of strange towns and had his wife fly in from New York. And Barnett told Russell that he was stepping out awhile to see the musician Chuck Jackson, a piece of whimsy Barnett indulged in in each city he visited, which never ceased to amuse Russell.

Not even Barnett could have conceived the strange circumstances that befell Cazzie the next day as he drove the highway back from Ann Arbor, the city where he had attended college. A policeman ordered Russell to pull over to the side of the road; another law officer lay sprawled across the hood of a patrol car with a gun trained on Russell. It was, it turned out, a case of mistaken identity. A black prisoner said to resemble Cazzie had killed a deputy sheriff while being transferred to another jail. If Russell attached racial significance to the incident, he did not say. What later transpired suggested he did, for that afternoon in a team practice at Detroit's Cobo Arena, Russell and May struck up fighting stances.

That in itself was not so remarkable. It was remarkable that when the Cap'n told Cazzie to save his anger for game circumstances, Russell called Reed an Uncle Tom.

Reed is said to have advised his fellows that Uncle was gonna whoop some ass if he heard more of that kind of talk.

The next night Cazzie came off the bench to score the crucial baskets in New York's 104–102 win over Detroit.

Two days later, the road trip ended in mid-season in Boston.

If the precepts of flower power did not dominate the Knicks over the final half of the season, neither did the spirit of crazy bullshit that had come to reside in them. There was a return to normalcy. So to speak.

The accomplishment of somewhat brotherly love was owed to a providential schedule and to the anterior portion of the medial ligament in Bill Bradley's left ankle.

What the schedule did was to permit the Knicks to play against lesser fives like Chicago, San Diego, Boston, Detroit, Philadelphia and San Francisco in the two-week period that followed the trip of fools. That fortuitous draw helped New York win nine straight games and regain its sanity.

What the torn ligament in Bradley's ankle did was to increase the playing time, and prolong the spiritual welfare, of Russell and Stallworth and, not coincidentally, the team. The aural sensitives among the Knicks found a decline in locker room decibels.

Bradley first injured his ankle against Boston on January 27, only a day or so before being elected to the board of directors of the Crystal City (Missouri) bank of which his father was president. He played the last four games of the streak, and several more. Then, from February 11 to March 13, he missed fourteen games.

The injury was complicated by the illness of Knick physician Dr. Kazuo Yanagisawa. Lacking proper diagnosis, Bradley simply assumed he could play. But the damaged ligament forced him to rely too heavily on his sound right foot and the imbalance it caused eventually strained his back.

Shortly afterward, Dr. Yanagisawa died, and Bradley went to Columbia-Presbyterian Hospital, where an ankle specialist informed him that the injury to his medial ligament was a rarity in a young man. So saying, he appropriated Bradley's x-rays for a teaching aid, and advised him to lay off basketball.

For a week, Bradley stayed in bed and elevated his foot. On February 14, he left his apartment on Manhattan's West Side for the first time since taking bedrest, and went to the Garden to watch the team against Philadelphia. "I was hesitant," he said. "I was out a week, and even in that amount of time, the kind of rapport that is built on constant association could be jeopardized by my absence. I was anxious about it. I missed the camaraderie and I missed Barnett and the kind of things he kids about, or the things he does to purposely create an impression for me."

Bradley got on. The Knicks had not regressed since the modest midseason streak to the earlier hothouse fevers. A measure of this was in the deference paid Russell for his work, even if parenthetical personal remarks accompanied some of that praise. Nonetheless, God's forward, as Russell was called in the out-of-town press, showed a blessed scoring touch after his restoration as a starter. In his first four games he scored 24, 35, 19 and 18 points, and remained prolific enough thereafter to make Bradley fret about the status he would have on his return. That fear moved Dollar Bill to plot a premature comeback, an idea for which DeBusschere reproached him. The absence of Bradley gave rise to speculative considerations of the relative worth of Russell and Bradley to the team. It took a sage's wit to fathom the jigsaw complexities and social dynamics of five Knicks in motion. But the prevailing sentiment among games scholars was for Bradley.

The virtues and vices of Russell sprang from the same source, his imposing ego. Teammates noted that on nights the press sought Cazzie's postgame words, he regularly brought out the Biotta carrot juice he kept chilled in Whelan's training room. Other nights he did not. The neon compulsion that made Russell eccentric in the locker room might make him heroic on the court, particularly in the short-run situations in which Holzman was accustomed to using him. Nobody in the pros made a game snap to the way Cazzie did.

But what impelled his game imperiled it. Under backboards, Cazzie liked to lash out for the ball with one hand, as the fancy-

dan first baseman does for an errant peg, a habit that won over
partisans of flash but lost a crucial rebound or two. In those in-
stances Bowman and Stallworth would claw the air with two
hands rotating, and Holzman would shout, GET TWO HANDS
ON IT, CAZ.

Holzman's advice for Cazzie on defense remained the by now
bromidic first principle of seeing the ball, dammit; and if Russell
was not only seeing but stealing it more and more, he still suffered
from the selective moment, an affliction that gave him to dance
mad cha-chas on the defense when the situation was conspicuously one-on-one or latent steal, and lighten up when it was
neither.

New York had a drabness even in victory when Russell was a
starter, but if people found proofs of Russell's catalytic inadequacy in that pudding, they were doing Cazzie a disservice. New
York had shown genius only in spurts since the first twenty-four
contests, and was no longer wired for the all-out game now that
the regular-season title seemed assured. Had Russell played for a
team that ran pell-mell as Baltimore did, or a franchise that
required a powerful lift as Chicago or Detroit did, he would have
fit team needs better than Bradley. The self-serving game did not
suit Bradley, who was convinced of the ungentlemanliness of
1-on-1. In its schematic connections, the Knickerbocker game
approximated Bradley's concept more than Russell's. New York's
communal defense relied on individual persistence that Russell
shirked in a game's anonymous moments. Its offense needed the
sacrificial vision. Cazzie's turn-ons required a glorying goose.

Bradley had team awareness that Russell lacked. When Los
Angeles stacked four men on the foul lane to give Jerry West a
broad avenue of one-on-one court, Dollar Bill took the initiative
and broke from the crowd to help Barnett double West; that
move reasserted the magic of the defensive daisy chain. On
offense, Bradley was more conscious than Russell of the delicate
balance of pass and shoot. He cultivated Frazier's game by
abetting his scoring; easy points got Clyde sufficiently hyped to
take care of his mates, and plays like X got him up.

"Getting up," a term that alluded to pregame simmer, varied
with the man. At Princeton, Bradley had played "Climb Every

Mountain" just before leaving for the gym. As a pro, he switched to "Sergeant Pepper's Lonelyhearts Club Band," and then tuned off altogether, finding the trick worthless by the time he arrived in the locker room. Frazier lived across the street from the Garden: he would put on Sly and the Family Stone, or Marvin Gay, and ride into the locker room on that rocking note. Reed used instant replay: he would lie in bed and visualize his man, *like, say, Jimmy Fox, I KNOW he's got a good outside shot, so I got to play him tight.* DeBusschere had the same device but conceded he found it impossible to psych himself for teams like Seattle and Chicago. Barnett went on like old man river. After each game he did exercises back in his hotel room—situps and pushups and 500 toe raises on a phone book for his once-injured Achilles tendon. Unable to sleep after games, he read until early in the morning. Game days he rested, ate, walked to get his blood flowing.

"A whole lot of ballplayers," he said, "don't give a damn until they throw the ball up. I mean, they never talk basketball. Maybe they're out all night, maybe they're out all day. They don't eat or maybe they eat a hamburger before the game or try to rush and eat something. Like me, I'm eating at this time because I know . . . everything is predicated around the game. So you're thinking about it all the time. Some guys go out and fuck before the game, you know, which affects their performance. A lot of guys drink. So they can't be thinking about basketball."

Once the players arrived for the game, Holzman took over. The way he consciously worked a room inspired few Knickerbockers. *There's something in psychology called parallel play,* said a player. *You can see it in little kids in a sandbox, the way they're both talking about different things at the same time and not listening to the other. That's the feeling I get when I talk to Red.*

Plainly, Holzman's locker room tactics did not possess the subtlety he envisioned. In relating how crucial Bowman was to team morale one night, Holzman was unaware of the disdain the player he addressed had for Nate. Since the Chicago incident, the pregame banter to which the coach was addicted was varyingly interpreted.

"I notice," said one Knick, "it's always Clyde and Russ and Nate . . . and Bradley. That's the way it is. It's always 'Bradley,' it's

never 'Bill baby,' theres no glad-handing there. He comes into the
locker room and says Dave the Rave and throws a piece of tape at
him. But never a word to DeBusschere or Hosket or Riordan or
May.

"He does it to keep the team light. He'll try to say all kinds of
things before a game. NATE, ARE WE SET? . . . CLYDE,
YOU'RE MY MAIN MAN . . . DAVE THE RAVE . . .
WHERE'S THE CAPTAIN. Sometimes he'll say something
that's really stupid. Or vulgar. I look over to Bradley. This shit to
him, this turns him off. But actually Red's pimping these guys.
Like he thinks Clyde has to be kept loose 'cause . . . this star
treatment . . . Clyde is real conscious of the publicity in the papers and he's sensitive . . . 'Clyde, you're my right-hand man,'
and all this shit. Well to me it's sickening and what he doesn't
realize is that to even the blacks, this is getting sickening, although they don't say it. They laugh and joke around. But when I
talk to them, they say all that bullshit he does with us—they realize what's going on—and they look at it the opposite way. They
think he's pimping them whereas he doesn't say anything to Bradley and DeBusschere. But like to us, it seems he bends over back-
wards for the blacks. Like why doesn't he say, 'Goddammit, Bowman, learn those plays. You're getting paid for it. If you go out
there and fuck up again, you're going out.' Red thinks that by
pimping Nate, by keeping him loose, it keeps the whole team
loose. He's got some attitude that all the other colored guys look
on Nate as the class clown, but that isn't so. Willis thinks it's a
bunch of bullshit. Willis doesn't like that garbage at all. It's like
Red feels he's putting something over on them, but to them he's
not putting over a thing.

"And once something like Chicago happens, deep in the guys'
minds I think they realize that it will never be the same. I know
I'll never feel the same about the man. I know Bradley won't. I
know how DeBusschere feels. Well, like Dave . . . let's see, what
do we run? We got the D play, the New York play, the Barry, the
2-3-F for Bradley. The only offense that we run that's Holzman's
is the 2-1-F where Nate comes in the game, because that's all he
can do. See, when DeBusschere came we didn't really have an
offense because our offense was geared around Bellamy and be-

cause Willis was so big. So Dave gave us the offense. But then like he had a thing about Clyde, that Clyde has to let his points come and just quarterback us and hit the open man, and not be a ball control guard like Oscar or Monroe. Dave kind of mentioned this to Red a month after we went stale, and it finally came out. Red thought he was getting critical of his teammates.

"Red taught Dave a helluva lot on defense, but at the other end of the floor it's all Dave's. So up to that point where Red thought he was getting critical, Red accepted Dave's suggestions. When it was an easygoing suggestion like a later practice time because of traffic. Just little things. How about having the guys swing out this way on this play instead of that way? Something like this. And Red won't take any more advice from him. It's bugging Dave now and Dave says I can't talk to the man anymore. It's just got to a point where, like I said, Red thinks some of his authority is slipping. I can't explain it really. Like, in the papers, he's constantly saying, I don't do anything, it's the ballplayers and all this . . . that's bullshit."

"A guy might want to mention something," said Cazzie Russell, "and Red'll start in talking even before you finish. In other words, 'Scratch it, you don't know what you're talking about.' He may not say it, but I don't need to be spoon-fed to know when a guy doesn't want me to say something. . . . Now if the coach doesn't give a damn about your feelings, then you say the hell with him, you see. Like for example, if he gets ready to give a peptalk and he'll say something basically supposed to be funny, he'll look at me. I'll look at him but I won't crack a smile. You see the feeling is that you don't care about me, why should I care about you?"

Holzman's humanity was treated more kindly in other quarters. The Hawks' general manager, Marty Blake, remembered that Red had given Milwaukee owner, Ben Kerner, money from his own pocket to keep the franchise solvent in the impoverished days of the league's infancy. In the road world in which he traveled, he was leader of his drinking group, a benevolent despot whose gruff retorts, FRANKIE, YOU DUMMY, were sought as tokens of the hardy affection that was communicated in that group of writers and management people. But even here, Holzman coveted authority. Should newcomers like Sly reply to his one-liners with too

incisive a wit, the coach resorted to power plays, YOU KNOW,
WE DON'T HAVE TO LET YOU DO THIS STORY OF
YOURS, a method he did not hesitate to employ in the locker
room. One pregame night, Holzman remarked on the grooming
habits of a player who was combing his hair. The player replied
that at least he had hair. It was noted that the player did not
receive his accustomed playing time that night. Such experiences
led players to call the coach names other than Red.

Coaches had estranged their players before and made use of it.
A player-coach of the Syracuse Nationals, Al Cervi, was so thoroughly disliked that at the end of one season his athletes voted not
to give him a share of playoff money, an unprecedented move that
resulted in a rules change making a coach's cut automatic. What
Cervi did was to verbally whip his charges. *He had just one philosophy of coaching,* said Dolph Schayes, *and if a guy was going
to sit down and cry after he got bawled out, Cervi didn't care. He
was raw but very effective.* Incensed players released anger in
games.

Holzman provoked smaller passions, but nevertheless controlled games from the bench. The defense consumed him in
contests. *Between you and I,* said Cazzie Russell, *he told Willis
the other night—'If you're going to be loafing, loaf on the offense.'
In other words he doesn't care about the offense, he thinks playing
the defense is going to make the offense but you have to be disciplined on both ends of the floor.* The offense Red left to his players. *Remember the game we won in Milwaukee in the last seconds
[December 10]? Well I was the one who called the play,* said
Reed. *We came in and, y'know, it was kind of like, well, what we
going to do? So I said, well, let's go with the 2-3-F for Bradley.
And it's been like this a lot of times, y'know.* When the team
added plays to its repertoire, Holzman was not the inventor. *I
would say,* said Stallworth, *a couple, three of the plays were derived by Red but the rest of them by the players. DeBusschere, he
has experience in coaching in a professional level, so he picked up
a couple of plays.*

That no public mention was made of Knick conflicts at this time
bespoke the immunity that professional sport had from such

investigation rather than any discretion with which bickering may or may not have been carried on, and suggested the care that management took with appearances. If the Knickerbocker image was a shadow of its reality, this was merely part of a fine old tradition.

Image was a many-splendored thing.

DeBusschere drank beer like a stevedore, but when a sporting journal named *Jock* published a color photo of him doing it, Blauschild phoned its offices and expressed displeasure on behalf of management. Bill Powers, the miscreant who snapped the shot, was advised not to do it again. What made the affair more curious was DeBusschere's reaction: he agreed that it was a blight on a player's image. Such concern for public appearance did not apply to all the Knicks, but was representative enough. The cultivation of image led some players to ask authors to bowdlerize language attributed to them, but in their attempt to avoid appearing prudish they sanctioned certain profanities and not others.

Most black Knickerbockers didn't give a ——— about obscenity; but then their consuming interest in clothes was not shared by whites. Barnett was the elder statesman of fashion on the club. The *Post*'s Lewin recalled that the first time he saw Barnett was when Dick came to the Garden with the old Syracuse Nationals team. That night Barnett was wearing a homburg, a cape and spats. Barnett and Frazier went to a tailor named Lester. Lester had offered either of them free merchandise for bringing Bill Bradley into his shop. Frazier felt that a thousand dollars would get the Bradley wardrobe *to-gethuh*. Bradley said he would think on it, but poor Lester never did boast of Dollar Bill as a patron.

Bradley's dress was infamous among Knicks. On a team that fancied matching underwear of exotic cloths, Bradley sometimes wore a Knick tee shirt. When a shabby raincoat of his was deemed unfit, it mysteriously disappeared. And so it went. "Like during the exhibition season, he walked around the airport with a big hole in his socks, in the heel of his socks," said Bowman. "Every time he walked this big hole would come up. I mean anybody could see that big hole. I saw it and so I started sneakin' around tellin' everybody about it, and, uh, different guys just went to whisperin' about it. They didn't really want to say anything, 'cause Bill he's a real good guy, y'know. And no one really wanted to talk up and say, 'Man, what you doing with that hole in your sock?' So I walked up to him and I said, 'Man, you gotta do something about your socks.' That's all. He didn't think anybody had noticed it, y'know. So he say, 'You better, you better keep quiet about that.' So I said, 'Man, you know I wouldn't tell anybody.' "

Others had backgrounds that made them more conscious of clothes. May was mortified when years ago Hosket listed the few shirts he owned. Barnett used to slip into his brother's clothes in a barn on the way to school rather than wear his own. That concern for outward appearance, Garden photographer George Kalinsky said, made the Knicks cooperative camera subjects, Bradley not excepted. Bradley had Kalinsky comb his hair and worried about a tendency to appear crosseyed in pictures. Frazier wanted new shots to record the mossy Victorian sideburns he had grown since the last season. Bowman had the greatest facility for striking poses, and Kalinsky claimed that, had he never seen any of the players, he would judge Bowman a star from the action shots of him he had taken.

For the Knickerbockers, however, the pens were mightier than the lens. In particular, management cultivated the metropolitan area newsmen, or "daily guys" as they were called. Most of these writers had their expenses covered during road trips by the team, the representatives from *The New York Times*, the *Daily News*, and *Newsday* being exceptions. Blauschild, Wergeles, Holzman, Whelan, and the daily guys were fraternal; their habit of traveling together led the players to call them the Rat Pack. The Pack occupied the choice locations at the press table and got gratis courtside seats for their families and friends. Prose writers from magazines and book publishers and no-account news sheets were not held in the same esteem. Management was suspect of journalists from these bastard prints.

Once, several years ago, Vic Ziegel, a writer filling in for Leonard Lewin on the *Post*, discovered over breakfast table chatter that a Knick named Art Heyman wanted to be traded and wanted to be quoted to that effect. Ziegel quoted him. The story was a sports page headliner. Management retaliated by not informing Ziegel that Heyman had been fined the next day. The ludicrous part of the whole affair, Ziegel discovered, was that Heyman had been grousing for weeks to the daily guys that he wanted to be dealt away, and was politely ignored by all.

More recently, Phil Jackson had received a standing ovation at an exhibition game at Muhlenberg College after a story appeared in the *Post* that had him on the demonstration lines at the 1968 Democratic National Convention facing Cazzie Russell's fixed bayonet. Jackson found the applause exhilarating but regretted he was not in Chicago that summer. When Jackson first came to New York from North Dakota, media scholar Riordan had advised him that he would get on with reporters if he told them he was a cowboy back home on his uncle's ranch. The year he was at Allentown, Riordan would read headlines like, JACKSON LASSOS 15 POINTS, and so on. Only when Jackson commenced to wear mod clothes and talk of Kant and Gertrude Stein did the press give up the six-gun image.

One day Barnett asked, "Did you read that shit in the paper by Leonard Lewin? I told him about one of my boys down in Harlem. He had an El Dorado Cadillac. And you know how you pick up four wheels hot. The cat says, 'I got four dual 90s which cost approximately $90 to $100 apiece. I can get you four for about $100.' And the cat says, 'Bring the tires and I'll give you the money.' So the guy brought the tires. He gave him the hundred. And when he went around to put them in the trunk of his car, his car was sitting on bricks, the guy had took his tires. Now this cat ends up being me. So this is the whole boolshit that you get from the sportswriters. This is one reason I don't like to talk to 'em because half of the shit that they write is boolshit. But like Lenny, he's still my man. I didn't say nothing about it to him. This is what I expect, you know, so it doesn't bother me."

Lewin's account of Knick success led some players to question his interpretative faculties. "Like, you can't pick up an article that Lenny writes," said a Knick, "that doesn't give practically all the credit to Red. Like, it's Red Holzman's making of a dynasty, the genius who's got the Knicks in form, and all this. And the players feel it's a combination of things. I don't know if you read that article, it was in the scorecard. Lewin's fabricated piece of BS. About how Red would always flip a key to Frazier and say, 'Walt, you're my key man,' which was true. And then when Bradley got down in the dumps, he reversed the process and did it for Bill, called him the key man and threw him keys. That's BS. He never did that. It's like Lewin saying, 'He did this for a black, now wait a minute, he's got to do this for a white. I'll work it in here with Bradley.' He just tried to fabricate an article and make it like the picture perfect team."

Lewin, senior member of the daily corps, was a cousin to Blauschild and held stock in the Garden corporation. A small dapper man whom the players pointedly referred to as the Dean, he was thought of as a fringe management figure. In a Baltimore locker room one night, Lewin overheard Bowman tell *Newsday* writer Jeff Denberg that the Bullets would never ever beat the Knicks and, envisioning the fury to which Baltimore would be roused by the quote, advised Denberg not to print it. Bradley offered, in a theoretical way, a concept of the sportswriter as a legitimate critic. Lewin did not even abide legitimate critics. "I can't understand these guys on TV, can you?" he asked. "They're esoteric, just interested in their own words. All they're doing is putting the spotlight on themselves. If I was a critic, I'd go and ask the producer what he was trying to do and find out what went on from the eyes of the people who were in charge."

The hard-core Pack writers were Lewin of the *Post*, Joe O'Day and Phil Pepe of the *Daily News*, Rogers of the *Times*, Denberg of *Newsday*, Murray Janoff of the *Long Island Press*, Borgi of the *Bergen Record*, Bob Harding of the *Newark Star-Ledger* and Paul Horowitz of the *Newark News*. On the road, most of the Pack often congregated in either Blauschild's or Holzman's room, where they'd drink and watch TV. Holzman was devoted to movie trivia; he, O'Day and Rodgers had a running competition identifying bit players in old films. For writers not affiliated with the Pack, Holzman had Blauschild serve as an intermediary. Blauschild informed them that the coach did not mind their recording quotes issued by his players but got edgy at locker room notetaking that aimed at mood and perception. Red's feeling was that it did not make for a relaxed atmosphere.

Many Knicks saw postgame interviews as artificial situations in which they were expected to flesh out writers' preconceptions, a process they found singularly dreary. At these times, Barnett and Bradley were indifferent. DeBusschere and Riordan hid out in Whelan's quarters. The talkers were Reed, Frazier and, in good times, Cazzie Russell. Like Russell, Frazier enjoyed talking to the press, and had an authentic gift for the memorable phrase or snappy one-liner that brightened newspaper copy and Clyde's reading. Reed's answers were not as inspired as Frazier's but he had a sense of responsibility even toward the press, and worked at questions until the daily guys were satisfied.

The mild condescension with which the players held the Pack was directed more to the institution than to its individuals. Barnett, for instance, occasionally played cards with Pepe and Harding. Borgi and DeBusschere discussed the stock market. Players consulted Janoff in their choice of restaurants, dining places being Murray's idea of landmarks. Players and writers alike were entertained by the pornography that one writer casually flashed about.

A reference made to the Pack's capacity for mixed drinks in the Sunday magazine of *The New York Times* agitated the group; the feeling was that it deserved the same exemption from forthright scrutiny that it granted the team. The author of the piece, Larry Shainberg, was marked as an unscrupulous sort and thereafter was *persona non grata* in the locker room. At one point, management considered (but eventually rejected) the idea of barring from the locker room renegades not attached to dailies.

Writers felt an affection for the team (Borgi named his son David William after Stallworth and Bradley) that limited barbed commentary on players' ability. Sly could understand it: after the close associations he'd had on road trips, he welcomed getting away from the players so that he could ponder them more objectively. On the troubled January trip, he had jettisoned early to escape it all. Bradley recognized that the foremost impediment to critical sports reportage was the hesitance of writers to incur disfavor. "Writers," he said, "want to be liked." Risks, to be sure, were engendered by unflattering reference to a Knick performance. Lewin's implication one night that the scoring production of John Tresvant and the defensive talent of Russell were connected caused Cazzie for many weeks after to issue "no comments" to the Dean, and speculate on his character. "You can't make a statement derogatory toward a guy and then expect to come back and sit up in his face and laugh," he said. "I'm not that kind of individual."

Critiques did not go down well with players even when spoken softly. Bowman refused to acknowledge his faulty memory of the plays; his intricate excuses drew titters from teammates. Once when Asofsky remarked in candor on Russell's defense, Cazzie wondered what kind of friend he was. The inability to confront personal flaws suggested some limits of the athletic process, the nuances of which Bradley could articulate better than anybody on the team.

"Athletes live in a very insulated sort of world," he said. "For one thing, you have to be very careful of the physical things you do. If you are a so-called conscientious athlete, you make sure of sleep and food, and do things that restrict your personal freedom. That limits your physical adventure, and your awareness. At Princeton, I would never take chances with myself. It was one of the things I was consciously glad about when I finished college basketball and went to Oxford. Now I didn't have to worry about sprained ankles. I could take a chance with drinking water. If I got a disease, who cares? The only person who cares is me. So I'd take a chance. At Oxford, I played soccer, wrestled, and wasn't hesitant about climbing the Dolomites in Italy or trudging through the woods.

"On another level, you become very self-conscious which leads to introversion, or narcissism-egotism, both of which militate against a kind of quiet experimentation or militate against something outside of yourself which you have to try to embrace or understand. Some of these people grow up in situations where everything focuses on them and how they perform. As a result they are not interested in other things, because they become so pleased with themselves.

"Then there are the social forces. Society molds you by its vision. Either the athlete doesn't realize the alternatives or isn't strong enough to take them because his ego-narcissistic thing is out of control, or he finds it easier to embrace the stereotype that society has of him. When you are a seventeen- or eighteen-year-old person who says he wants to become an athlete, you're unaware of social influences. You're just pushing along. Maybe you realize it later, but then the choice is already made for you. What society does is to socially process you into a mold that you unconsciously accept. A guy is not strong enough to break through the stereotype society has of him. He either lacks the foresight to see beyond immediate rewards, or he finds it easier to accept that athletes should be hard workers rather than struggle with the same problems of identity and awareness others do."

To fans, it appeared players had an immunity from defects. In the valley of these giants all was safe and sound. Even the Oscar-winning screenwriter William Goldman preferred that that microcosm dear to him be unassailed by critical words; he confessed to Hosket that he feared one of the numerous books being written about the Knicks might undo the public image of the team.

The perspective that led most fans to sanctify the players promoted the outrage of a lunatic few. When Barnett played for Los Angeles, he was notified in correspondence that he was a nigger for depriving a white teammate, Jerry West, and a black one, Elgin Baylor, of the umpteen shots a game he took. Phil Jackson kept as a reminder of his tortured professional start a missive urging him to solo sexual congress. And Bradley had in his files from his debut year epistolary trash whose syntax required heavy blue pencil.

Damning kooks were a decided minority. Fans, Knick fans especially, had inordinate passion for the contestants. The Garden crowd was both hip and heated. No gallery in the NBA had a quicker reflex to the inevitable errors that referees committed or omitted, or greater vocal muscle. Enthusiasm for the Knicks habitually obscured the last bars of the national anthem, and lasted a full forty-eight minutes for the home club.

Frazier loved that noise, some nights it gave him goose bumps. New Yorker Riordan had a feeling for its origins, and could distinguish between a hard-core midweek crowd and a Sunday playoff crowd diffused with family sorts. Only Bradley mentioned the kicks that crowds gave him on the road. He likened his role to that of the wandering gunfighter: *In Salt Lake City*, he said, *the crowd was different, it was like we had to conquer a new world.* He preferred a large hostile audience to a sparse apathetic one.

Knick fans were rarely apathetic. John Condon, the public address announcer at the Garden games, recalled one enthusiastic woman who, years ago, attended with a more reserved spouse. "She was raising hell and the man sat there with his arms crossed the whole game, didn't utter a sound. When the game was over, his wife got up to go, straightened herself out and then turned to him. She gave him a tap on the shoulder and he toppled. . . . He'd been dead, they estimated, since the first quarter."

Back in the old Garden, Condon liked to torture those fans who wagered on out-of-town games. "When I'd introduce a score you could hear a pin drop in the place if the money was big on it." Luxuriating in that kind of absolute power, Condon remained consistently inconsistent in his method. "They never knew whether I'd give the loser or the winner first. I'd say, 'Here is an NBA score from Philadelphia . . . at the end of the third quarter, Philadelphia, 71' . . . then a good long pause to let them mull it over . . . 'and Boston, 83.' Man, those guys wanted to kill me. One night there was a shocked silence after I finished and some guy up in the mezzanine screamed out so loud you could hear him all over the arena: 'What are you, some goddamn wise son-of-a-bitch?' "

With the team's success, the bettors became absorbed into the mob of corporate vaudevillians, pretty people, and legitimate fans, some of whom were memorable to the players. "This night Hos, Donnie and I were out early for three-o'-cat," Riordan said, "and Donnie got off to a 7–0 lead. Then I came back and scored six in a row. There were maybe just a couple hundred people in the place at this point, and just after I hit the sixth one, this guy way up in the stands hollers in a loud voice, 'C'mon, May, you're only up one basket.' "

Garden history was filled with such rabid sorts. In the old Garden there was the dancing fat guy, a butterball in baggy sweater and trousers who would come down from the stands and, at end court, break into a terrific frug before leading the crowd in cheers that he invariably finished on his knees. One time Asofsky spied the dancing fat guy in coat and tie at the Queens Plaza subway stop, and went over to introduce himself. The dancer's eyes narrowed, and he asked where Asofsky knew him from. Stanley told him the Garden, and the guy turned his back. That was the end of the conversation.

The dancing fat guy didn't show anymore, but the Chinaman was there once in a while, still hell to sit next to. A night with the Chinaman required ripaway jerseys; he sat in a blue topcoat and eyeglasses with rubber bands, and when the action got hot, he grabbed at people. A man needed a good tailor to risk the Chinaman.

A guy named Sid Hietzler impressed Asofsky and Klein the night he took on Wilt Chamberlain, a confrontation that qualified him in their minds for instant superfan. "He was giving it to Wilt unmercifully," remembered Klein, "calling names . . . you big stiff, you lemon, this and that. At the end of the half, this photographer walked over and said to Sidney, 'Wilt Chamberlain sends a message: the next time you open your mouth he's walking over.' So there was a big silence, a lull. The second half started. Chamberlain walked out, and it was like the whole Garden was quiet and Sidney yelled out, 'Chamberlain, you stink.' Wilt looked at him, shook his head and walked away."

Jack Needle was considered by Asofsky and Klein a far-out baskets man. Jack Needle was a middle-aged schoolteacher who worked in a ghetto neighborhood and wore his hair in the Harpo Marx fashion. On school days, he would arrive with a basketball an hour or so before classes started and scrimmage with the students. Other times he would walk around town dribbling a basketball. Friends of his would see him going to the St. Anthony's festival in the Village, or in Times Square, or at a party in an artist's loft, and Jack Needle would have his basketball with him. Even Asofsky was puzzled by Jack Needle at times.

Asofsky was thirty-three and balding but had credentials from earlier days. When Nat (Sweetwater) Clifton was New York's first black player back in the 1950s, Asofsky would carry his shaving kit to the locker room. One night he inquired what was in it, and was told that it held a toothbrush that Sweetwater used while the Knick coach was giving his pregame talk.

Asofsky met Fred Klein at the Ninety-second Street YMHA in a "pickup" game in which they almost came to blows for elbowing indiscretions. The burly Klein is remembered at that institution

for combat he did have with former Knick Art Heyman several
years ago. "We took the ball away from him twice. The third time
he came down he tried to back into me—he's six-five, I'm six-one
—and turned around and said, 'You're pinching me.' I said,
'Pinching?' and at that he took a swing and missed and I took a
swing back and I just missed his head by about an inch and I tell
you I'd have knocked his head off if I'd hit him. . . . The funny
thing is that Art Heyman was Jewish and I used to root pretty
hard for him because he was one of us."

Fervor alone did not "entitle" a fan; more important were the
names and games he could drop. Their front row baseline seats
gave Asofsky and Klein an advantage. It enabled Klein, for instance, to flip a stick of gum to Walt Bellamy on a night he scored
thirty-two points so that for games afterward Bellamy would demand his Juicy Fruit lest he fail to score so prolifically. Klein and
Asofsky helped the Bells another way. It was Walter's habit to
make a toilet run just before each game and, should he forget,
Asofsky and Klein would remind him, 'Walt, Walt, you got to take
a leak.' And he'd say, 'Oh, yeah,' and dash to the locker room.

When Russell worked out at the Ninety-second Street Y, Stanley aided him by pointing out the house psychos so Cazzie would
not be caught unawares and injured. One of Russell's more remarkable offcourt performances occurred the night he drank out
the orange juice supply at Topsy's, a Queens restaurant in which
Klein had served as the brokerage agent. When big Fred was
involved in a restaurant called Montmartre the Cap'n came in and
ended up talking basketball with the patrons. *He left the girl he
was with and talked for two hours. She just sat there like she was
never there. It was unbelievable.*

One night Klein was showing a friend a tie that his father had
made. Then he saw Frazier staring at the tie. "And I said, 'You
like the tie?' And Frazier said, 'Yeah.' This was before the start of
the game, the warm-ups. He usually quits warming up about five
minutes before anybody else and sits down. So he saw the tie and
he said, 'Yeah, man.' So I brought it over, it was a wild flower tie.
I said, 'Do you like it?' He said, 'I have to get a suit to match it.'
When I told him my father makes ties as a hobby, he said,
'Really? Get me some solids, solid ties, wide ones.' So the next

time, I forgot to bring them, so he walked over during the warm-ups and said, 'Where's my ties?' So I said, 'I forgot, we'll make up some for you.' So that was the night he scored forty-three points against San Diego. He was tremendous and when they took him out he sat on the bench and I hollered over, 'Good game, Clyde.' And he said, 'Good game, shit. Don't forget the ties.'"

In the section from which Fred Klein dispensed ties and gum, Asofsky often was as much a show as any Knickerbocker. Whereas Klein slumped into his seat and puffed on long stogies, Asofsky was up and down; at tense moments when Holzman moved to the edge of his seat so did Stanley. Klein swore Asofsky had a cult of people who came to the Garden just to watch him and to whom big Fred regularly directed an apologetic expression. "Some of the things he says are so off the wall. Like the referee makes a call, Stan all of a sudden will say, 'It's not your call! It's supposed to be Gushoe's call 'cause he's at the point!' And he's standing over there and screaming and people look in amazement, and also looking in amazement is Nate Bowman. He constantly hits Stallworth and they point to Stan."

Asofsky conceded he was not your ordinary spectator. He warmed up mentally for games directly on leaving the publishing house at which he worked. "I'm thinking. I say, 'It's a Jerry West game. They're going to go one-on-one on us,' or let's say they're playing Frisco and I say, 'Gee, Willis Reed's not going to get away with that corner shot 'cause Nate Thurmond plays him clean. He goes through that pick.' And I think Stallworth can drive on [Joe] Ellis if they put in Ellis at the same time as Stallworth, and things of that sort. I'm part of the game."

Asofsky and Klein were bachelors sworn to celibacy in game hours; experience had taught Stanley that his work suffered if he took women to the Garden. "It's different when I take a chick to a tennis match and I say, 'Hey, Pancho is stalling for time because he's tired.' I can explain things. It's a different type of game. I remember one chick, François, a French girl, I took her to a Charles Aznavour concert the night before in Carnegie Hall and she went through her shenanigans. She jumped up as if Elvis Presley was on the stage or Jagger from the Rolling Stones. And I didn't understand what was going on on stage, I couldn't

understand the words. I'd heard some of the stuff, he sang some
Jacques Brel tunes. But then when I did my bit at the Garden, she
didn't sort of appreciate it. I yell, I'm verbose, I stand up. I don't
do it for David Merrick or theatrics, I do it for myself. Actually,
Freddie couldn't sell me on going to the end of the court at first. I
used to sit upstairs and do this stuff. I used to yell and scream and
there used to be quite a few of us around. Now, I like to be right
here, I like to hear what the ballplayers say. I like to hear Red
Holzman yell, 'Stay with him, stick with him . . . give one
. . . take it deep into Willis . . . 22,' things of that sort. I
enjoy that stuff. And like this François, I sensed her thinking, like
this is the real you, you're on your best behavior when you're in a
restaurant with me, but this is the real you, you're floating like a
zeppelin, this is your nirvana, you have an orgasm in the Garden."

Asofsky and Klein's proximity to the floor gave them access not
only to the home team but to the opposition and referees. Baiting
the aliens was sport for them. Sometimes it was undertaken in the
spirit of fun. "I know this girl from Detroit," said Fred Klein, "her
name is Dimples and she's a business girl, a hooker. And she said
to me, she met me once, she was talking to me and she said, 'If
you see so-and-so [an NBA ballplayer], tell him that Dimples says
hello. So this guy she knew came driving in for a layup one game
and I said, 'Hey Dimples sends regards,' and he blew the layup
and smiled at me. And he came back after and said, 'Where is
she? Where is she?' And he was screaming at me. 'Where is she?' I
said, 'I don't know.' And he threw his hands up in despair and
walked away."

Other times Asofsky and Klein were more provocative. They
saw their job as that of unsettling the visitors. And they did.
When referee Mendy Rudolph flicked sweat off his brow at them,
or Emmette Bryant gave them the finger, or Manny Sokol asked
how they knew about Sokolofsky, these were events of transcending importance for Asofsky and Klein. In their fashion they were
in . . . the . . . ball game.

In a day when theater, music, therapy espoused more involve-
ment, games kept pace with the times. Fans reflected in a sporting
facility the inadequacy of their lives out of it, and the lunacy of a

society. At hockey rinks, they called long-haired players fags, in baseball parks they ran onto fields to shake hands with center-fielders, at boxing matches they threw bottles and chairs. There was a thin line where feeling for a game became soft-headed. Its existence among New York fans was acknowledged in a prospectus for a Knick fan organization.

ARE YOU A BASKETBALL NUT NUTTY ENOUGH TO PAY $200 TO SIT AT THE NEW YORK KNICK PLAYERS' TRAINING TABLE?

You are invited to apply for a charter membership in a Club for *insiders*. A Club that is more than just a group of fans or boosters. Much more.

To begin with the Bench Warmers Club is run by the Knick players and they will be present and part of every meeting.

Right from the first meeting you'll be on a first-name basis with the players. And by the second meeting you'll feel like a sixth man on the regular team.

You'll rub elbows with them. Eat with them. Ask them anything that's on your mind. Yes, anything. Like asking Willis Reed how he plays Lew Alcindor or Wilt Chamberlain. Sound good to you? Of course it does.

What the game held for the fan was not necessarily the same for the player. "Basketball," said Phil Jackson, "is an illusion, it's a funny life. You live it for ten years and you're gone, and that's no time really at all, ten years in your life. It's not a real life, you're traveling, you're home, you're traveling, you're home. It's star-worship kind of stuff. Crowds. Running. And your body is always active, and it's good, it's healthy. And it's a good life, I'm not knocking it, or anything else, but it's an illusion. And we're basically not people that should be looked up to and said, 'Ah, there's my idol. There's a nice body running down court.' I like to be a nice athlete out there running but I hate to be looked up to just because I'm an athlete."

The hoo-rah that the fan gave the game's player animated his nights and conferred on his work a blessed immediacy that solitary artists never had. But the blood that was pumped up by the clamor and became better (or worse) by it turned still in the aftermath. Whatever rough love there was between mob and player lasted the forty-eight minutes of the game's duration, and not much more.

The public, be sure, tried to prolong it. When Jackson was hospitalized, he had an adult visitor who wore a New York Mets baseball cap and jacket, and spoke of the basketball trunks with Knick piping that his mom was making for him. After he was discharged from the hospital, Jackson got a message from the Garden to call the fellow. He did, and was connected with the mother, who proceeded to break down in tears on discovering who the caller was. She gave Jackson another number at which her son could be reached, and urged him to call directly. Jackson did as instructed, and found out what the hustle was: the young man wanted Frazier's room number at the Hotel New Yorker.

A Knick's notion of himself did not always coincide with the public's. "Like, most people that don't know me," said Frazier, "they don't believe I'm for real because I'm regular. They can't see a guy with my status just being normal people. They put you on a pedestal. Like, I usually go to Harlem and I hang around the joints up there. So my friends tell me that these guys think I'm phony, you know, because they can't see why I would mingle among them when I could be going other places, meeting better people there, I guess they think. So friends tell me that guys up there talk about me and say I'm not that good a ballplayer, I guess because I associate with them. I don't know what it is, but they can't see me just because I'm regular and I speak to everybody and I'm friendly."

No matter what a player did, it was subject to public interpretations. "I got a letter from a black lady in Brooklyn," said Reed. "Like what she said was . . . you out there telling everybody that you giving all these scholarships to your (boys) camp and everything, and still in reality, most of your campers are still the white kids, because these are the kids that can afford it. And like why aren't you in Bedford Stuyvesant teaching these kids.

"So like I had to kind of shake my head. A man can only do what he can do in his own way. I know like this New Year's Eve, I had like twenty five kids that came over to my restaurant, the Beef 'n Bun. And well, it was a social club. I know this guy who runs the club and he wanted the kids to come down and meet some of the basketball players. So I said, 'Yeah, bring the kids by,' and I give 'em hamburgers and cheeseburgers and malteds and sodas and everything. And I charged them half-fare, 'cause the club pays for it, y'know, which may not have meant nothing to a lot of people but I think to those kids it meant something. I charged half-fare because that's about what it takes for me, you understand . . . so I won't make anything on the deal."

Such experiences made a man cautious with the public. A player's regard for fans roughly coincided with his particular impulse to life. Reed and DeBusschere had the tact and cool grace that at once acknowledged and distanced the fan; boundaries were sensibly set. Russell was more responsive and so more inconsistent; multiple moods colored his reactions. Frazier was drawn to and repelled by adulation and in the end cared more for easy comfort than for changing a hotel dining locale at which the public hounded him. Barnett was not so equivocal, he allowed no breach of privacy. In the exhibition season he did not so much as swing his eyes onto an airport policeman who inquired if he was a ballplayer; he looked straight ahead and said no. Bradley had not evolved to such flaming disinterest, but he no longer felt the onus he once had; the change was owed to Oxford.

"In London," recalled Bradley, "I remember walking up streets subconsciously expecting 'pssssst, pssssst,' and nobody was saying it at all. And I began to realize what freedom was and that I was now part of the right perspective on life. You now are about serious things and not the victim of the superficial and plastic kind of treatment which the press often bestows on an athlete. Then I'm back [in the States] and put back into the glass cage and it doesn't bother me, because I have a fuller sense of self. I just do what I want to do.

"Before, at Princeton, I felt a little more false responsibility to the public. Toward the end, it got to bother me. The whole thing, walking down the streets of New York and 'there's so and so,' and someone comes up to you and asks for an autograph. And I didn't realize it until England, the imposition the public makes on the private areas of your life. Like appearances. Not only was it the kind of thing a public figure did, but it was supposed to be fun.

Only it wasn't so. I found it in most cases to be boring. Take the usual banquet thing. Banquets are essentially bores, a product of a certain attitude toward sport. And they include examples of what sports supposedly can do for you, as it did for me. I found it hypocritical to say to them, which in effect you do, 'You too can be in this position if'—and then list things. My presence at these banquets, in a way, kind of said, I'm agreeing with the coach, and I didn't even know who the coach was, and whether he was thinking of the welfare of his players.

"I still go out of my way for smaller kids. I do it because I can remember how I was, and because I feel sports is a legitimate activity for them. When you get to adults, you wonder whether they admire sports or the celebrity aspect. If they admire the celebrity aspect, then it's not too good. Then you ask yourself if there's something heroic about you. If so, then maybe the admiration is good. The immediate question is: is there something heroic?"

The question became rhetorical once New York won the divisional title a week before the season ended, and moved into the mad business of the playoffs.

♛ CHAPTER THREE

RIGHT BEFORE the playoffs, Asofsky had palpitations.

It happened on the tennis courts at Marine Park in Brooklyn. Asofsky's heartbeat accelerated, he became faint. Stanley's game was not so furious nor his health in such disrepair that he figured his body was in trouble. But on the chance that it was, he visited his good friend Dr. Elliot Levine. The doctor took blood analysis, chest x-rays and cardiograms and pronounced him in splendid condition. The palpitations puzzled Asofsky and only days after did it dawn on him what the problem was. The truth is Asofsky was worried as hell about the Knickerbockers.

It was a valid concern. The momentum that sportscasters embraced as a game's mystique had swung to other teams. In the months following the record streak, Milwaukee and not New York was the most effective team in the NBA. In that period, New York won 37 of 58 games. Milwaukee over the same span won 43 of 59, a record that suggested the giant strides its Lew Alcindor had made as a matriculating professional. Western Division teams were stronger, too. Atlanta beat the Knicks the last four times the teams met, and at Los Angeles Chamberlain was ready to play after rehabilitating his knee in a program that included volleyball on Santa Monica beach.

The night New York clinched the divisional title in San Diego, there was no celebration. "The feeling was," said Bradley, " 'So we clinched it.' I didn't feel anything. I don't think anyone else wanted a big celebration." Toward the end, the season went flat for the Knicks. They finished the year losing four straight games. The assumption was that come the playoffs the game's muse once again would slip through New York locker room doors and sanctify Knickerbocker nights. It was under that sort of impression that another local sporting combine, the New York Jets, had labored in the autumn. Week after week the Jets won with uninspired effort which gave the theoreticians among their backers to espouse the concept of selective adrenalin. But that theory was exposed the first time the Jets played for reeee-ul, in the league championship games against Kansas City. New York lost, 13–6.

The Knicks did not even have history to support illusions. What playoff tradition they had was folly. As far back as the 1950s the Knicks were preempted from the Garden at playoff time by the circus, whose dates were then inviolable. No franchise had waited longer to win an NBA title than New York. Only two other teams, Boston and San Francisco (the Philadelphia Warriors until they moved after the 1962 season), had survived the original league that began in 1946–47. Each was a previous winner.

Now the game superseded the circus and on playoff nights circus rigging hung above the courts. Pro ball was no longer a penny ante spectacle. When Holzman played on the 1950–51 champion Rochester Royals, total NBA playoff take was $50,000. Two decades later, the amount was $400,000—$118,000 for the winning team alone.

In olden times, money was tighter for players. For leading the Knicks in scoring in 1947–48, his rookie year, Carl Braun was offered a raise of $1,500, to bring his salary to $5,500. Finance was a more casual subject then. "Like, we only played forty-eight games," said Braun, "so we had maybe two, three nights a week where you'd be hanging around New York, so they sent us out on clinics. They'd give us $12.50 in expenses or pay, whatever you want to call it. We'd wind up playing ball with the kids after the clinic and really enjoy it. The one thing we didn't realize was what a great promotion this was for the Knicks." And what a cheap one. "You'd get a free supper after the clinics," Braun said. "We took a cab up to the Bronx and they would set up a meal at one of the hotels. So you'd get supper, $12.50 and cab fare, and man we used to kill 'em on that meal 'cause we wouldn't eat any lunch. Two steaks, three shrimp cocktails. But we only got away with that for a couple of weeks and then they started to limit us, to limit the amount of money we could spend."

Before pro leagues were popularized, Bill Hosket's father had commercial teams that would barnstorm the Dayton area. "He used to have one that had a meat packing company in Dayton called Sucher's as sponsor, and we have old uniforms at home that say 'Bill Hosket's Sucher's.' He used to promote the game himself in the Dayton Coliseum, seats 2,500, 3,000. And it'd be on Sunday afternoon and they'd have, like, fifty cents a head top price, that was for a doubleheader. And they'd bring in teams like the Harlem Globetrotters. And he would go up to Fort Wayne and play and to Columbus and down to Cincinnati and sometimes into Kentucky. He did this for about four years, till about 1938.

"Another team he had during that span was the Waterloo Wonders. They won the high school state tournament the same year my father graduated from college, I believe. My father gave these guys their first pro start, he brought them into Dayton. He would round these guys up down on the farm and they wouldn't have shoes, they would just come barefoot, and they'd put on basketball shoes he would get from other guys that he knew, or go out and buy them. He was like their playing coach and promoter, and I guess my uncle took care of the tickets, kind of like a family deal. But, like, the Wonders used to come in and a lot of times they would be half-loaded, on corn liquor or something like that. And I can remember people telling me how this guy named Drummond used to go over and sit in the stands and eat popcorn. The Wonders would play with four guys, and stuff like this. My mother said they had a big game one week and one of the Wonders was in jail and another one they couldn't even find. So my dad got some old guys that played together in high school, and they got beat bad and people got mad and wanted their money back. It was tough times and they went through a lot of business like that.

"My dad started a near riot in Dayton one Sunday afternoon. They had the Phillips 66ers in, and the trademark at the time for Phillips was to get 66 points and then stall and let you score when you get the ball. And they used to win all kinds of ball games like

66–42, 66–30, and they took a lot of pride in this. They really tried to hotdog it once they got to their 66—66 was like 125 points is today. Anyhow, my father eventually took the ball down and put it in their basket and gave them 68 and a couple of guys from Phillips jumped him, I guess. The place really went crazy."

Players were more sophisticated about money matters these days. They had attorneys barter for their salaries, and representatives to contract for endorsements, public appearances and book deals. The literary plunge into the game led *New York Times* columnist Bob Lipsyte to envision the day when teams would charter airplanes that had separate compartments to accommodate each player and his agent, ghost writer and editor. It was not too surreal at that. Seeking to interview Frazier, Sly first had to contact his autobiographical ghost for permission, a situation for which Clyde was apologetic. Once, in an interview, DeBusschere whipped out a notepad on Sly and scribbled into it for a book *he* was co-authoring. The game was the thing but not the only thing. Playoff booty was not confined to what the league put up.

Bradley disdained fringe commerce. When the team was used for a Vitalis commercial he would not appear. He refused to endorse products, even for the $500 Vitalis paid each Knick. Bradley and Russell were said to be the only New York players making more than $100,000. Reed was expected to earn it next season. If management did not give Reed his due in salary, it served him nevertheless. Up in 4 Penn Plaza, Reed had lookouts who channeled fringe moneys his way. Reed reciprocated: in discussing the reality issues of basketball life he was more cautious than anybody on the team but John Warren, his roommate. When publishers bid for his autobiography, he made Wergeles his agent.

Few people begrudged the Cap'n the returns of his working days, especially at playoff times. Reed had a knack for transcending himself then: in the 20 playoff games in which he had appeared the past three seasons, he had averaged 24.8 points per game, or five points more than he had in regular-season games. Reed thrived on his burdens.

"I know one of the greatest thrills I ever had," he said. "I made twenty-five dollars in one day cutting grass back in Bernice, Louisiana. I cut about four or five yards in one day. I started at sunrise and my last lawn I cut . . . it was a church, a little church and the lady had to . . . she left her car lights on so I could finish cutting the yard. Like it was about eight o'clock at night. I was about fifteen, sixteen then."

Q: Was Reed the leader at Grambling?

(GRAMBLING COACH FRED) HOBDY: Not at first. As a freshman, he played a ball game in New Orleans during the Christmas holidays. And I had been raising a lot of hell about Reed getting to the goal to get the offense and defense rebounds. But all he was doing was shooting because the teams in high school had played him a zone. So I said to the person who was working with me, a fellow by the name of Howard Willis—and I said to him, I said, "Gee, we have a lot of trouble with this boy. He's going to be a great ballplayer but it's just a matter of him learning what to do and when to do it." So we played Savannah State in New Orleans. The team whipped us, and I told him that night, I said, "Boy, you'll never play basketball."

Q: Said to Reed?

HOBDY: Yes. And I think he cried a little that night, you know.

Q: Literally cried?

HOBDY: Yes.

Q: In front of you?

HOBDY: Yes. I think this was one of the growing up periods, you see. And then we had a game with our archrival, Southern University, in Baton Rouge, and the assistant coach, Howard Willis, said to me, "Which one of these guys do you want me to start?" Well, I had a guy by the name of Bowens, who is playing with [ABA] New Orleans now, a colored boy who's playing with the Buccaneers, and Willis. So I said, "Oh, it doesn't make any difference." See, neither one was getting the ball. Then I turned to Willis, I said, "Boy, I'm going to give you a chance tonight. You go out there and get that ball." And he gritted his teeth and said, "I'll get it for you," and when this happened I never shall forget it the longest day that I live, he went out that night and he got me 21 points and 20 rebounds.

Q: What kind of leader was Willis his four years there?

HOBDY: Well, if anybody got out of line, I'd go to Willis. He'd take care of it. Then we'd sit down and go over the game plans together. How we were going to try to play the team. I would do this with him, and I wouldn't do it with the other boys.

Q: Why was that?

HOBDY: Because he and this boy, Herschel West, they were students of the game. They were more or less like grown men. Relevant to these other kids, these other kids were a little bit immature and all that. Reed was a mature person in terms of understanding and you could get him to do anything in the world for you. Like if we were on the road, I'd say, "Well, Willis, have the boys at so and so time at such and such a place." "Okay, coach." We didn't have any boys to rebel against him. Now Willis was the kind of person, like, he'd tell you two or three times plus the fact he would demand that they do it and it was no problem on that.

Q: Nobody ever said to him, like, "the hell with you"?

HOBDY: No. He would say to me, "Now look, coach, you need to do something for this boy," if the boy was goofing off, "you need to call X in and talk to him." We have a situation where we . . . out in Texas, out in Houston, we had kids that had gotten out of line and we were playing Texas Southern.

Q: What do you mean, "out of line"?

HOBDY: Well, you know, they blow curfew. So he told me, "Kids didn't get in on time last night. We're going to have trouble this game, this is a good team." And sure enough he was right. So after the game, I said—

Q: Did you lose?

HOBDY: We won, I think by a point. And after the game I said you have these boys by my room. And usually a boy does this, breaks curfew, and the guy tells on him, and they'd be pretty mad with him, not with Willis. He had so much rapport with the guys and they respected him so much. He could *tell* and they would still respect him. He was always the spokesman for the group. I remember when we went down in South America, we were down there on a tour, I think it was in '62. And we were playing a team that came in third in the Olympics, whatever it was, in '60. There was only seven of us and they had something like twenty guys. And you talking about big people, they had some big people. And we were really being taken, you know. At the half, I was all destructive because we looked very poorly in the first half. And Willis, you know—they got in before I did, and Willis is in there talking to them that it was embarrassing to Grambling to play that poorly in front of about twenty thousand people down in São Paulo, and Willis is doing all this talking. Well this is the same thing that I was going to say, so I never said but two three things. We were down by fifteen points at the half. And to my surprise, we went out and beat the team by two points, 82–80. And this is the type of guy that he was.

Knickerbocker management had Reed's faculty for "getting up" for the big games, most notably at the box office where tickets were scaled down from a record $12.50. New Yorkers hardly blinked at the prices, to quibble about dollars at a time like this was sacrilege for a Knick partisan. Fans shut out at the box office did not necessarily accept this. Up on the fourth floor of 4 Pennsylvania Plaza secretaries Dinoia and Bloomfield were besieged by callers who felt it their right to sit in the Garden for the championships. Denied, they would shout obscenities at the girls and hang up. When Fred Klein went to pick up his clique's thirteen tickets, he was accosted by a man he described as a "seedy-looking Zero Mostel type" who grabbed his lapels and, with wild-eyed outrage, demanded to know what right he had to so many tickets. More softly, he said at least maybe give him one.

Ticketholders were no less on edge. Bernie Brosniak, who sat with Klein and Asofsky, found himself snapping at the patrons in Hudson's, an East Village army-navy store in which he worked. One day he read in the pop music column of the *New York Post's* Alfred Aronowitz an account that Beatle George Harrison gave of the rudeness he had suffered in Brosniak's shoe department at Hudson's. Brosniak remembered Harrison and the lovely girl he had come in with that afternoon; and had the Beatles had priority over the Knicks, he might have been properly shamed. Regrettably for George Harrison, he had come along in the stress time of playoffs.

A voodoo strangeness came down on people at playoff time.

Asofsky took to parking his Volvo in the same place, in front of
the Breslin Hotel on Broadway and Twenty-ninth. Holzman's
wife Selma wore the same orange and mauve striped dress to
games and hung it by the same window at home. She did not dare
send it to the cleaners for fear that the hocus pocus in that gar-
ment would be gone on its return. Her husband was just as super-
stitious. When the Cap'n's sneakers were falling apart during the
eighteen-game streak, Holzman advised him to persevere with
them until the string was broken.

Baltimore had not yet discovered any supernatural agency to
help it against New York. The Bullets were third in regular-season
play in the Eastern Division, a finish entitling them to face the
Knicks in the playoffs' best-of-seven opening round, and to bear
unendingly the dark humor that surrounded Baltimore teams in
competition against New York's. What the Jets performed on the
Colts, and the Mets on the Orioles, would have been sufficient to
give a city a complex. But the Knicks' success made it seem dia-
bolical: of the last ten times New York and Baltimore played, the
Knicks had won nine times.

In midseason Bullet fans had worn "Kick the Knicks" buttons to
games. But now the sight of one on Bowman's warm-up jersey
was just another reminder of the cruelty that the inscrutable
sporting life had visited upon them. Fans and players alike became accustomed to the comic assaults on their city, the frequency of them rivaled those directed against its leading citizen,
Spiro Agnew. By the playoffs, the populace was resigned to more
embarrassments. From Sweeney's on Greenmount (boasting a
cocktail "twistologist") to the honky-tonk bars on East Baltimore
Street, the sentiment was that Baltimore would be swept in four
games by Holzman's team.

The Baltimore entourage, from Earl the Pearl Monroe on down
to the team's rabbi, arrived in New York with higher hopes. The
rabbi was a friend of Bullet owner Abe Pollin's, and after games
his praise was equally spent on the Deity and the Bullets. That the
Baltimore players believed in their powers to play New York in
spite of massive proofs to the contrary evidenced remarkable
faith.

The players of Baltimore had more nicknames than the Dead

End Kids. Monroe was varyingly referred to in his baskets lifetime as Black Jesus, Magic, Doctor, Slick, the Savior and, in the pros, as the Pearl. Kevin Loughery was Murphy for the murphy bed he had slept in as a rookie at Detroit. Rookie guard Fred Carter was tagged Mad Dog in training camp by teammates for his furious play, a name he initially resisted but now answered the phone with. The team's leading rebounder, Wes Unseld, was the Chairman of the Boards. Gus Johnson was Honeycomb. Forward Jack Marin had no nickname but the congenital reddened area on his upper torso led teammate Ray Scott to speculate whether the white of Marin was the birthmark and he was indeed a latent redman.

On the Baltimore team, Marin had a reputation as a marathon orator whose socio-political diatribes were egged on by the poker-faced teammates he amused when he talked nonstop. But times when a Bullet was in a hurry to get some place he did not linger in Marin's vicinity: Jack was said to be an insistent talker. His game was as assertive as his politics: he cast a left-handed jump shot in the eye's blink and was not hesitant about firing toward the basket on a drive. Marin, a valedictorian in high school and chemistry major at Duke, was matched against Bradley.

Gus Johnson fancied the showtime moves that his competition, DeBusschere, spurned. On drives to the basket, he would swing the ball through the air in lovely twirls that gave his soaring transit majesty that DeBusschere lacked. A favorite move of his was to pivot to the basket, cup the ball in one enormous hand, rise off one leg and give it an imperious flip from 10 to 15 feet away from the basket. Johnson had, in his NBA career, unhinged baskets in rebound tussles and once the force with which he dunked a ball busted a backboard. On a high school team in Akron, Ohio, that had 6–11 Nate Thurmond on it, 6–6 Johnson jumped center. He was the strongest, leapingest fancypants in the league.

Baltimore relied on Unseld to, as the pros put it, "get the boards." Unseld, a thick-muscled man who stood 6 feet 7½ inches —more with the Afro he had grown since last season—not only got the ball but dispatched it with the greatest of ease. His quick release of it was what made Baltimore run. He could shoot too, but in the gimme-gimme game the Bullets played, shots for him were scarce. Against Reed, Unseld was to play with a cool visage that belied his generous nature. In Baltimore he was a frequent visitor to a local children's hospital where he had installed portable basketball facilities bought from coach Shue's sporting goods store at a cost of $80. On a USO trip to Vietnam, Unseld had told the cashier in a snack bar that the treats were on him for the GIs waiting in line behind him. The bill was said to total more than $100.

It cost Kevin Loughery broken ribs and a punctured lung to play out the season, injuries suffered when he had run into Alcindor. Before the series against New York was to commence, trainer Feldman read of a lightweight protective vest that a hockey player for the Boston Bruins wore. But there was not sufficient time for flying Loughery to Boston to have him fitted and the device constructed. So it was Loughery's lot to play with his ribs trussed by five pounds of aluminum and sponge. That resolve was familiar to Baltimore. When the Pistons traded Loughery to the Bullets, he drove all night from Detroit to Baltimore for the next day's team practice.

The sprightly Carter was expected to play ahead of Loughery. He was a perpetual motion athlete whose boyish face reflected the joys and sorrows of being Mad Dog in games, an expressiveness that made him a favorite of the galleries. In Baltimore locker rooms, Dogg, as he liked it spelled, took special glee in flexing muscles before Gus Johnson and baiting the big fellow with remarks. His game had the same kind of daredevil flair to it: he hurdled through crowds on reckless drives, sneaked up on rebounders to snatch the ball from their hands and made himself a general nuisance to foes. He was Barnett's assignment.

That left the Pearl to Frazier. When he was hot, the Earl of Pearl brought royalty to the court. In the Bullets' only victory against New York in the past 10 games, Monroe had put on leaning twisting in-your-eye gymnastics with which not even Clyde could cope; 37 points in all he scored against the best defensive guard in the pros. Contrary to his public image, Bullets' people said he was reserved and thoughtful off the court. The year before, Monroe had worn a black patch on his jersey in his own memorial to Dr. Martin Luther King. On road trips, the books he read frequently were about blacks.

When the Bullets were on their game they could hurt any defense. The quick draw of their shooters made a man prudent about doubling for fear he would be considered derelict in his own assignment. Monroe was especially cunning at foiling the double that was the Knick genius; he could writhe and sway in crowds and make shots that mocked the honest labors of the best defense in continental America.

Opening night, March 26, he was, in Barnett's terms, dooo-in' it. Jump shot . . . a steal and lay-up . . . a drive: Baltimore led quickly 10–2. So it went that night, Monroe working with his rump to Frazier, pumping the ball and eying over the floor, like a man peeking around a dangerous corner. When he went, he moved casually one way before whirling the other in pivoting spins that required superplasm in his ankles. Sometimes the moves left him wide open for the shot, but not often against Frazier. When they didn't, he'd lean back and flick the ball from behind his head.

In the Philadelphia schoolgrounds in which Monroe had learned the game, half the fun was, as Frazier put it, "showing" on a guy, making shots come off as attitudes. Riordan had seen Detroit's Jimmy Walker dribble downcourt against a schoolyard player, back him toward the basket, turn and release the ball like a man does a homing pigeon, declaring as it left his hands FAAAAY and, as it went through the hoop, SHOOOOOL. FAAAAY-SHOOOOL. For facial. Right in the poor guy's face. And so did Monroe declaim his own sinuous beauty with shots.

He also passed the ball, a strategy he frequently had overlooked in the Bullets' four-game disaster the season before. On a team with the trigger finger the Bullets possessed, pass amenities from the Pearl were not wasted. And shots hit off Monroe's passes made the New Yorkers less nervy on defense.

On the other end of the court, Baltimore was sabotaging New York's offense. Riordan had seen the Bullets' assistant coach, Bob Ferry, at Knick games toward the end of the season, and from the first quarter it became clear that Baltimore had foreknowledge of

New York plays. From the pivot, Unseld alerted mates to *Barry, New York, Trap* and so on, pointing to places on the floor to which they should hie. The first time Bradley and Frazier ran the *X*, a Bullet was there to intercept the ball.

What Baltimore did in the first game of the series was nullify the team virtues New York's game had. Bullet marksmanship forced the Knicks to play their men "honest." Lacking pigeons, the defense risked becoming the routine whirlaround it was with other teams. And Baltimore's ability to "read" the offense forestalled the motion that the New York attack required.

New York *had* new plays. The *B-F* or *B-C* was set up like the *Trap*, with Reed and a forward parked next to each other at the lower end of the lane. The weak-side forward flashed to the foul line to get the ball and then turned to pass it. If it was *B-F*, the ball went to the forward, stepping back of Reed; on *B-C* it went to Reed. The Knicks also had a new *19* or isolation for Reed. It started from a *D* situation where Frazier passed to DeBusschere and came behind him to take the ball. DeBusschere went toward Reed in the low pivot. The Cap'n used him for a pick to get the ball deep, and DeBusschere cleared out. Then Reed did what he wanted. Occasionally, the *19* became *19-F:* DeBusschere would go through and then come back along the baseline, as Bradley did on the *Barry*. New York would have preferred to run the old standbys if Baltimore let it. But at both ends of the floor, Baltimore was forcing New York to play its one-on-one game.

Down the stretch on opening night, the man to whom Baltimore went was Monroe, whose doctrine was not so much "see" as "shoot" the ball. Ah . . . he shot. A jumper from the side . . . another in the lane . . . a free throw . . . again the jumper . . . a free throw: eight straight points and at 0:24 in the game, it was Baltimore 102, New York 102.

Baltimore gave Monroe the ball for the final 24 seconds. He was a slouched figure moving the ball up and down and waiting to go. Barnett made a try at doubling him but the Pearl slipped away. Then, just before the buzzer, he leaned back from Frazier and let the shot fly from the rear of the key. This time it missed. Afterward, Monroe was to confess he thought that the third quarter and not the game had ended. The evening had the kind of dislocating force mad dreams do on the just-awaked sleeper. It would get weirder. In the last minute of the overtime it came down to Frazier and Monroe again. Monroe was working toward a 39-point performance but Frazier was used to long nights on the defense. *At Southern Illinois,* he once said, *defense was the name of the game. We had drills that were similar to football drills, reaction drills. Move lateral and back and forward, all the time crouched. About one minute at a time. You'd get a pain in your thighs like there were pins in your legs. Your feet would blister. Sometimes it was so bad that you couldn't straighten up right away.* This time from a crouch, Frazier lashed at the ball and sent it rolling downcourt. Barnett picked it up and was fouled driving to the basket. His two free throws made the score 110–110, at 0:23.

Now the Pearl had it again, dribbling out the seconds, and waiting to put his move on. Frazier sprang for the ball and got it to bounce free. Barnett fetched it and drove for the basket in his flatfooted way. Up he went for the shot but here came Mad Dog angling in just at the buzzer to

block

or

goaltend

the shot.

Referee Mendy Rudolph said it was a legitimate block, that Carter had put his hand to the ball before it started its downward flight. The opinion of the Knickerbocker gallery was hotly contrary to Rudolph's. Debris flew out onto the floor. Asofsky and Klein stormed to the edge of the court to scream at the ref. Rudolph paid no mind to Holzman, the Knicks or fans. His court bearing was that of the headwaiter at a class restaurant. For years, Asofsky and Klein had saved their choicest remarks for the aristocratic Rudolph. "Who's watching the newsstand?" they'd shout. Or, "No more marijuana for you, Mendy." Once, big Fred ran into Mendy in the Garden lobby and asked, "Who's gonna win tonight, Mendy?" Rudolph told him the team that scores the most points, shmuck. In games, the ref would flick his sweat at

them and not change his haughty expression. Now he ordered the
Knicks to return to the bench and the second overtime to begin.

It was an unsettling night. Even Holzman's cool was affected.
Minutes into the second overtime, New York led 117–112 when
Holzman got up from the bench and called, "Mike, Mike," for
Riordan. Bowman and Russell smiled. Again Holzman called for
Riordan, this time more impatiently. When it was pointed out to
him that Riordan was in the game, Holzman allowed as how he
guessed he wanted Bradley, not Riordan. One Knick clutched at
his throat to signal that the coach had "choked" or erred under
pressure.

In the upper tiers of the Garden a chant started: *DEE-fense
DEE-fense*. It reminded sports observers of frigid afternoons in
Yankee Stadium when New Yorkers had hollered at footballers
named Huff, Robustelli, Modzelewski, and Grier. It was defense,
or the lack of it, that decided the game. At 117–117, the Knicks
called the *2-3-F* for Bradley. DeBusschere moved into the lane,
Bradley came off him and swung around Reed but Baltimore was
waiting. So Reed went out to get the ball. Gus Johnson came with
him and gambled on stealing it. *Johnson was too Johnson was too
late,* it said the next day in a typographical error in the *Baltimore
News-American*. Reed turned with the ball and hooked it through
the basket at 0:31. Frazier made Monroe force a shot. DeBusschere hit a foul shot. That was it, 120–117.

For Asofsky the win was so exhilarating he wandered the city
that night in the rain, a walk that was to bring on an arthritic
condition in his back that got worse as the playoffs progressed.
But when doctors recommended he fly to the Caribbean for a
while, Stanley gave them a strange smile and said he'd see, he'd
see. What did doctors know of Cleveland Buckner and Popeye
and long sad nights in the Garden?

The teams flew to Baltimore that night. The Knicks stayed at
the Holiday Inn, walking distance from the Bullets' Civic Center.
The Civic Center did not have the game's tradition the Garden
did, a $6.25-ceiling on playoff ticket prices being some small
measure of that. Baltimore was characterized by Bullet trainer
Feldman as "an industrial, neighborhood, beer-drinking town"
that supported only football. Baltimore management had in-

dulged that small-town spirit in its early days with imitative bullet blasts after particularly thrilling home-team goals and now by allowing its mascot, Alex the Bullet, an eleven-year-old, elevenpound dachshund, to lug around a little cart on one of whose sides was printed, THERE IS NO SUBSTITUTE FOR VICTORY. Alex's master was a retired naval officer. Bullet programs contained lotsaluck messages from local business patrons like VIP Travel Bureau and Johnny Orsino's Sporting Goods Store, and a face-in-the-crowd photo that entitled the encircled fan to a $15 gift certificate from "one of Baltimore's finest clothiers, Phil Kolodne Jr.'s on Reistertown Road, Pikesville."

Nevertheless that was progress from the days when the Baltimore management drafted Gus Johnson sight unseen. After a national magazine printed a story on the University of Idaho player, Baltimore had a local writer phone the daily paper there and find out whether Johnson was worth drafting. The newsman in Moscow, Idaho, mentioned that San Francisco had talked to Gus. That was recommendation enough.

For three quarters of the second contest New York had little to recommend its game. DeBusschere would come out of the game, see the offense bogged down and shout from the bench, MOVE THE GODDAMN BALL. In huddles Knicks complained about that and the failure (WHY AREN'T YOU HELPING ME?) of the defense. Bradley was especially vociferous in huddles, *He comes in time-outs,* said a Knickerbocker, *and hollers like an insane man. He's such a perfectionist. Red would say, "Take it easy, take it easy." I don't think Red grasped the seriousness of the trouble we were in even though we were winning.*

That evening, Mike Riordan, who had suffered as Asofsky had with earlier Knick teams, came to the rescue of this one. Growing up in the schoolyards, he had emulated Dick McGuire, and, at home hung Richie Guerin's photo on his wall. At nine, he played center for a Police Boys Club team in a benefit game against Knickerbockers like Braun, Gallatin, Sears and Connie Simmons. *For the center jump, they put me up on a chair. Score? Yeah, I got a couple driving lay-ups.* Now, unaided by elevating props, Riordan took the fourth quarter tap directly to the basket and scored, and next time sped by Monroe on a baseline move that narrowed

Baltimore's advantage to 83–81. For the rest of the game, Riordan kept scoring and pressured Monroe on defense. The Pearl's knees required icepacks on trips to the bench, but bad knees or not, he had managed 18 points in the first three quarters. He got only one more against Riordan for the game. Riordan scored 11 of his 13 points in the same period.

The second game also was decided in the last minute. New York had possession of the ball at 1:20, leading 103–99. The strategy was to consume time and make the clock work against the Bullets. The clock did hurt Baltimore but not as New York intended. With just over a minute left and the 24-second period to shoot expiring, Bradley took a desperate shot that struck the side of the backboard. The buzzer to the 24-second clock went off. Baltimore players froze, thinking the ball was theirs for not hitting the rim. But the rule required only that it touch part of the backboard or the rim. Bradley got the rebound.

The Knicks set the ball in motion as the clock ticked away. Bradley had it again when the 24-second span was finishing, and this time his shot was what pros call an "airball": it touched nothing. Unseld reached for it but DeBusschere came from behind him and spiked the ball with his fist ("I didn't slap it because Unseld is too strong") into Reed's hands. Just before the 24-second buzzer, the Cap'n dunked the basketball, for a night's total of 27 points (he'd had 30 in the opener). Barnett added a free throw. The final was New York 106, Baltimore 99.

Baltimore rooters seated behind the Knick bench berated the players for their luck. One fan had shouted at Hosket all game. "I couldn't hear much of what he was saying earlier," Hosket said, "but every time I'd look at him he'd be redfaced and shaking his fist at me. He kept finding a seat closer and closer to the floor. At the finish he was right behind the bench and screaming, 'I'm gonna kill you, you and May, next year in Buffalo.'" Knickerbocker success in the first two games was enough to make a man funny. Baltimore had scrambled New York's game, and still lost twice, the second time on particularly suspect heroics. So it went. Baltimore looked ready to be swept.

The next day Baltimore's troubles continued when its Allegheny flight to New York was cancelled because of the air controllers' strike. The Bullets chartered a bus. No feeling of doomsday rode with them. Marin was said to be in top oratorical form: he engaged players and the team doctor in conversation and, several hours and several sleeping Bullets later, still had the goodnatured doctor for an audience.

But the mood in the locker room before the third game struck Baltimore trainer Feldman wrong. Feldman had this theory that in Bullet locker rooms the team either got up or didn't in the five minutes prior to taking the court. Once, in a losing streak, he had heard the Pearl shout, "We're gonna beat these bastards." And the streak ended that night. Now, in the Garden, he was worried. There wasn't anything going.

Then Loughery stood. In his cumbersome brace, he began walking around the room, banging his teammates on the head and screaming, "Be an animal. Be a goddamn animal. I'm tired of losing to these guys." And suddenly there was new blood in the locker room. "Be an animal. Be a goddamn animal." Everybody started to fall in.

Murph himself stripped the corset he wore around his ribs at the end of the first quarter. By then Gus Johnson had swung at Bradley for pushing, Unseld was using his heft beneath the boards and the Bullet bench was roused by every questionable call.

The tolerance of the Garden crowd diminished in playoffs. What human comedy it had found past times in Bowman ceased. Bowman's two personal fouls less than a minute after he entered the game brought booing. The Knick partisans hitched their wagon to what moved the team. Hosket's three straight shots as Reed's backup were not forgotten. When Bowman rose from the bench to spell Reed the next few games, the crowd chanted, "We want Hosket, we want Hosket." The playoffs located true passions. They brought out the spartan in Asofsky. His aching back needed sunshine but he refused to consider it. Instead he started on a cod-liver oil diet recommended for arthritic joints and got to games early to "get the feel" of them. And in the press section, Sly, who had sat objectively through a season's games, began to raise his fist at Knick baskets and profane referees he had earlier interviewed.

On Fordham Road in the Bronx, Kevin Loughery's mother moved her fingers over rosary beads and rooted more quietly for the Bullets. Her son was giving the beads a good time. In the second half he scored 13 of his 17 points, Marin and Monroe each hit 6 of 7 shots, Unseld accumulated rebounds at a rate that gave him more (34) by the end of the game than the entire New York team (30). And Baltimore won, 127–113.

The New York game that had given Bradley fits even in victories had him pondering nights later when the Bullets tied the series at two games apiece. At midnight, short hours after the loss, he had a solution to New York's dilemma when Hosket and Riordan came by his room.

"He didn't have any notes," remembered Riordan. "He had it all in his head. The big trouble was that the wrong man was trying to double-team Monroe. See, that night Monroe had hit the big baskets at the end. I was on him real tight, and he'd hit 'em in my face. We knew we had to make him give the ball up.

"What was happening when Monroe took it down the side of the floor, Gus would cross over to the other corner, giving Pearl the whole side of the floor to work. Then Carter would exchange places with Marin so that Marin at the side of the key became the outlet and Carter became the second outlet. That meant that since Bradley was guarding Marin he had to be the one to double Monroe. Before, the guard on Carter was trying to double. They'd swing the ball and get an open shot."

There were corollary points.

—Monroe was standing around on defense. It gave him a chance to edge upcourt for the outlet pass after a New York shot. If Barnett moved through the lane, the Pearl could not linger on the perimeter of play, waiting to kick off the Bullets' running game.

—Unseld occasionally came to the high post, got the pass, dribbled toward Marin and put a screen on Bradley for Marin's jump shot. The play had worked again and again. But if Reed just suggested a switch (SHOW YOURSELF) and Frazier sagged toward the ball, it might inhibit the play. The weak side forward, DeBusschere, had to cover if Unseld rolled free toward the basket for the pass from Marin.

—To revive the attack's motion the Knicks had to concede Baltimore the *Barry, New York* and *Trap* and rely on the *B-F, B-C, 2-1-F* and *2-1-G.* Or, on the *New York,* have Reed roll toward the basket for the pass from Barnett.

So much for the plan.

It was a dandy enough strategy but Bradley worried how he was going to convince Holzman to try it. "See Red has this authority thing," said a Knickerbocker, "so Bill asked a bunch of us to talk it up in practice. Red was getting real gruff with him 'cause Bill had been complaining so much all this series. Like, guys would be screwing around in practices, making funny passes, and Red wouldn't say anything. Then Bill'd throw a bad pass and Red would stop practice and show him. Like he was a little kid. And there were comments during the Baltimore games. Bill wouldn't answer back, he'd just look away. The longer the season went, the less it took to aggravate each other. It was exasperating for Bill because he couldn't communicate with the guy."

Players were not the only ones to note Holzman's sentiments toward Bradley. After *New York Times* columnist Lipsyte did a three-part series on Bradley, he happened to engage Holzman in a conversation on the distinction referees made about namecalling. Lipsyte had heard Holzman call an official a "plumber" and wondered, in a wry way, what reaction "truck driver" would provoke? Holzman eyed him darkly and asked if he intended to write an article about *that?* Yes, said Lipsyte jokingly, a five parter. That, said Holzman, must make me more important than Bradley.

"Like over a year ago," said a player, "two of us were hitting Danny [Whelan] up for a cab ride and, like, Danny owed us six dollars or something. We were asking Danny for the money, and Red said something about you guys always complain about your money. He says, 'Here, you want your six dollars . . . I'm the one that got you this big contract. I was scouting at the time.' Well, I don't like to talk contract with anybody on the damn team and I especially didn't want to hear that from him, it made it sound like he was jealous of our money and I think . . . this to me is the deep-rooted feeling he has against Bill Bradley. Because he knows that Bill signed for a half-million and I think it took Red a long time to appreciate Bradley. He was forced to start him. He didn't

like . . . there was no way in a lot of ballplayers' estimations that
Bradley could be playing behind Cazzie . . . that knew the game
and knew their attitude."

Bradley's attitude toward the game sometimes appeared equivocal. Months before, in Windsor, Ontario, he had sat in a restaurant sluicing the wine and watching the Detroit River from a picture window. "When I get tired," he'd said, "I tend to become
most reflective about being in the game. Like last night in that all-
night diner I was thinking about it. 'Here you are in Windsor
eating eggs after you've already eaten hot dogs, chili, ice cream
and whatnot.' When I say, 'What am I doing here?' it's not that I
shouldn't be here. It's just I want to remember the strange feeling
I sometimes get. There *are* times when I wonder about myself
being here, I wonder if I'm kidding myself. I don't think this is a
waste, I don't think it detracts at all from more analytical alternatives. But there are times when I look around and see guys my
age, like you or friends practicing law or business. They are
doing something they can do forever and what they do now will
contribute to what they'll do in fifteen years and what I do won't,
in a solid sense of learning something."

Recalling his days at Oxford, Bradley took what seemed a morbid delight in the woeful basketball conditions there and remembered with mild amusement the school's forfeit in the quarter
finals of the English championship on a day when the squad chose
to hear Robert Kennedy speak rather than play the game. And yet
he could in private workouts on that Oxford court create in his
mind, as schoolboys do, the crowd, foe and game circumstances.
That sort of response to the game once led a Princeton friend of
his to say, "The deepest thing he feels is playing basketball.
Maybe he wanted to change, become a mainstream Princeton
man, but he still has that small-town streak. He's like the guy from
the small town who comes to Princeton and goes to the deb
parties and says, 'Ah, this is me.' Then the little girl back home
writes and he goes running back to her. Well, that's the way
Bradley is with basketball."

At practice before the fifth Baltimore game Bradley and his
chorus presented the game plan. Holzman okayed it. *Bradley put
himself on the line,* a teammate said, *he had to prove he was right.*

And by gametime courtside observers sensed something was up. As columnist Larry Merchant put it, "From the start of the fifth game of the playoffs—actually, said Bill Bradley, from the time the Knicks were practicing lay-ups—it was clear that the Bullets did not have a friend at Crystal City State Bank." Merchant went on to describe Bradley's flushed face in terms of cherry lollypops, stop signs and so on. In the early moments of the game Bradley hit New York's first two shots and established the team concept of defense that gave him so much satisfaction. When Bradley came to double Monroe, the Pearl rushed his shot and missed. The Knick defense became the sprawling brainy piece it was in autumn.

By the third quarter, and for the first time in the series, New York broke Baltimore down. DeBusschere got Johnson to shoot an airball. Bradley tied up Monroe on a drive into the lane. The Knicks tripled the Pearl and made him force a shot. Johnson shot another airball. DeBusschere blocked Monroe's drive. Barnett and Frazier doubled Monroe and stole the ball. The Bullets were to make only 10 of 59 shots in the second half. Offensively, it was all Reed. At Grambling teammates called him Wolf for the way he would gobble up basketballs near the boards. This night he had 36 points and 36 rebounds, which led the press to speculate whether the shot injected into his knees was cortisone or something stronger. When it was over New York had won 101–80. And in the locker room, Hosket taped to his dressing cubicle a sign that said, *PRIDE . . . and a little defense.*

In the playoffs, the emotional peaks to which teams were roused came and went. Consecutive furies were rare. Feelings could not be bullied. In the first quarter of the sixth game neither team was "up." Errors abounded. All the while Bradley was fuming. What bothered him was the ball. Bradley liked the ball soft, inflated to the 7½-pound legal minimum rather than the 8½-pound pressure maximum. It was an easier ball to shoot. When it hit the rim, it "gave." It was a shooter's ball. At home New York kept its twelve balls soft. Sometimes the opposition complained. For a jumping team it paid to have the ball springing off the rim. On the road, Whelan carried a needle to deflate the ball. Since the visiting team had its choice of ball, it was no devious ploy. But this afternoon, the ball Bradley wanted could not be found. And the veins on his neck showed when he ranted at officials Powers and Sokol to get him a good one.

Had New York shot any ball with its accustomed accuracy, it could have put the game away early. Baltimore made 4 of 26 shots in the first quarter. But New York put in only 7 of 23 over the same period. That allowed Baltimore to stay close until the second half when Johnson and Monroe started to make baskets. Gus had 21 points and the Pearl 19 in the second half. For the game, Bradley made only 1 of 9, DeBusschere 2 of 11 and Reed 2 of 14. Baltimore won, 96–87. The series was tied, 3–3.

Voices were hushed in the locker room afterward. Frazier stared at the floor. Bowman slipped into a shirt of floral purple and pink. Phil Jackson walked about the locker room in cowboy boots and a mod suit, and quietly snatched up three beers for later. A ballboy with metal hooks for hands dispensed towels. Bubba Smith, the Baltimore Colt player, came in and talked with Cazzie Russell; a golf putter was in Russell's dressing cubicle. Players whispered to each other. The game was gone but not forgotten, save by the old man, Barnett. He said, "That mutha fucka in the books."

The seventh and final game against Baltimore was at the Garden. New York had won the home court advantage for any series it might play by its regular-season record, the best in the league. In Whelan's room, Russell walked nude to the scale and adjusted the weights on it. Reed was on the training table being rubbed down. Whelan touched his right knee and Reed said, "Ow." Inside the locker room, Stallworth was pumping his foot to Sly and the Family Stone. *Hiiigh-er, Hiiiigh-er,* rock 'n' roll Sly was singing. On the side of Stallworth's locker was a standard posed shot of the Rave that was doctored to include convict stripes, a ball and chain and the notation "Dangerous."

Bradley was getting dressed. On the shelf of his locker, there was an orange and blue tie that had hundreds of words on it. All the words said, LINDSAY. On the side of his and Bowman's lockers were posters for Odyssey House, a drug cure center. Riordan was already on the court, shooting. Asofsky was out there to watch him. He was saying he'd bought his ritualistic pretzel from

Raymond the Pretzel Man. Raymond had the freshest pretzels in town and was a baskets man. Asofsky remembered him from City College games. Raymond the Pretzel Man was a boisterous fan; if officials saw him at courtside before a game they would ask the police to escort him somewhere else.

Inside the music stopped. Riordan came in to shower. Holzman started pacing. It was silent. Barnett sat on a stool before his locker staring ahead. A guy called Say It Loud came in. He wore a button that said, I'M BLACK AND I'M PROUD, SAY IT LOUD. Say It Loud went to Barnett for his customary acknowledgment. Barnett did not look at him. Say It Loud tried Bowman for a hello. Nate did not even raise a brow. Say It Loud turned and walked out.

The crowd was hopped up. It stood when the team was introduced and set a Garden record for shorting the anthem. Earlier, Knick secretary Dinoia was so nervous that she had asked the New York hockey team's trainer for mild codeine tablets to calm her.

Holzman made one tactical change: he had Barnett bring the ball upcourt to preserve Frazier for defense against Monroe. The strategy had a reviving effect on the Knick ancient, too. For six games Barnett had averaged only 12.5 points a game, but this night he discovered he could get by Monroe. Coiling and uncoiling like a snake, Barnett moved through driving lanes and scored, or stopped curtly for the jump shot. The jangling rhythms with which he played once caused two Bullets to leap simultaneously on a fake of his. The veteran ducked betweeen them, emerged on a well-lit piece of court and stuck the shot in. His shooting roused the Knicks and the crowd. New York fans booed when the dachshund appeared on the floor at a time-out. At the half, New York led, 62–47.

Then DeBusschere came on. *Baltimore,* said Asofsky, *had worried me because it was the only playoff team I could imagine that wouldn't be at a disadvantage against DeBusschere. DeBusschere's matchup is usually worth something in most games. But against Gus, who could say?* For six games, it'd been Johnson and then DeBusschere, but at the end it was a triumph of modest craft over the eyecatching game. The beauty of DeBusschere was in his impartial distribution of energies; he worked the quiet corners of a game as vigorously as any pro, the evidence of it was in his face. As photographers were to discover in the playoffs, DeBusschere was the coverboy of the game's agony. *When I was a kid,* De-Busschere once said, *I'd play any sport going. But I can remember that I'd play so hard that every night, right after dinner, I'd be so exhausted I'd just drop off and go to sleep. Almost every night.* In the second half, DeBusschere was to score 18 points.

Cazzie Russell, recovering from an injured knee, got hot for the first time in the series. Early in the third quarter, New York leading 68–53, he made a jump shot (70–53), blocked a shot of Marin's, got a follow-up basket (72–55), sank another jump shot (74–57) and worked the crowd up. *The Hawk* [high school coach Larry Hawkins] *used to say I had charisma, that people would react to me no matter what I did.* The Hawk knew a thing or two.

So did Asofsky. *Nobody believed me,* he said, *but I figured Baltimore would be as tough as anybody in the league for the Knicks, and forget the loser's thing of Baltimore teams. It was in the matchups.* It took seven grueling games to bear Stanley out, but by the end Barnett and DeBusschere each had 28 points, Russell 18, and the crowd was chanting, "It's all over now [clap, clap]." New York won, 127–114, and Eddie Layton, the Garden organist, played "Happy Days."

Back in the locker room, the flashbulbs popped. Stallworth danced to radio rock. Barnett drank canned Fanta. Bowman was on the phone in Whelans' room, writing down a number. In Baltimore's dressing room, Monroe slipped into a red shirt with white clocks, red trousers, red shoes, threw a black tank top and red leather jacket over, adjusted tinted scarlet shades and walked onto Thirty-third Street. The season was over for him.

The prospect of 7-foot 1-inch Lew Alcindor playing in their cities had NBA franchises salivating even before he turned professional. Just prior to the league's draft of college talent last year, the management of the Phoenix Suns staged a poll to let fans determine how to call the coin toss that would decide whether Phoenix or Milwaukee was granted the rights to Alcindor. The Phoenix people chose heads, and shortly thereafter Alcindor purchased a Ural Mountains hat and the longest scarf in captivity and trundled off to Milwaukee.

Alcindor came in from the cold to a luxury apartment complex called Juneau Village, from where he made intermittent pronouncements on Milwaukee and its benighted culture. The feeling of Milwaukee, curiously enough, was not mutual. What Alcindor did for civic pride on the nights he worked for the local team privileged his remarks. In his first year, he scored 28.8 points a game and led the Bucks from last place to second.

The basketball consciousness he gave the city was not in all cases welcomed. An alderman named Clarence M. Miller was forced by his constituency to propose an ordinance prohibiting late-hours basketball in the alleys of Milwaukee, a craze for which Alcindor and his $1.4 million contract were responsible. "Every father," said Miller, "had his son out playing basketball because he felt that if Lew could get all the money, so could his son."

That parochialism marked the fans who came to the Milwaukee Arena. A local purist named Jack Rusnov considered them among the more boorish ones he had seen. Rusnov, a Marquette alumnus who had roomed with a former varsity player named Brian Brunkhorst, said, "They don't even know NBA rules. They don't know what the hell they're screaming about. Like on the give-one foul, they jump to their feet thinking it's something malicious."

The twenty-five-year-old Rusnov, a burglar alarm salesman, cited case studies. "There's one guy who brings a bullhorn to games, I call him Bullhorn. He sits four or five rows behind the Bucks' bench. Every time there's a call against the Bucks, he's up into the aisle with that bullhorn, screaming at the refs. He's a big hero to these people. There are scattered dummies who pattern themselves after him. They take a step onto the floor and shake their fists. The Bullhorn went on the road with the team, down to Atlanta. And the management there took the bullhorn away from him. Around here they kind of smile on him.

"There's another guy I call the Sneak. He looks like a stockbroker. Sits behind the visiting team bench. His thing is he throws a peanut shell or something at the visiting team and when they look around he's sitting there like an angel. One night he threw a

paper cup at [Atlanta coach] Richie Guerin and Guerin went into
the stands after him.

"These fans are easy to psych. There's a group of guys I call
Bookie Row. One of them weighs about five hundred pounds, no
exaggeration. When he's betting on the visitors, he gets his kicks
psyching the fans up. He stands in the aisle so they can't see and
gets them all riled.

"The guy that perpetuates all this is the local radio announcer,
Eddie Doucette. Actually he's a real nice guy. I've met him in the
bars. But when he gets behind a mike . . . it's like Dr. Jekyll and
Mr. Hyde. He's real excitable. He yells and screams, and baits the
officials and tells the fans the refs should have their heads exam-
ined. One night he called Luke Jackson from Philly a gorilla, a
hatchet man."

Game rites were ruled by a small-town perversity. After the
anthem was tendered in respectful silence, the arena became
charged with the blasts of a dixieland band, cheers that started
and ended as if on instruction and announcements in duplicate of
home-team scores ("basket by Alcindor, basket by Alcindor").
The baskets of foes were by contrast slurred over, and their artis-
try was unattended by applause, a provincialism not observed in
the Garden. A writer named Frank Dedford said that Buck fans
were the sort who, if they were automobiles, would all be wearing
STP stickers.

When New York arrived in Milwaukee for the playoffs, the
Knicks led the series two games to nothing, a lead as much owing
to the failure of Alcindor's teammates as anything else. Their inability to score allowed the Knicks to become bolder on defense
against Alcindor.

The failure of Flynn Robinson, Milwaukee's second-leading
scorer, was regarded as crucial. "This is a complex moody guy,"
said Bob Wolf of the *Milwaukee Journal*. "He's more easily
affected than most when things go wrong for him on the court. It
started in the [playoff] series against Philadelphia. Flynn doesn't
like hands on him on defense, and Philly found out that when
Wally Jones handled him he didn't score. In the Philly series,
Jones handled him a lot, his hands were all over him. Robinson
takes it as a personal affront. When Archie Clarke did it, he went

after him. Not only did he let it get to him and lose his poise, he also would not work as hard to get the ball. He almost made himself useless." Milwaukee's other guard, Jon McGlocklin, was less perplexing but no more effective than Robinson against New York. A standup shooter, he had trouble penetrating.

What scoring Milwaukee lacked in the backcourt it needed from its forwards. But the reputation of one of them, Greg Smith, was not made on the shot. As a rookie last year, he was under advice not to shoot the ball from distances that were routine for other players. He was, though, a lively enough rebounder and defender. "This is a guy," said Buck publicity man Jim Foley, "who really wanted to play NBA ball. His brother Dwight was considered an even better player than Greg and was on his way to Los Angeles a few years ago to sign a contract with the Lakers when he was killed in a car crash. The ABA wanted Greg real bad, but he wanted to play in a more established league, maybe he had a thing about his brother. Anyhow, he wanted to play here so much that when he was drafted by us, he called [Milwaukee coach] Larry Costello to say that the ABA was after him but he preferred the NBA." Milwaukee's other forward, rookie Bob Dandridge, was lean and quick, but on most nights no match for DeBusschere.

The night he was, in the third game of the series, he shot 10 for 15 from the floor and forced DeBusschere away from the boards. That gave Alcindor the privacy he needed against Reed, and Lew proceeded to snatch 31 rebounds, more than he had gotten in any professional or college game. When Lew got a little help from his friends, he was very tough. And so was Milwaukee. That night the Bucks won, 101–96.

To galleries, Alcindor appeared more aloof from the game's emotions than Reed. He spoke of doing mental exercises beforehand "to get myself in harmony with the universe," and used the music of Freddie Hubbard and Red Clay to orchestrate them. On the court, he would sit down after abbreviated warm-ups and stare at the court with the indifference he affected in games. Reed was more a traditionalist. On the flight to Milwaukee, he lingered over a news story whose headline read, REED HAS A JOB: STOP ALCINDOR. In the locker room he would relax before going onto the floor by reading *Field and Stream,* and come onto courts with a purposeful step and earnest demeanor. Reed was a blue-collar pivotman.

In the Milwaukee series Reed made Alcindor conscious of the strength he had. "Against Baltimore," said Phil Jackson, "Unseld and Willie really laid on each other. They're both big strong guys, and in a way it was good for the Milwaukee games, see, because it set a precedent for the referees. Like in the regular-season games the refs didn't let Willis get away with much against Lew. Now they did. Reed used it. In this league, you have to have a center who can intimidate—not specifically intimidate, but I don't know what other words to use. It was something Willis couldn't do against Unseld. But against Alcindor he was capable of doing it. He let it be known he wasn't gonna take any shoving. It was important. Like the six-foot hook becomes a nine-foot hook. Don't let anybody tell you that guys can't be intimidated, particularly rookies. My rookie year, I kept taking Paul Silas underneath the basket one game, and because I did it he kept putting blows on me, telling me in his own way that he didn't like it. Then he threw a blind punch on me and knocked me down, and for the rest of the game I was really shook."

Reed had the same affect on people. Recalling the second game, Greg Smith said, "I hit Reed in the mouth with my elbow as I came down with a rebound, and I apologized fast . . . as quick as I could get it out of my mouth. I'd almost hooked up with Reed in Milwaukee earlier this year, and he straightened me out fast. He said, 'I own this court when I'm out here. I'm the king bee.' I had to agree. See, I saw a picture in a magazine showing Reed knocking out Rudy LaRusso a few years ago, and I don't want to be knocked out in front of 19,500 people and a TV audience back home."

Against Alcindor, Reed needed every advantage he could get. At 7–1, Alcindor was remarkably agile; sometimes he dribbled through his legs before making a move to the basket. Near the basket, he was impossible to stop. It was to Alcindor's credit, and coach Costello's, that he had kept his maverick nature out of his work. "Lew," said the *Journal's* Bob Wolf, "does things pretty much his own way except on the court. He's one of the few guys I know who eats hot dogs half an hour before a game, or refuses to sign autographs. But when it comes to team things, he's just another guy. Not like Elvin Hayes, who won't carry his own suitcase on roadtrips."

Costello was a compulsive basketball man. He would take his wife to the Copacabana in New York and talk shop with assistant coach Tom Nissalke during the show. In training camp, he gave each player a fifty-page bound volume of his intricate systems, and had rookies take a written test on them. At games he would use a yellow, lined legal pad to keep notes that he would transcribe onto the backs of boxscores and store away in voluminous files. "He's totally without humor," said Terry Bledsoe, another *Milwaukee Journal* writer. "He tells jokes that are not funny and which are, I think, a reflection of his dedication. He talks basketball almost exclusively. There aren't too many coaches who rely as heavily on drawings; he draws up plays on that yellow pad he has, sometimes improvises them during the game. He's a very businesslike coach, and players regard him that way." Said Wolf: "That's right, he's strictly business. He's not a charmer like, say, van Breda Kolff. He's known as a particularly hard worker. On days off he rarely misses a chance to hold a practice. He works constantly. On the plane, he takes papers out of his attache case and starts figuring strategy."

After the first two losses, Costello's strategy was to start Fred Crawford rather than Robinson, the team captain. When Robinson got into the fourth game Milwaukee had scored 16 straight points to cut New York's 20-point halftime lead to 69–67 and cause Dick Barnett to mumble as he passed the Knick bench, "This shit gotta stop." It did when Robinson forced a shot, and Russell and Stallworth started hitting shots that Cazzie, in pharmaceutical confusion, said were like penicillin for the lift they gave the team. Though it was Russell's three third quarter shots that sent the Knicks on to a 117–105 victory, it was to his second missed dunk of the series that Barnett addressed himself. "I wonder," he said afterward, "if they got that mutha on instant replay."

A night later, Barnett enlivened the Garden with a burst of jump shooting. He scored 9 points in less than three minutes, 16 points by the end of the quarter, and seized the game from Milwaukee in the first 12 minutes, 35–19. The tempo never let up after that, New York moved the ball as slickly as Holzman's old City College teams. Back door . . . give and go . . . pick and roll: the schoolyard academics.

It was an evening for team virtues. In the whirling astute game the Knicks put on, Alcindor no longer was the games player who could leap formidable teams in single bounds. What fear the Asofskys in the Garden had of Milwaukee was that Lew would expose the orderly beauty of the Knickerbockers by his unnatural gifts and so mock the baskets' verities. That fear lasted not much longer than the first half of the game when New York left the floor leading, 69–45. For fans, many of whom had had their own shots contemptuously handled in schoolyards by boyhood geniuses of leap, it was a vindicatory night. They ended up chanting and clapping, "Goodbye, Lewie, we hate to see you go."

And as the Knicks increased their lead, the Garden turned festive. The starters were treated to long, standing ovations. The clamor for the reserves reached such proportions that when the injured Hosket was called for, an announcement had to be made that he was unable to play. The crowd cheered him anyhow and, under Reed's prodding, Hosket brandished his fist in the air. In the upstairs seats, the gallery then chanted for the coach to put on a uniform. *Holzman, Holzman.* New York won the series, four games to one, on a 132–96 victory, and Eddie Layton, anticipating the finals against Western Division winner Los Angeles, played, "California, Here We Come."

Afterward, while Knicks sat and savored the win, chairman of the board Felt spied a lone player soaping up in the shower stalls. Felt was filled with proprietary pleasure. Big-eyed and beaming, he had the slight swagger of winning generals. Stepping toward the shower, he said, "Dick, you son of a gun." Barnett wiped suds from his eyes, looked out to see who it was, said in his ponderous sleepy way, "Yeah, all right," and went back to his shower.

Shortly before the Los Angeles series, Danny Whelan got a phone call. It was from a guy he had known in the navy while stationed at San Pedro, California. Whelan had not heard from him since 1946. But it did not surprise the trainer when he was asked for a ticket. People were in a hard way in New York; only this city of wild dances could inspire the cutthroat fevers that arose the morning of the final ticket sale. In the milling lines people pushed one another and knocked over barricades to gain a better station. One man caught in the crowd yelled at an idle cop, "You lousy bastard, get on that fucking bullhorn and help us." A man moaned that he was having a heart attack; another stooped to help him and had tickets snatched from his trouser pockets. A kid waved his tickets at friends and was the next moment empty-handed. People who had waited overnight in sleeping bags had to fight for their places in line.

A young lady, Alice Radosh, was moved enough by the crazies in the lobby to recount her experience in the *Village Voice*. Others avoided the hassle altogether by hiring stand-ins from places like Office Temporaries and Manpower. Fans who had missed their shot at the ticket window went for the rebound among players. Riordan would alight from the Long Island Railroad and have kids beg him to sneak them in. At the employees' entrance, 8 Pennsylvania Plaza, he would find a Dominican brother of slight acquaintance looking for a ticket. Upstairs, in the dressing room, a priest down from Providence would phone an hour before the game asking for ticket dispensations. Even while Holzman gave his pregame talk, the phone was still ringing for Riordan. Knickerbockers had neither the tickets nor the foolproof plan Walt Bellamy used to have. Bellamy, they remembered, would promise tickets to anybody who asked. But when envelopes were delivered to the lobby, only a select few would have a ticket in them. If disgruntled friends of his asked Bellamy what had happened, invariably Walter would say, "Goddamn ballboys. They mess things up every time."

The ticket hustle went on right up to gametime. By the championship round, even Raymond the Pretzel Man was in. Raymond still drove up to the Garden in his car that had the back seat knocked out for the pretzel van. But he didn't come for business. Raymond the Pretzel Man was looking to get in, he even hit on Asofsky. At playoffs the only guys who got people in had a ticket in one hand, a bribe for the gate man in the other.

If Knickerbocker patrons lacked impeccable manners outside the arena, they were irreproachable inside it, saving their best moves for the finals. Riordan had an affinity for the fans that not even instructional words from them on foul shots could alter. Granted, he had never heard advice before from the gallery. But then it had been a long while since New York had come so far.

Each time the crowd stood for the national anthem the odds were that organist Layton's rendition was obscured many bars from its conclusion. At questionable calls, solidarity chants of BULLLL-shit BULLLLL-shit came down from the stands. For their part, Asofsky and Klein worked on keeping Reed's foe, 7–1, 290-pound Wilt Chamberlain, out of the foul lane by shouting for three-second violations every time he lingered there. Chamberlain was sensitive about that; later in the series he snubbed, then shouldered by columnist Milton Gross for Gross' allegations that refs let him overstay the three-second limit. When Klein mocked his foulshooting by advising him to study the Cap'n's shot, Chamberlain turned and swore at him.

Chamberlain was the greatest scorer in NBA history. In a game against the Knicks in 1962 he made 100 points, a record for a single game. After he had injured his knee this season, doctors advised him not to play until next year. But Chamberlain had disregarded their advice and worked long hours to come back and help his teammates in the playoffs.

Yet among the Lakers, Chamberlain was a puzzling figure whose fitful quirks alternately amused and annoyed them. Chamberlain was said once to have refused to play unless a ballboy ran out for some 7-Up, a refreshment he took in game pauses. Not long after, another Laker, Elgin Baylor, mocked him by threatening a sit-down unless he got his grape soda.

Chamberlain was obsessed about personal statistics. When van Breda Kolff was coaching LA, Chamberlain phoned the press booth at half time of a San Francisco game in which the Lakers were losing by 20, and said he had been shortchanged in rebounds. After victories, he would grumble about statistics, too. To teammates he was a moody distant man. When the club's wisecracker, Baylor, had the season before lovingly insulted a plodding Laker named Jay Carty by calling him Golden Wheels,

Chamberlain interrupted the laughter by asking couldn't Baylor say something nice about people? The remark threw a pall over the room, and suggested the dreads that moved Wilt and his game.

Wilt was perplexing. On monogrammed shirtcuffs he had the nickname "Dipper" rather than the gookish "Stilt" the press used; "Dipper" conferred a grace that when affronted made him over-react. A Laker man spoke of Wilt's "fear of failure." It was most conspicuous at the foul line, where the hooting of crowds unnerved him. Teammates swore the only Laker who could shoot fouls better than Wilt in practice was Jerry West. A Laker official had seen him a month or so prior to the playoffs make 23 in a row at the foul line in an empty Forum. In games, he could not make one of every two free throws.

Baylor was better for the crowds in the stands and on the floor; the moves he made were so spontaneous he could not do them in quite the same way outside of game circumstances. Once, a photographer from the *Los Angeles Times* had Baylor try it in private, and when the drives came off poorly before the camera, he thought Elgin was putting him on. Fanciful humor was not alien to Baylor. When Barnett was at Los Angeles, Baylor and Rudy LaRusso engaged in outrageous debates that Barnett often instigated. Barnett would pose such conundrums as, "Which is faster, the sardine or barracuda?" LaRusso and Baylor could argue it at length, each offering proofs that grew more spurious by the minute. One time Baylor confounded LaRusso in a coin flip for a quarter. He called heads and when it came up tails, LaRusso announced, "Sorry, baby, it's eagles." Baylor grabbed the coin from his hand and, justifying it, replied, "Eagles have heads, my man."

Against people like DeBusschere, Baylor was not so flip. In fact he was once referred to as the only man who could look dignified in basketball shorts, so stately was his carriage. The team's star, Jerry West, did not appear that prepossessing at first glance. Thin and crooked-beaked from a nose broken nine times, he looked like a hillbilly Ichabod Crane. The Lakers called him Tweety for the high-pitched nasal twang he had acquired in his native Cabin Creek, West Virginia. West had so unheroic an aspect that a woman spying him in the Forum lobby mistook him for a ticket department employee and asked him to exchange some concert tickets she had bought.

The cheery disposition West had at those moments lasted only until games. Game days brought on stomach upsets and, his wife swore, the only fights their marriage had suffered. For his digestive tract West took his pregame meal shortly after noon. For the sake of his marriage he usually got to the arena before the dressing room was open.

Swiftness and arms that required a 37-inch long sleeve made West more fit for the game than the casual observer suspected. He was so quick at taking the ball off the dribble and sending it into the air that he appeared to get his shots at will: in 1969–70, he led the league in scoring with a 31.2 points-per-game average. By now, his easy grace was considered one of the natural wonders of the game. What injuries he still got, he took pains to hide, at times he refused to be taped for an injury if the tape was visible to the public.

The intensity West had was new to Keith Erickson, the long-haired Laker forward who was Bradley's matchup. Erickson grew up on the beaches of El Segundo, California, where volleyball and easy living are the games people play. His origins inclined him to choose volleyball rather than basketball as his sport in the 1964 Olympics, and made him at first a perfunctory pro. Erickson had, so the story went, revelations at the end of last season's playoffs of his wasted career and, over the summer, shot 200 shots a day that he had his wife shag for him. The season he'd had in 1969–70 was good enough to make wifely care worth it.

The slavish dedication Mrs. Erickson had for her husband, Los Angeles rookie Dick Garrett had had for the defense at Southern Illinois, where he was a teammate of Frazier's. The two of them had wagered a $200 party at the campus on the outcome of the series, and it was Clyde's opinion that Garrett had been had. "He said okay. Spoke up quickly. Just like a rookie."

In playoffs, the Lakers had been had, too. In the past eleven years they had reached the finals seven times and not won once. In that span Boston was their nemesis, having beaten them in all championship rounds. The Boston era had traumatized Baylor; during the New York series he was to say, "This doesn't seem

completely real anyway. It seems to me that even if we get by the
Knicks, the Celtics must be waiting for us somewhere out there."

The series figured to be a struggle of tempos. As Los Angeles
coach Joe Mullaney said, "Baby, when they get us running, even
I can't run with them, quick as I was." The Lakers' Chamberlain
made it unlikely that Los Angeles would run of its own volition.
The condition of his knee prescribed a more pacific game. It also
required him to occupy space other Lakers might have preferred
for their own. Forward Happy Hairston, a prolific scorer in
Wilt's absence, was so crimped by him that he was nullified as a
threat and benched. But the virtues of Chamberlain's stretch
were considered to outweigh his assorted faults, and when he was
properly disposed, he could gain Los Angeles the board pre-
dominance to make its game work. Outrebounded, New York was
not as apt to turn a court chaotic and disrupt the Lakers' one-on-
one eminence, Jerry West.

But when the Knicks were playing their disarming defense, or
shooting bull's-eyes from outside, the game speeded up and became more hellish for LA. The nub was keeping it going, any
slackening let Chamberlain restore the snail's pace that was Laker
preference. Knickerbocker tempo relied on Frazier and Reed, but
Frazier had his game moods and Reed his hurt knees, both of
which could attenuate the motion New York had to have on the
attack. What was pivotal for both teams was what Reed and
Chamberlain did to each other. Before the series, Chamberlain
made it plain he would not be drawn away from the basket, saying, "If Reed's shooting 20- and 25-footers and if we get beat by
them, I'll still let him have them." If Chamberlain did camp at the
basket, Los Angeles had a defense that switched a Laker onto
Reed and realigned elsewhere in a kind of zone. To stop the Los
Angeles big man, New York would rely on Chamberlain's wither-
ing skills and its own doubling. What was apparent from the first
was that whatever defense Los Angeles devised Reed could shoot
the bejeezus out of it, and Chamberlain could shoot only what
was called his "finger roll" shot. Nights after the series started, a
member of the ABC-TV crew, a short potbellied fellow, mimicked
its execution. Cupping an imaginary basketball, he puffed his
chest out to confer on himself the grandeur of a seven-footer. Next

he stooped and squatted over the ball, back to the basket, and approximated two stiff dribbles to his right. Gathering himself together a moment in an obscene crouch, he rose up from it like Nureyev, the right arm flinging out past his shoulder and the body stretching toward the rim of the envisioned basket. That was the finger roll. At ABC, it got a lot of laughs.

Whatever advantage Reed gave New York in the first two games at the Garden it still managed to squander them. Opening night his 25 points in the first two periods sent New York to an 11-point half-time lead that it lost by the end of the third quarter. In that time, West and Baylor scored with shots so traditional that the gallery hardly stirred. By contrast to Baltimore, Los Angeles made quiet points. West did not have the *la-la* Monroe did, and Baylor no longer possessed the lightning bolts to rattle rims and boards as Johnson did. They worked like dinner guests pocketing the silverware.

Not in this game, or the next one, was there a sense of the furious exertion for control that marked the Baltimore series. Both New York and Los Angeles showed a notable restraint at wiping the other out. *It's just such a long season,* said Hosket. *Like, by the LA series guys were tired of it all, it was a strain. You know, the sun's shining and you're thinking about what you're going to do in the summer and stuff like that. I mean, guys wanted to win but . . .* Both games were decided on last quarter spurts. In the first one Russell hit eight points in a five-minute stretch that saw the Knicks pull away for a 124–112 victory.

Cazzie's performance was overlooked for Reed's game total of 37 points, an output that made Chamberlain and Mullaney reexamine the entrenched pivot position upon which Wilt was insisting. A few days later both of them watched films of the game and issued mixed reviews. The coach tactfully suggested that Chamberlain move out on Reed. Chamberlain came away convinced he had been the victim of shotmaking miracles. A photographer at courtside, Martin Blumenthal, remarked on the interpretive faculties of Chamberlain. "He screws up, blows a play," said Blumenthal, "and you can hear him muttering and cursing to himself like it's some supernatural forces that are making things go wrong."

Those sovereign agents delivered the Knicks right into Chamberlain's hands in the closing minutes of the second game, and gained him heroic notices in the next day's press. Wilt made Riordan bail out on a drive, and then blocked Reed's shot in the lane to hold off New York in a 105–103 Laker victory. Neither play was as remarkable as it was made to appear. Riordan's open throttle got him into trouble as much as Chamberlain did, and Reed first had to reach back for a pass before taking his shot. Nevertheless, the series was tied a game apiece.

The Knicks headed for the West Coast on a charter flight. The mood was relaxed. Ned Irish took off his jacket and exposed striking red-white-and-blue suspenders. Players and writers indulged the bottled spirits. DeBusschere was cultivating the look of a literary figure, letting his hair grow out. Holzman thought it could use some barbering but DeBusschere was leaving it long awhile. Johnny Warren's hair was sprouting too—into a full Afro cut that led teammates to nickname him Mod Squad. Cazzie Russell took onto the flight a book that, on disassembling, flattened down into a simulated putting green. In hotel lobbies, he and Bowman would hunch over putters in spirited competition. Some pornographic photos were handed about. At the front of the craft, Barnett, Jackson and newsmen played cards. A stack of bills was in the pot. The wives of various writers were at the rear of the plane. Two movies were shown: *Topaz* and *The Reivers*. Bowman and Russell laughed at the love scenes in *Topaz*, Holzman fell asleep during them. Warren read *The Autobiography of Malcolm X*. Don May declared that his season was over, what was there good to do in LA?

Los Angeles was not a basketball town. It was an endless highway to spectacles. Topless and/or bottomless. Arby's. Sunset Strip. Grauman's. Lawrence Welk. Wilt Chamberlain. The Forum, the arena in which games were played, was peculiarly fitted to that Californian whose notion of mixed media was tits and the luncheon special. In the lobby of the Forum, a pretty girl hawked scorecards with an affected British accent, a voice more fit for the opera house than the arena. There were girls like her in mini-fits to dispense liquor and Mexican or American food, or show the patrons to their places. Should a fan need to leave his seat during the game, the commentary of Laker announcer Chick Hearn was piped to him in the lobbies. Let Frazier pick up a loose ball near the basket and score and the fan heard Hearn say, "Garbage play by Frazier. He was just standing there straightening his moustache." A showtime spirit reigned in the Forum. The organist there was presented as "the incomparable Gaylord Carter," an introduction whose disclaimer was issued by *Newsday*'s Denberg. "Eddie Layton," he said, "would take him out in sixteen bars."

Los Angeles fans were a strange breed. For them the game was just another spectacle in smorgasbord city. Some measure of that was their response to the Lakers in pregame introductions: Chamberlain consistently got a bigger ovation than West and Baylor. Sixty-one hundred season tickets were sold, but many to corporations. Clearly, there was no consuming passion for the sport. People left games early to beat the traffic.

Jack Kent Cooke, the millionaire owner of the Lakers, dispatched the press to the stands for all games, and filled the vacated floor perimeter with customers. League rules stated that fourteen seats be relegated to each team. Cooke conceded ten, and sold the rest. Often celebrities sat at courtside. In earlier Laker days, Doris Day and Dean Martin had attended. Now Rhonda Fleming, Andy Williams, Shelly Berman and Walter Matthau showed up when they were in town. In warm-ups before a game on the Coast, Hosket spied used-car salesman Ralph Williams, whose fast-talking commercials he had seen on TV. Hosket shouted to him: "How much will you give me on a '68 Buick?" Williams was not mixing business with baskets: he waved and kept going.

Barnett drew West as his defensive assignment in the third game, and stayed with him for the rest of the series. The change gave Frazier more of a chance to gamble on defense, Garret not being the threat West was. What threat Clyde held as a scorer was diminishing with each playoff game, at some cost, it seemed, to the attack. No longer was he working as boldly as he had early in the season when he had provoked comparisons with the master of one-on-one, Oscar Robertson.

Frazier did not covet the shot the way most pros did, or worry about locating its groove. *It's like a buzzer inside of me when I'm ready. I warm up very slow, shoot some free throws and maybe three jumpers from the top of the key. If they go in and they feel alright, then I think I'm ready. So I'll sit down and rest and, like, during the game I get in the groove. But really, shooting's never interested me that much.* In the Baltimore series, Holzman had advised Frazier to move the ball and not worry about his shots, a notion Clyde had by now rendered *reductio ad absurdum*. In the first two games he took a total of 14 shots and on the Coast he was to pass up open shots.

Barnett's switch on defense forced West to play against a more physical defender. Barnett bumped and pushed where Frazier did not. Over 48 minutes, it might tire West. The success the veteran was to have with West came as a surprise to casual observers but not to Barnett. "I've been playing defense for ten years. I mean, you know, when you're winning, everybody suddenly is great. Like they said, we got the greatest bench in the world. But you let the same sucker get out there when you're ten down and see how great he is. Sportswriters can make a monster out of you, and they can make shit out of you. As long as I'm rewarded financially, that's the main thing now. I'm past caring."

In days when Barnett was a Laker, announcer Hearn would call out into his microphone "Fall back, baby," every time Barnett hit his fragmented shots. It became a rallying cry for Los Angeles partisans when he came off the bench to play. Such attentions did not much faze Barnett, he was busy trying to get his fair share from Laker management, a process his bench status impeded. As a sub, Barnett served Los Angeles the way Russell did New York for instant points. In three seasons on the Coast, he averaged 18.0, 18.4 and 13.8 points a game and, he figured, $5,000 a season less than he would have as a starter. *The general manager gave me the argument that I wasn't as great a ballplayer as I thought I was and ran down all my weaknesses. But you know general managers give you the same old boolshit every time. I didn't counter to it at all. I just asked to be traded.*

The Laker general manager, Lou Mohs, was now long gone from the front office, but Barnett the Knick was still conspicuously around. Zero for seven in the first half of the third game, he led the team back from a 56–42 half-time deficit. The high tight dribble, the irregular body rhythm, the shots from all angles of his person, Barnett got it all together in the final four minutes. He went by West on a baseline move for a three-point play to cut Los Angeles' lead to 90–88. Two foul shots at 3:06 . . . a 20-foot jump shot at 2:42 . . . a 10-foot jumper off the drive at 1:58. Nine straight points for Barnett. And moments later, at 96–96, the rush was on to beat the traffic.

Meanwhile, back in the Forum, the Knicks and Lakers had themselves a finish. The score was tied 100–100 when DeBusschere took a jump shot from behind the foul line. On the way up LA's Hairston hit his hand and DeBusschere fought the ball to the peak of his ascent. The shot came off like a knuckleball, floated toward the hoop and in. Three seconds were left. New York 102, Los Angeles 100.

When Chamberlain picked up the ball, he never bothered to step off the court before making his inbounds pass, a rules infraction that Los Angeles televiewers could see on the next night's news but official Jack Madden could not during the game. Chamberlain's pass went to West at the left of the lane. West took three dribbles and, from a crouched position, bounded off the floor 63 feet from the basket, his right arm swinging straight out, his momentum carrying him to midcourt.

On the New York bench, Whelan reached for his trainer's satchel, Phil Jackson raised a victory fist. Stallworth had grabbed his sweat pants, Russell a towel. The whole team was up. As the ball traveled on a direct line to the basket, Holzman raised both fists over his shoulder and tensed. Riordan's eyes went wide. The shot went in, causing DeBusschere to drop where he stood, under the LA basket. "What's amazing," said Hosket, "was that West was concentrating on his followthrough. I was watching him and he shot the thing like he really figured it was going in. I looked over at him just before the overtime period and shook my head. He got embarrassed and just shrugged."

It was West's parting shot. Weary from playing 48 straight minutes of regulation time, he missed all five of the shots he took in the overtime. Barnett sat until 1:40 was left in that period and then gave the Knicks the big basket at the end. New York's final offense was intended to go to Reed, but the Cap'n gave the ball to Barnett. Barnett started to his left, stopped and, ten feet from the basket, kicked into the air and shot his jumper in a crowd of Lakers. It dropped through to give New York a 111–108 victory. When a newsman asked him later if that shot left him with a special feeling, Barnett looked up, said, "Not really," and went to take a shower. Whelan, advising him that there was no hot water, quipped, "Mullaney shut it off."

Mullaney had other problems. West had hurt his left thumb in the first half when he banged it against Bradley's leg. The swelling made him a doubtful starter for the fourth game. That, at least, was the Laker party line. "That's what I had to say for the press," said LA publicity man Jim Brochu. "That's what the doctor told me to say. But I knew and everyone knew he'd be there for the fourth game. He always had been before." Over breakfast at the Sheraton Inn the next morning, the Knicks looked at the headlines, WEST DOUBTFUL NOW FOR . . . FOURTH GAME, and had not the least doubt that Tweety would show. *Eh, it's newspaper crap,* said DeBusschere. *No way he's not going to play.*

When the Lakers arrived at their locker room for the fourth game, there was a telegram from a fan named Russell E. Carr, saying: FOR WEST'S HAND EPSOM SALTS AND HOT WATER THREE HOURS. It was not the cure Laker trainer Frank O'Neill elected. For three and a half hours the afternoon of the game, O'Neill packed the hand in ice and soaked it in a whirlpool. There was still swelling in the fleshy cushion by the thumb and on up to the index finger. But, as expected, neither rain, sleet nor a swollen metacarpal phalangeal was to stop West from his appointed playoff rounds. He had 37 points and 18 assists in a 121–115 overtime victory for Los Angeles witnessed by those at the Forum who did not mind the traffic. The series was tied at two games apiece.

Even though two of the three remaining games of the finals were scheduled for the Garden, the homecourt advantage warranted no premature celebration among the Knicks. New York was struggling. Erickson was crowding Bradley's shot and using quick hands on him when he dribbled. In the two Coast games, Bradley had made a total of 6 of 24 shots. Frazier was yet to bust out at either end of the court. And Reed's knees were hurting.

In 16 playoff games against the games best big men (Unseld, Alcindor and Chamberlain) Reed had averaged 25.9 points and 15.3 rebounds on knees growing progressively more painful. The Cap'n had tendonitis in both knees, a muscular strain that had bothered him on and off since before midseason. Speculating on the strain the final games would put on those knees, the *Times'* Leonard Koppett wrote the day before the fifth game: ". . . as of tomorrow night, he will face two games in three nights and possibly three in five. There is no question Reed will play, and probably play well, until and unless he actually collapses."

The next night Reed collapsed. With Los Angeles leading 25–15, Willis fell trying to drive by Chamberlain at 3:56 of the first quarter. Even before he hit the floor, he had strained two muscles in the thigh of his right leg, damage serious enough for him to leave the game. Shortly after, he, Whelan and Dr. James Parkes went to the locker room.

When Willis Reed limped off, big Fred Klein did not panic. He sought medical advice. Klein's boss was sitting several rows in back of him. The boss' son was a doctor. What the son-the-doctor told Klein was that Reed was through for the series. Informed of that diagnosis, Asofsky and the boys did not lose faith but rather stated their own unprofessional opinion. The doctor, they said, was full of shit.

What Holzman said, and did, revealed a less augustinian outlook, but was surely as crucial in working out Knickerbocker destiny. He found a lineup whose fighting chance was a 6-foot 6-inch matchup against Chamberlain. At 4:31 of the second quarter, the former guard and forward of the Detroit Pistons, Dave DeBusschere, became New York's fourth pivotman of the evening, succeeding Reed, Bowman and Hosket, and preceding the hope that the Cap'n might still play. But when the Knicks came into the locker room at half time, trailing 53 to 40, Reed was lying in pain on the training table in Whelan's room and Dr. Parkes, the team physician, was attending him. Reed was finished for the night.

The strategy was revised. Defense was obvious: New York had

to double-team and gamble and corrupt the gentleman's leisure with which Los Angeles played. Bradley recommended the offense, a 1-3-1 alignment that college teams used against zones. In this offense, Frazier would be out front feeding the ball to a high pivot or the wingmen at the sides of the foul line. But the virtue of the 1-3-1 was its service to the back man, designated as the *rover*. The rover would be the man Chamberlain had to play, and what the 1-3-1 did was to force Wilt away from the basket against a smaller, more agile foe. Should Chamberlain choose not to go outside, he left the rover, DeBusschere, with an open shot. Only one problem remained: who to pair with Barnett on the scoring flanks, Bradley or Russell. Bradley suggested Russell, saying Cazzie was the more accurate shot in the first half. That was it but for Holzman's sober words about winning it for the Cap'n.

In the Lakers' dressing room, less inspiring words were spoken. Wilt Chamberlain was saying, "Gee, I hope we don't lose it," a remark that struck teammates as sufficiently morbid to remember long after the series was ended. *Guys,* said a Laker man, *mentioned its having a disturbing effect.* That it did was as much a commentary on Los Angeles' games soul as Chamberlain's. Neither had the blood for changes or strange entertainments.

Eleven years a pro, Chamberlain was no more subtle or cunning than when he had come into the league. Moreover, public embarrassments appeared to have exorcised not enraged the closet beast that players require; that the beast was well fed and exercised seemed to suffice now. When big Freddie Klein, who would have knocked Art Heyman's head off if he could have, saw Chamberlain work against DeBusschere in the early minutes of the second half, he thought, *Lookit him, lookit him, he can't push people around. He's not an animal, he's not an animal.* In the second half, Chamberlain took only three shots.

Nor was Los Angeles especially spirited. In recent years, the team had relinquished something of its nerve and wit to West; the better he got, the more he was made to do, particularly at finishes, times when spirits are renewed. Night after night, the soul of the team was stashed away in fourth quarters while West performed one-on-one. In a way it was necessary and natural. Baylor was old and graying in his sideburns. Chamberlain was invalided. The others were routine talents. But the consequences of West's necessity came down on LA in the fifth game.

The team that ran smooth in leisure came apart in the chaos of 1-3-1 and the *DEE-fense, DEE-fense* the Garden crowd chanted. "They sped it up like a fast movie," Mullaney was to say afterward. "We've been playing a certain style of game. All these playoff games have been nearly the same. Then, all of a sudden, it switches around a hundred percent." Los Angeles was forced to respond like a team and couldn't. The crowd, sensing its little bit could help, gave. *DEE-fense, DEE-fense*. Lulls made the mob edgy; at one such interlude a kid screamed at the Garden organist, "Come on, Eddie Layton, you faggot. Play."

The Knicks defensed. They ran Lakers into those dead ends of the court where bad things happened. They made the Lakers improvise ways out but LA was unable to. Los Angeles could hardly get a shot off. "I've seen two good drinkers take more shots than that in one evening," West said afterward. Clyde was at his ease in the defense, sliding, sliding, coming up on a dribbler, steal or not he never changed expression, very cool was Clyde. He came in on little cat's feet to steal an inbounds pass, and then took another straight-on from West. Bradley, whose upturned brow was forever referred to as satanic, was more violent on the defense. Big-eyed and flailing he doubled when he could. Russell was just as emotive. His forehead would wrinkle into worry folds, he would crouch and sway, reaching out with two hands upturned and moving. One night late in the season a fan came down to courtside, a leather-lunger, and critiqued every defensive move of his so vocally that the Knick bench looked over and Asofsky, sitting nearby, turned away. But here was Russell stealing the ball in the last minute of the period and passing to Barnett for the jump shot. At the end of three quarters the score was Los Angeles 82, New York 75.

DeBusschere, working up a massive beer thirst, was leaning on Chamberlain from the lane side, conceding him the baseline, a route he infrequently took. Wilt preferred the turn-in move and finger roll shot instead. When Chamberlain got the ball, DeBusschere retreated and shaded him toward the middle or, if the pass was not expertly thrown, tried to deflect it. But at 9:17 of the fourth quarter, DeBusschere drew his fifth personal foul, and the crowd fretted.

Stallworth became the pivotman. He chose to play Chamberlain the way Bill Russell did, keeping off him and swinging from side to side to hide his whereabouts. It worked. By now Chamberlain was tranquilized. *He's not an animal. He's not an animal,* mused Klein. *We've got 'em, got 'em.*

The Knicks kept coming on. The Garden crowd was ecstatic. In the upstairs press box, Sly shouted "one time, baby," on every Knick shot, an expression the equivalent of "make it." At 7:43 Bradley made it, a jumper from the left of the key on a pass from Russell that tied the game, 87–87. The sound it set off would have raised all the sad ghosts of twenty-four Knickerbocker years had they waited around. Goebel Ritter in the snowbank. Buckner and the long running dunk. Popeye. Walter Bells. At 5:19 Bradley hit another jumper at the left of the key to give the Knicks the lead, 93–91. The fans were rapturous.

From that point Los Angeles went reeling through the final minutes in a stupor so consuming that neither players nor coach had the presence to repair it with a time-out. The game drifted away from them like a cloud. Stallworth and Russell had the mad moments that suited their runaway game and they snapped to it. Russell scored six points in a row. Stallworth did it at both ends, here driving by Melvin Counts, there stealing a pass to Chamberlain. The *coup* was the piece of work he did on Chamberlain when he loped by him on the baseline and padded off the wood for a striking reverse lay-up to up the Knick lead to 103–96 with 1:32 remaining. Stallworth was so taken by that shot he bounced up and down, and shot his fist to the air. At courtside big Fred Klein's friend, Jack Needle, the ghetto schoolteacher with Harpo Marx hair, had come downstairs from his seat to root the team in. He had tears in his eyes. Ninety-two seconds later, it was over. New York 107, Los Angeles 100. In the locker room a man was saying, "And they made the point spread on top of that."

Reed, who'd heard John Condon's account of the game in the locker room on a special hookup, made the trip to the coast for the sixth game, but his playing status was in doubt. The morning of the game, John Warren issued a breakfast report. He said the

Cap'n had woken, got out of bed and, in BVDs, tried to jump to
the ceiling. Failing that, he'd retired to bed. It was no surprise.
The surprise was what Holzman did that night. He announced
Bowman as a starter, news that led Barnett to speculate whether
Christiaan Barnard was on hand to revive him should he be required to go the distance. "That sucker gonna need a hearse," he
said. Jokes aside, the game plan was dispiriting to most of the
players. *Like the day we flew to LA, said a Knick, on that afternoon we had a practice first. And, like, Red had used the guys
who'd done it the other night. So everybody was figuring we'd
take it to them again. You know, guys were up for it, talking
about it in the hotel in the afternoon. We'll do this and that, that
kind of stuff. Then Red says "Bowman" and it's like he's conceding
the game. The guys lost their psych as soon as he did that.*

When the team went onto the floor, Bradley and Holzman
stayed behind. Bradley tried to convince the coach to use the
lineup that had worked in the fifth game. *He couldn't do it,* said a
teammate. *He told us, "I couldn't talk to him."* What Chamberlain
failed to do at the Garden, he did at the Forum. He shot the ball,
45 points' worth, and Los Angeles romped, 135–113. Bradley
played so listlessly that Ned Irish asked Dr. Parkes afterward,
"What the hell's wrong with Bradley? He's playing like he's in a
fog." The doctor conceded he didn't know. Only Phil Jackson got
anything out of the evening: he made $75 for photographing the
game for the *New York Post.*

The Knickerbocker loss affected people in different ways. Back
in New York, a woman sent a telegram to the team's office right
after the game. It read, *Thanks a lot for losing. Thanks to you our
children won't get to see the circus.* The championship game
bumped the circus on the last weekend of its engagement. So it
went. New York's worries were about Reed. The Cap'n flew home
immediately after the game. In his absence the Garden switchboard took more than 250 phone calls from people inquiring
about his injury or recommending cures. The callers included legitimate physicians and a few quacks. One man sent what he
called a "sacro-sack" and attached a note, reading, THIS WILL
HELP WILLIS. Whelan looked at it and laughed. Reed had a

leg problem and the sacro-sack was for the back. Whelan used more conventional means, three hours of whirlpool and hotpacks and massages and ultrasound. Afterward, Reed slept the day away in his Rego Park, Long Island, apartment.

On the flight to New York, Los Angeles suffered Chamberlain's second rhetorical turnover of the series. Recalled a Los Angeles man: "We're going to New York, right? Well, they passed out the *Herald-Examiner* and there it is on the second sports page. In headlines. 'WE AMERICANS EMPHASIZE WINNING TOO MUCH.' Wilt's quote. Nobody says anything but you could tell by the looks on their faces that it was the wrong thing to say. A guy like Jerry, you gotta figure he's thinking, 'Here we are again and I'm going to have to do the whole thing.' It wasn't what you'd call a healthy attitude." Teams wounded different ways came down to the final game of the season.

It was a warm and sunny day. At his office, Asofsky was analyzing inventory figures and trying to stay cool. But he was, as he put it, scared shit. He divined foul things from his day. Leaving work early, he took the KK train to Brooklyn, and it was late. Anticipating a meat meal, his mother made dairy. Uptown, Joanne Dinoia stepped outside Penn Plaza and a man with a walking cane offered her $100 for the ticket she had. She refused, and he told her she was crazy. All across the city people were making plans for the game. Ticketholders were taking early dinners, and slipping into lucky wardrobes. Others headed straight from work to the bars on the east side of Manhattan, where the game was to be shown on cable television.

Sly bought all the local papers to get the blood going, accepting what Barnett referred to as boolshit for the exhilarating effect the words had. Newspapers on big game days were instant movies, reviving hopes and glows and other outmoded sentiments of children.

He read:

Like the cavalry thundering over the hilltop at the moment the beleaguered frontier fort is about to fall, or like Superman exploding from a telephone booth when Lois Lane is face to face with villainy of the worst order, Willis Reed (in the fantasies of thousands of fans of the New York Knickerbockers) will bound onto the court of Madison Square Garden tonight and save his team from worse than death.

And he loved it.

The Cap'n met Whelan at the Knick dressing room at two. He wore a red, white and blue shirt, a vest, a black and white bandana, blue and white trousers and a bush coat. His leg was treated with heat for ninety minutes in Whelan's room. Then he and the trainer dined at the Penn Plaza Club in the Garden. The place was empty. Reed ate a steak and a salad and, from time to time, told the kitchen help who wandered out that, yes, he would play.

At courtside, ABC was setting up for its national TV hookup that night. The network's Chet Forte, once a basketball star at Columbia University, and Ned Irish were discussing camera emplacements. Security chiefs were informing their aides to have extra men stationed near Eddie Layton's organ in case fans wanted to disassemble it afterward. Maintenance men wet-mopped the floor. The early arrivals among the press sat on a bench in the hallway outside the Knick dressing room, where Reed was now resting. When Holzman passed by, Koppett pointed to the writers on the bench and said, "Ellis Island." Holzman smiled. Minutes later, the first of the security forces trooped through the corridor. Many of them were in the social security bracket, others were young and undernourished. "These guys," said a writer, "are going to keep 19,500 away?"

At 6:03, Reed came onto the court. He spun a lay-up on the rim and, when it dropped in, ushers applauded him. With Don May feeding the ball, he slogged to spots on the wood for his arcing shots, favoring his left leg on liftoffs. In the aisleway to the locker rooms stood an interested observer. "Don't look, Wilt," a guy hollered. Wilt Chamberlain looked. Shortly after, Reed returned to the dressing room. On this final night of the season, it was closed to visitors and press.

The Knicks took the floor without Reed. He stayed inside trying to pinpoint his pain for Dr. Parkes. Once it was localized, the doctor would give him a shot of cortisone, an anti-inflammatory agent, and a shot of Carbocaine, a pain-killer. Cazzie Russell was with him. Meanwhile, Knick fans were wondering about the Cap'n. The word over the airwaves during the day was that he would play. But as the crowd eyed the foyer through which the teams moved, there was still no Reed. When a figure in a Knick warmup suit appeared, a roar went up. It turned out to be Cazzie Russell. Speculation grew.

Then, minutes later, Reed was there. He looked straight ahead, his lips pursed, his step deliberate. It had the melodrama of the cinema death-row walks. Nobody cared. When Willis Reed moved through the cordon of security guards and onto the court, the crowd lit up. They cheered even his warm-up shots, an enthusiasm whose precedent was Bradley's pro debut. At the Laker end of the court, players turned to watch the Cap'n.

In a series turned adrenal, New York had the trump in Reed. Yet no move of Mullaney's was to suggest a sense of the gut forces at work or to acknowledge that some very weird stuff had gone down the last time in the Garden. Mullaney stood pat, even when it was soon apparent that Reed had to drag his right leg to defend and was vulnerable to motion. On his bench Mullaney had Counts and Hairston, either of whom would have given him a more nimble big man than Chamberlain. Counts or Hairston, particularly Hairston, might have accomplished on Reed what the rovers, DeBusschere and Stallworth, did on Chamberlain. The wonder is that at no point early in the evening did Mullaney take the cue New York had given him and use the 1–3–1 that had exposed his own Chamberlain. On psychology alone, it was worth trying for a team whose verve in strange entertainments was questionable.

Instead Reed established credibility at both ends of the floor in the first two minutes. Trailing the offense, he hit the first basket of the game from behind the key and another jumper from 20 feet on the right side. On defense he had enough agility to contend with the finger roll. As the game wore on, and shots proved more difficult for him, Reed signaled Knicks to use him as a screen for their shots. The Knicks shot. From the official play-by-play sheet (with the score 5–2, New York):

	NY	LA
Chamberlain fouled by Reed—misses both tries. DeB		
rebds		
Frazier fouled in act by Erickson—makes 2	7	
DeBusschere one-hander from top of the key	9	
(Time out Los Angeles @ 9:42)		
Baylor uncontested one-hander from left of lane		4
Bradley quick spinning one-hander right of key	11	
(Erickson walks under pressure by Bradley)		
(Barnett loses it)		
West driving lay-in from the right		6
Frazier fouled by Garrett—makes 2	13	
DeBusschere off-balance one-hander from left baseline	15	
(Lakers lose to Reed)		
(Reed throws it to Garrett)		
Chamberlain flies thru to stuff rebound		8
Bradley with arm wide outstretched lays it in from left	17	

What Reed did, and Los Angeles didn't do in the early minutes of the game gave New York an emotional edge that time and place and Walt Frazier sustained. Frazier was working the left side of the floor, using his gliding suggestive motion to con a step from Garrett so that he could cuddle the ball at his shoulder and shoot it. Five straight times in the first quarter Frazier swung room for his shot, and hit.

It was ironic that it should be Frazier who gave the Knicks the magic the last night of the year. When New York was at its worst after the 18-game streak, it was Frazier upon whom criticism fell for his dribbling excesses. Teammates thought he'd had show-time blood in the club's first national TV appearance when he dribbled behind his back four times in the opening minutes of the game. It was not the only time. But in the playoffs he underwent changes: when asked by Holzman to move the ball and not worry about his shots, he became so sacrificial a player that he appeared to lose his homing instincts for the basket.

Other writers referred to the subtle game direction he was giving the Knicks in the playoffs, but Sly could remember only the assessment the hero of John Updike's *Rabbit, Run* had made of the self-effacing game. "On a basketball team, you see, whenever you have a little runty clumsy guy that can't do anything he's called the play-maker. I don't know where he's supposed to be making all these plays." Frazier was playing toward the end as if he had contracted the runt's mentality and was servicing the team accordingly. Sly was convinced that it was no accident that on this night when Frazier felt compelled to go to the basket, the attack became the furious show it did.

It was not by shot alone that New York brought Los Angeles down. The defense accomplished incredible things. The Knicks stole the ball from Chamberlain and Erickson and Baylor, and even West. Frazier, lurking behind Riordan, came off him like a linebacker on a stunting move, and took the ball cleanly from West at the middle of the floor. Eight seconds later, Riordan harassed West and made him step over the backcourt line for another violation. By the end of the first half, the Lakers had committed 15 turnovers (to New York's 7). And the Knicks led, 69–42.

The Knicks did not suffer letdowns they'd had earlier in the series. They were, in a phrase Frazier had used about the playoff state of mind, "psyched to kill." Asofsky had seen that even before the game: when the pop vocalist Steve Lawrence had gone to the Knick bench to shake hands with DeBusschere, DeBusschere had given him a limp hand and a vacant stare. *I'll bet,* said Asofsky, *DeBusschere never knew who the hell it was.* What Reed accomplished for morale was in the Oral Roberts tradition. In a game in which he was to score only four points and grab three rebounds, it was nevertheless inconceivable to think of New York winning without him. When he came onto the floor for the second half, Bowman, already announced as the starter, left the court for Reed and vigorously whacked him on the rump. In that gesture was Nate's affirmation that all was right in heaven. The Cap'n and the Knicks would carry on.

The crowd had to affect the adrenal processes too. Asofsky and the rest were crazy with joy. Asofsky would look down the row and shout over to William B. Williams, the disc jockey, to forget about his voice and let's hear it for the Knicks. Sly's unprofessional ardor caused out-of-town writers around him to cast critical eyes at him. The Knicks responded, particularly Frazier. In the third quarter, he went on another tear: he hit a jump shot, a free throw, got West to charge, stole the ball from Garrett and scored, stole the ball from Chamberlain and scored . . . all in a matter of minutes. By the end of that surge, the Knicks led, 79–54. Shortly after, Reed left the game for the night. The rest was for savoring. For some it was not easy.

When Mullaney had made no changes at the start of the second half, Asofsky, a thirty-three-year-old Knickerbocker fan whom history had taught circumspection, nevertheless thought it in the bag. But however keen a baskets dialectician Asofsky was, the years had trained his biology to fear and no amount of rational powers could change that. In the final 24 minutes of the game, Asofsky said yes yes yes, it's happening, and tried to relax. But when it was over and the Knicks were at last the champions, 113–99, Stanley Asofsky had his underwear slipping and knotting against his legs. It was a small price to pay for this night.

Yes yes yes, it had happened. The Knicks were the champs. **At last.**

♟ EPILOGUE

SOME KNICKS didn't know how to open the bottles. That lesson learned, the champagne flowed.

•

A man came around with championship rings.
Riordan said he'd never worn a ring in his life, not for college or marriage.
He allowed as how this damned well would be his first.

•

In one corner of the room, an old Knick named Tom Hoover stood watching.
He'd played in less honored years.
A touch of sadness was on his face.

•

In another corner, DeBusschere, Riordan and May huddled and, faces lit with smiles, talked in conspiratorial whispers and nodded to each other.
Seizing bottles of champagne, they stalked into the coach's offices and doused Red Holzman with the bubbly.
Ssssst.

•

When the press was gone, Willis Reed struggled to lift his leg and get his trousers on.
Seeing him, Cazzie Russell wordlessly moved over and helped.

•

Sly watched the celebration and felt apart.

In the end, the joy of the moment was theirs, not his.

He had not thought of endings.

When he turned and left the locker room, he felt the feathery sense of loss that follows finished loves.

He went to a party and got very smashed.

•

The next night, Knick management held a party honoring the team.

A newsman in attendance got up and spoke.

He said he'd waited twenty-five years for this evening.

He said he'd raised a son without a Knick championship until now.

When he sat down he had tears in his eyes.

What bullshit, several players thought.

•

At the same affair, Dick Barnett had a thing or two to say.

He said how he'd heard that for just getting into the playoffs, the management of the Phoenix Suns had sent its players to Hawaii for rewards.

He said inasmuch as the Knicks had won the championship of the . . .

It was reported that the only man not smiling at Barnett's rambling delivery was the chairman of the board, Irving Mitchell Felt.

•

Days later, Riordan was making a personal appearance at a Hicksville, Long Island, shopping mall.

A stranger who'd heard he was going to Vietnam the next month for the USO came up to him and said, "Do me a favor. Why don't you take those two dummies [referees] Rudolph and Powers with you and leave them there?

Asofsky, who'd celebrated the championship by watching the game again on the delayed tape broadcast, would have liked that.

TWENTY-FIVE YEARS LATER . . .

DICK BARNETT had earned a Ph.D. in education from Fordham and headed the Athletic Role Model Educational Institute in New York.

NATE BOWMAN was the only member of the 1969-70 Knicks not still living. Bowman died of a heart attack in December 1984.

BILL BRADLEY was a United States senator from New Jersey.

DAVE DeBUSSCHERE was a vice-president of corporate development for the New York-based real estate firm of Williamson, Pickett and Gross.

WALT FRAZIER was a color commentator on Knick radio broadcasts and appeared on television doing pre- and post-game analysis of Knick games for the Madison Square Garden Network.

BILL HOSKET was general manager of Millcraft Paper Company in Columbus, Ohio, and did color commentary on television for Ohio State and Big Ten regional games.

PHIL JACKSON, who travelled with the team in 1969-70 but did not play because of an injury, was coach of the NBA champion Chicago Bulls.

DON MAY was a purchasing agent for Mosier Industries in Dayton, Ohio.

WILLIS REED was executive vice-president and general manager of the New Jersey Nets basketball team.

MIKE RIORDAN owned a restaurant in Annapolis, Maryland.

CAZZIE RUSSELL worked regularly as a coach in the Continental Basketball Association; during the 1992-93 season he was head coach of the Columbus (Ohio) Horizon.

DAVE STALLWORTH worked in the aircraft industry in Wichita, Kansas.

JOHN WARREN was a New York-based attorney.

RED HOLZMAN was a consultant to the Knicks.

STANLEY ASOFSKY and FRED KLEIN continued to occupy their baseline seats and to attend all Knick games. Asofsky managed the tennis operation of a country club in Roslyn, N.Y. Klein still worked as a restaurant broker.